in company 3.0

UPPER INTERMEDIATE Teacher's Book

B2

MACMILLAN

Macmillan Education
4 Crinan Street
London N1 9XW
A division of Springer Nature Limited
Companies and representatives throughout the world

ISBN 978-0-230-45538-2

Text, design and illustration © Springer Nature Limited 2014
Written by Pete Sharma

The author has asserted his rights to be identified as the author of this work in accordance with the Copyright, Designs and Patents Act 1988.

This edition published 2014
First edition published 2005

All rights reserved; no part of this publication may be reproduced, stored in a retrieval system, transmitted in any form, or by any means, electronic, mechanical, photocopying, recording, or otherwise, without the prior written permission of the publishers.

Design by emc design Limited
Page make-up by MPS Limited
Cover design by emc design Limited

The publishers would like to thank the following people, schools and institutions for their help in developing this third edition:
Pat Pledger, Pledger Business English Training, Hamburg; Louise Bulloch, Intercom Language Services, Hamburg; Elbie Picker and David Virta, Hamburg; William Fern, KERN AG IKL Business Language Training & Co. KG, Frankfurt; Belén del Valle, ELOQUIA, Frankfurt; Katrin Wolf, Carl Duisberg Centren, Cologne; Andrina Rout, Fokus Sprachen und Seminare, Stuttgart; Gerdi Serrer, ILIC, Paris; Sylvia Renaudon, Transfer, Paris; John Fayssoux; Kathryn Booth-Aïdah, Araxi Formations Langues, Paris; Fiona Delaney and Allison Dupuis, Formalangues, Paris; Francesca Pallot and Susan Stevenson, Anglesey Language Services, Chatou, France; Paul Bellchambers, Business and Technical Languages (BTL), Paris; Louise Raven, marcus evans Linguarama, Stratford-upon-Avon.

Many thanks also to all the teachers around the world who took the time to complete our *In Company* online questionnaire and who have contributed to the development of the *In Company* series.

The author and publishers would like to thank the following for permission to reproduce the following copyright material:

Excerpt from 'The Ultimate Business Presentation Book' by Andrew Leigh. © Andrew Leigh 1999. Published by Random House. Used with permission; Excerpt from 'The Accidental Tourist' by Anne Tyler. Published by Random House; Excerpt from 'Contemporary Public Speaking' by Courtland L. Bovee. Published by Rowman & Littlefield 2003. Reprinted with permission; Excerpt from 'You have to Start Meeting Like This!' by Gina Imperato. Published in Fast Company Issue 23, 1999. Reprinted with permission; Extracts from 'Innovation Intraprenuring-The Five people of innovation' Published on www.pinchot.com; Extracts from The Worst Case Scenarios series website, reprinted with permission of Quirk Books, Philadelphia, USA. www.Quirkbooks.com/Worst-Case-Scenarios; Extract from 'Effective Decision Making' by John Adair Pan Macmillan, 2009. Reprinted with permission; 'Coke Products Banned in Belgium' published by The Associated Press. 15.06.1999. Reprinted with permission; Extract from 'What are the Biggest Email Mistakes?' by Tim Sanders. Published by Krup NYC. Used with permissions; Extract from 'SEND, The Essential Guide to Email for Office and Home' by David Shipley and Will Schwalbe. Published by Knopf Double Day / Random House 2007. Reprinted with permission; Extract from 'I Have a Dream' speech by Dr Martin Luther King Jr. Reprinted by arrangement with The Heirs to the Estate of Martin Luther King Jr., c/o Writers House as agent for the proprietor New York, NY; Extract from Conservative Party Conference Speech, by Margaret Thatcher 10.10.1975. Reprinted with permission from the Margaret Thatcher Foundation; Extract from Nelson Mandela Inauguration speech 10.10.1994. Reprinted with permission from the Nelson Mandela Foundation; Material from 'Jet Lag Hater's Guide to Business Travel' by John Cassey / George Mackintosh Originally published in the Guardian 14.9.1999. © Guardian News & Media Ltd 1999. Reprinted with permission; Extract from 'Should Genetic Tests Decide Job Prospects?'. Originally published in The Sunday Times, 24.01.1999. Reprinted with permission; Extract from: "In a high-tech world, it's a cinch for employers to spy on workers" by Liz Stevens, Knight Ridder Newspapers, originally published December 6, 2002. © McClatchy-Tribune Information Services. All Rights Reserved. Reprinted with permission; Extract from 'Creative Way to Better Management' by Francis Beckett. © Francis Beckett. Originally published in The Financial Times, 08.11.1999. Reprinted with permission.

These materials may contain links for third-party websites. We have no control over, and are not responsible for, the contents of such third-party websites. Please use care when accessing them.

Printed and bound in Great Britain by Ashford Colour Press Ltd.

2019
10

Contents

Contents	**3**
Student's Book contents	**4**
Introduction	**6**
Teacher's notes with answers	
01 Business or pleasure?	12
02 Information exchange	18
03 People skills: Rapport	24
Management scenario A: Culture clash	26
04 Voice and visuals	29
05 Problems on the phone	34
06 Leading meetings	40
07 People skills: Coaching	45
Management scenario B: Coach crash	48
08 Promoting your ideas	51
09 Relationship-building	57
10 Making decisions	63
11 People skills: Stress	69
Management scenario C: Pitch and persuade	72
12 Emailing	75
13 Making an impact	80
14 Out and about	85
15 People skills: Delegation	90
Management scenario D: Change champion	93
16 Teleconferencing	96
17 Negotiating deals	101
18 People skills: Mediation	107
Management scenario E: Moral quarrel	110

Student's Book contents

Unit	Business communication skills	Reading and listening	Language links
01 Business or pleasure? p6	Discussing corporate entertainment Sharing information to select appropriate corporate events for clients Avoiding saying 'no' Paying and receiving compliments **Fluency** Keeping up a conversation	**Reading** Information on four corporate events in the UK **Listening** People chatting at corporate events Discussing corporate entertainment	**Vocabulary** Small talk **Grammar** Tense review **Phrase bank** Making conversation
02 Information exchange p13	Describing attitudes to and content of meetings Paraphrasing information Pointing out discrepancies Dialogue-building using the language of meetings **Fluency** Breaking bad news and writing a report In company interviews Units 1–2	**Reading** Meeting: breaking bad news **Listening** A meeting: problems with a product Five meetings: discrepancies The language of meetings	**Vocabulary** Meetings **Grammar** Conditionals **Phrase bank** Debating issues
03 People skills: Rapport p20	Strategies and techniques to build rapport **Fluency** Building rapport with a colleague	**Reading** Top tips for building rapport Training manual checklists **Listening** Two meetings to discuss teleworking	
Management scenario A: Culture clash p22	Identifying potential cultural differences Avoiding a culture clash **Fluency** A meeting to discuss a merger	**Reading** Cultural sensitivity checklist In company in action A1: A culture clash A2: Positive cross-cultural understanding	
04 Voice and visuals p24	Doing a quiz on how to command attention Giving feedback on a presentation Using visuals in a presentation Analyzing the voice in presentations **Fluency** Giving a speech	**Reading** Articles on voice and visual impact **Listening** Voicemail Presenters giving information in different ways Radio programme: drama for business A Shakespeare speech	**Vocabulary** Presentations **Grammar** Modal verbs **Phrase bank** Describing and commenting on visuals
05 Problems on the phone p31	Discussing phone usage and its usefulness Dealing with 'chatterboxes' Complaining and dealing with complaints Toning down 'flames' Speculating about a problem **Fluency** Solving problems on the phone	**Reading** Article on 'chatterboxes' **Listening** Someone dealing with a 'chatterbox' Someone dealing with a customer complaint People discussing a problem People solving a problem	**Vocabulary** Phone, tablet and email **Grammar** Complex question formation **Phrase bank** On the phone
06 Leading meetings p37	Discussing dynamics of meetings Disagreeing diplomatically **Fluency** Chairing a meeting In company interviews Units 4–6	**Reading** Article on behaviour in meetings Disagreement strategies **Listening** Radio programme: alternative approaches to meetings Managing meetings	**Vocabulary** Companies and capital; The financial pages **Grammar** Linking and contrasting ideas **Phrase bank** Chairing meetings
07 People skills: Coaching p44	Discussing the role of a coach The GROW model of coaching **Fluency** Coaching your colleagues	**Reading** Article on professional coaching **Listening** Four extracts from a coaching session	
Management scenario B: Coach crash p46	Giving feedback on a presentation Coaching dos and don'ts **Fluency** Past-present-future presentations with coaching	**Reading** Coaching dos and don'ts In company in action B1: A failed presentation B2: Successful coaching	
08 Promoting your ideas p48	Discussing attitudes to public speaking Discussing national stereotypes Describing what makes a good talk Discussing innovation in your company **Fluency** Presenting an idea for a product or service	**Reading** Website extract: *Intrapreneurs* **Listening** Presenters talking about what makes them nervous People comparing audience expectations of presentations Presentation: a new business idea	**Vocabulary** Phrasal verbs **Grammar** The passive **Phrase bank** Pitching an idea
09 Relationship-building p55	Discussing first impressions Completing a questionnaire on networking Practising networking skills Getting out of the office **Roleplay** Visiting a colleague's home	**Reading** Questionnaire: Are you an effective networker? Article on sport and business **Listening** Three small talk conversations People chatting at golf Conversation: visiting someone's home	**Vocabulary** Social English **Grammar** Multi-verb sentences **Phrase bank** Networking

STUDENT'S BOOK CONTENTS

Unit	Business communication skills	Reading and listening	Language links
10 Making decisions p63	Discussing making decisions in difficult situations Doing a quiz on life-and-death decisions Giving advice on worst-case scenarios or workplace dilemmas Inserting missing articles into two texts **Fluency** Holding a crisis management meeting In company interviews Units 8–10	**Reading** Website extract: Worst-case scenarios Company crises **Listening** Advice on surviving worst-case scenarios Decision-making meetings Case study: Coca-Cola crisis	**Vocabulary** Marketing **Grammar** Articles **Phrase bank** Decision-making
11 People skills: Stress p70	Analyzing attitudes to stress in the workplace Identifying techniques for managing stress **Fluency** Helping a staff member in a stressful situation	**Reading** Article on helping colleagues manage stress **Listening** Talk on stress management Eight managers counselling their staff	
Management scenario C: Pitch and persuade p72	Identifying effective pitching techniques Using Cialdini's six principles of influence **Fluency** Pitching a new project	**Reading** Article on building donor circles In company in action C1: A failed pitch C2: An effective pitch	
12 Emailing p74	Discussing how to deal with emails Correcting errors in an email Shortening and simplifying an email Adding the personal touch to an email Choosing an appropriate email style **Fluency** Writing and answering emails	**Reading** Extracts on emailing **Listening** Podcast: what your emails say about your career prospects Radio programme: The biggest email blunders ever made	**Vocabulary** Prepositional phrases **Grammar** Future forms **Phrase bank** Emailing
13 Making an impact p82	Identifying effective presentation openings Identifying rhetorical techniques Rephrasing to add impact Identifying ways of closing a presentation **Fluency** Producing a promotional presentation for a new country	**Reading** Book extract on opening a presentation **Listening** Presentation openings Extracts from political speeches Closing remarks from four presentations	**Vocabulary** Metaphor **Grammar** Rhetorical techniques **Phrase bank** Opening and closing a presentation
14 Out and about p89	Discussing business travel and packing habits Identifying ellipsis in conversation Striking up a conversation Telling an anecdote **Fluency** Chatting over a business lunch In company interviews Units 12–14	**Reading** Extracts from *The Accidental Tourist* **Listening** People talking about their worst flying experiences Conversations over lunch	**Vocabulary** Storytelling **Grammar** Narrative tenses **Phrase bank** Sharing anecdotes
15 People skills: Delegation p96	Identifying information needed for delegation Discussing management styles **Fluency** Effective delegation and appropriate management styles	**Reading** Blog post on delegation **Listening** Presentation on management styles Three managers delegating tasks	
Management scenario D: Change champion p98	Discussing implementing change successfully Identifying the stages for managing change **Fluency** Meetings to implement change	**Reading** PowerPoint slide on managing change In company in action D1: Imposing changes D2: Managing change	
16 Teleconferencing p100	Discussing potential uses of tele- and videoconferencing facilities Discussing action in a crisis Completing the minutes of a teleconference **Roleplay** Holding a teleconference	**Reading** Website extract: Business benefits of *TelePresence* Emails about a film shoot **Listening** An unexpected phone call An emergency teleconference	**Vocabulary** Teleconferencing, Personnel and production **Grammar** Reporting **Phrase bank** Teleconferencing
17 Negotiating deals p107	Negotiating a tricky situation Identifying negotiating tactics **Fluency** Negotiating a contract In company interviews Units 16–17	**Reading** Analysis of a negotiation Article about the music business **Listening** Negotiations People talking about negotiating strategy Meeting: signing a new band	**Vocabulary** Negotiations **Grammar** Diplomacy and persuasion **Phrase bank** Negotiating
18 People skills: Mediation p114	Discussing the qualities of a good mediator Identifying the stages of mediation **Fluency** Mediating between colleagues	**Reading** Article about causes of conflict at work **Listening** Poor and positive mediation	
Management scenario E: Moral quarrel p116	Staying assertive in meetings Mediating to resolve a conflict **Fluency** A conference call mediation	**Reading** PowerPoint slide on assertiveness In company in action E1: A failed mediation E2: A successful conference call	
	Additional material p118	Listening scripts p139	

Introduction

A Business English classroom

As Stephen crosses the bridge over the River Main, the towering skyscrapers of Frankfurt's commercial district glitter with lights in the distance. 'Mainhattan' the locals call it, referring to a certain resemblance to New York. Stephen is on his way there now, to his last lesson of the day. But he's not happy.

The class itself is great. Otto, Wolfgang, Ernst and Liesl are a lot of fun. They often take Stephen for dinner at a nearby bistro after the lesson and he sometimes thinks they learn more English there than in the class.

And that's where the problem lies. The group speaks pretty good English already and, having had a succession of English teachers over the last three years, there doesn't seem to be a lot they haven't done before. The language of meetings, telephoning, presentations, negotiations – you name it, they've studied it. Stephen did a fluency activity with them last week only to discover they'd done it the year before with a different teacher. They laughed about it, but it was clear one or two of them felt they couldn't be making much progress.

Looking at the Upper Intermediate Business English materials in the teacher's room at his school, Stephen decides that most of them are really just going over old ground again, teaching the same basic functions and topics they taught at Intermediate, but sometimes introducing unnecessarily complicated language to justify the continued effort. 'What is Upper Intermediate Business English, anyway?' he wonders. 'What more is there left to teach?'

Then Stephen remembers a lesson he did with them a few weeks back. It was a roleplay in which they had to visit their boss's home for a meal, make a good impression and raise a rather delicate work issue without offending their host. They found it really challenging and liked the mixture of social and business language that came out of doing the activity. They said they felt this was more the kind of advanced English they needed. So, as Stephen catches his bus into the city, his mood is already brightening and he's beginning to think, 'Maybe I'm on to something here …'

in company 3.0

in company 3.0 is Macmillan's skills-based Business English series, aimed at professional, adult learners seeking to realize their full potential as speakers of English at work – both in and out of the office – and in social settings. This third edition builds on the success of the previous editions and has been enhanced and updated to reflect the realities of the 21st century professional. Business English learners now face a challenging, fast-paced, technologically-advanced workplace and the process of English language acquisition with in company 3.0 has been adapted to match this. In addition to a comprehensive Student's Book that offers quick and tangible results, the series now also provides students with a wealth of new material online via the Big Tree platform. This allows learners to extend their studies, not only within the classroom, but also outside of the traditional learning environment, on-the-move and in their own time.

Ten key observations regarding teaching English to professional learners underpin the in company series:

1. Professionals like to be regularly reminded why they are studying and what's in it for them.
2. They are used to goal-setting and time constraints, and tend to welcome a fairly fast pace.
3. They are motivated by topics which directly relate to their own personal experiences.
4. They expect to see an immediate, practical payoff of some kind at the end of each lesson.
5. It is English, not business, they have come to you for help with (but see 7).
6. They want to be able to actually do business with their English rather than just talk about it.
7. They appreciate texts and tasks which reflect what they have to do in their job.
8. They also appreciate texts and tasks which allow them to escape what they have to do in their job.
9. They don't regard having fun as incompatible with 'serious learning' (but see 1 and 4).
10. They like to see an overall plan and method behind the classes they attend.

At this level, learners can fairly easily cope with most everyday situations in English and, unless they have very special needs, there's a danger they may not be sufficiently motivated to continue their studies. Those who are motivated are driven by more than the need to be competent. They are already competent. They want to excel, to really 'look good' in English. Having worked for so long at improving their English, they think it's time their English started working for them.

For the upper intermediate learner, therefore, telephoning is less about learning set telephone expressions and more about solving problems on the phone; presenting is less about facing forwards and making sense and more about impressing and delighting the audience; meetings are less about coming in here and there with constructive remarks and more about taking the initiative and influencing the outcome. Social English in a real business context, where the boundaries between work and pleasure are not so clearly defined, is likely to be a priority. So too is the ability to talk perhaps only superficially, but articulately, about a number of topical issues.

Much so-called advanced English is really rather simple English used in advanced ways. So, as well as increasing the complexity of their utterances, upper intermediate learners need to learn that particular stresses, pauses and intonation can make simple expressions like 'Yes, but ...' and 'Well, okay, but look, ...' serve them very well in many business situations.

Skills-based approach

in **company** 3.0 Upper Intermediate is a practical course in how to do business in English. With target language selectively introduced on a need-to-know basis, each unit is a fast track to competence in a particular business skill. Recognizing that people need more than just phrase lists and useful language boxes to operate effectively in real-life business situations, each unit provides a substantial amount of guided skills work to give students the chance to fully assimilate the target language and 'make it their own', before going on to tackle fluency activities.

Target skills developed at this level include:

- making a strong impression on clients, colleagues and business partners in social situations
- introducing important business issues into general conversation
- expressing informed views on topics of general business interest
- leading and influencing the outcome of cross-cultural meetings
- tackling everyday problems on the phone
- acquiring a professional email writing style
- using the voice and visuals to their full potential in business presentations
- employing a range of rhetorical skills to get the message across
- dealing with crises and emergencies face to face and by teleconferencing
- being persuasive but diplomatic in negotiations

Student's Book

Structure for the third edition

in **company** 3.0 Upper Intermediate is organized into five sections. Each section consists of two or three 'Business communication' units, a 'People skills' unit and a 'Management scenario'.

Business communication units

These units deal with vital communication skills such as giving presentations, leading meetings and networking at corporate events. These units all contain grammar and lexis elements and are followed by *Language links* which offer extra vocabulary practice and grammar consolidation and extra practice.

Every second or third Business communication unit concludes with a video: In company interviews. These interviews showcase real business professionals discussing the preceding unit topics, and give a context for students' own discussion and additional worksheet activities.

People skills

Acquiring communication strategies for a variety of work-related and social contexts and developing interpersonal skills is the main emphasis of these units. The functional language required for interaction with others is presented and practised through dialogues and extensive listening practice. This is then consolidated through a comprehensive roleplay, where students put into practice the skills they have explored in the unit.

Management scenarios

A new feature of the third edition of in **company** are the five Management scenarios which provide learners with additional extended communication practice through a simulation of a real-life business situation. Most importantly, these business situations are illustrated through video, providing students with a visual support to the Student's Book activities which allows them to develop a range of different skills, including perception of body language, comprehension of various accents and an understanding of the importance of interpersonal skills.

Each Management scenario uses video as a prompt for discussion and then as a model for the students' own free roleplay. This fluency activity simulates a similar situation to the one the students have encountered in the video, but allows them the freedom to play their own characters. A self-evaluation form for every roleplay gives students the chance to assess not only their peers' performance, but also their own.

Vocabulary syllabus

in **company** 3.0 Upper Intermediate devotes a lot of attention to vocabulary, showing students how to build words, many of which they may already know, into larger, multi-word items they do not know. For example:

- compounds – *search engine, help menu*
- collocations – *sharp rise, go out of production*
- noun phrases – *cost of living, rate of exchange*
- phrasal verbs – *sell out, buy up, cut back*
- discourse markers – *above all, by the way, to sum up*
- fixed expressions – *Leave it with me, I'll do my best, I'm afraid we'll have to break off here*
- partial frameworks or scripts – *(a month) ago we were having difficulties with ..., which was also affecting ... and ..., not to mention ... . So, what was going wrong? Well, the problem we were facing was not ... but ... . Have a look at this ...*

Pre-constructed vocabulary chunks, like those above, are a crucial part of native speaker interaction and, if judiciously selected, can significantly speed up the language processing time of non-native speakers too, allowing them to sound more fluent and confident in situations they can predict they are likely to encounter.

Vocabulary, therefore, is given a prominent place in the units. In addition, each of the 13 skills units is followed by extra vocabulary practice in the corresponding

INTRODUCTION 7

Language links that follow the unit. These exercises effectively double the lexical input in each unit and can either be set for homework or made the basis of vocabulary-building lessons.

Throughout in **company** Upper Intermediate rather more attention is paid to the teaching of phrasal verbs and common idioms than was the case in the lower levels of the series. The aim here is to gradually build up student's ability to 'decode' phrases and expressions whose meaning cannot simply be worked out from their constituent parts, but which are, nevertheless, a common feature of natural spoken English. Students may not actually need to be able to produce such expressions themselves. Indeed, where they are working with other non-native speakers of English the occurrence of phrasal verbs and idioms will, of course, be much less frequent.

The reality is, however, that many students at upper intermediate level may be required to do business with native (or near-native) speakers, while having had little exposure to the idiomatic English such speakers use every day. There is much talk these days of aiming in the language teaching classroom for a less complex, more error tolerant and essentially de-cultured 'international English'. While this makes a lot of sense at lower levels where the students simply want to get by, we can safely assume that 'international English' is precisely the kind of English our upper intermediate students already have. And, surely, one of the reasons people continue studying English at advanced levels is to start to engage with native speakers on their own terms. If this was not their aim, they would only need to maintain the English they have. At higher levels, therefore, a grasp of idiom and natural conversational English is an important part of maximizing lexical power.

Some of the more difficult lexis in the skills material has been highlighted for pre-teaching. There is a variety of ways to approach this including: group discussion, peer teaching, definition/synonym matching, contextualization, real-life examples, etc.

Phrase banks

The *Language links* also include *Phrase banks*. These appear as exercises, which, once completed, act as a reference bank for useful phrases.

Grammar syllabus

Of course, lexical chunks are only useful in so far as our students are able to produce them in real time, as and when they need them. When, for whatever reason, they are unable to do so, they will fall back on the generative power of grammar and the simplest words in their vocabulary to get the job done.

The approach in in **company** 3.0 Upper Intermediate is to highlight target grammar as it naturally emerges in the activities, but there are no long detours in the units themselves into structural matters. This is where the grammar sections of the *Language links* come in. 13 grammar sections in the *Language links*, cross-linked to the 13 skills units, systematically address the usual questions of time, tense, aspect, voice, modality and conditionality as well as broader areas such as reporting and diplomacy, where grammar becomes as much a matter of choice as of rules.

In this grammar section, students are encouraged to explore grammatical use and, to some extent, fathom out the rules for themselves. Tenses are usually presented contrastively. Practice exercises are more commonly text- or dialogue-based (rather than simply sentence-based) to give a feel for the discoursal role of different structures.

In Company Online

The addition of a blended learning element to the course gives in **company** 3.0 a neat and compact learning solution for both students and teachers. For students, this means the opportunity to practise their language online, via the Online Workbook, as well as on-the-move by downloading the class audio and video. For teachers, this online product means the ability to track students' progress through automatic gradebooks, the opportunity to download the audio and video content, as well as gain access to additional photocopiable material, tests and worksheets.

Online Workbook

The in **company** 3.0 Online Workbook provides extra skills, grammar and vocabulary practice for every unit of the Student's Book. It contains interactive activities, audio for listening practice and automatic marking – making it perfect for self-study. Your students can instantly check answers and try again, as many times as they want. The Workbook is also linked to an online gradebook, which means you can see your students' marks for each activity as well as the progress they are making. Students will also be able to chart their own progress.

The Online Workbook contains 18 units to match the Student's Book. Students can read and listen to texts on topics similar to those featured in the Student's Book unit, and develop the reading, listening and writing skills that each Student's Book unit introduces. Each Workbook unit also contains lots of extra grammar and vocabulary practice, and there is a grammar reference section for students to consult if they encounter any difficulties.

Resource Centres

In addition to the Online Workbook, students and teachers have access to the Student's and Teacher's Resource Centres. These contain a wealth of additional resource material for use both in and out of the classroom.

Class audio

This includes all audio tracks from the Student's Book class audio CD, along with full listening scripts. Students and teachers can download all the material to a mobile device for listening on-the-move.

Video

In company in action videos accompany each Management scenario in the Student's Book. In the Teacher's Resource Centre, each of these videos has an additional classroom-based worksheet to fully exploit the audiovisual material, including teaching notes and answer keys.

In company interview videos showcase business professionals around the world discussing key business skills and topics. Each interview is supported by a self-study worksheet for students to complete at home.

All video material can be viewed online or downloaded to a mobile device for watching on-the-move.

Tests

Progress and placement tests allow teachers to assess their students' work throughout the course. The automatic gradebook on the Online Workbook also provides the teacher with instant feedback on their students' progress.

Additional student support

Students have access to the following resources to support their learning:

- Unit-by-unit glossary
- Student's Book answer key
- Student's Book phrase banks

Additional teacher support

In addition to the above, teachers have access to an additional 35 photocopiable worksheets which extend and/or revise elements in the Student's Book. The worksheets are written by ten practising Business English teachers, and they provide approximately 25 extra hours of material to supplement the Student's Book.

Fast-track map

An invaluable resource for the busy teacher is the new 'fast-track map' that accompanies every level of in company 3.0. This detailed map provides teachers with a fast-track route through the Student's Book, which is ideal for those students who have 30–60 hours of English lessons.

The fast-track map gives the teacher the option of following one of three routes (taster, language practice and language input), selecting the most relevant and useful activities to do in class. Each route also provides a comprehensive self-study plan, for students to enhance their learning outside the classroom.

Class audio CDs

Throughout the course, substantial use is made of audio recordings to input business expressions and grammatical structures. Indeed, very little of the language work is not either presented or recycled in a recording.

The recordings feature both native and non-native speaker accents, providing the students with extensive exposure to real spoken English. There is frequently an element of humour in the recordings which, besides entertaining the students, motivates them to listen again for things they may have missed the first time round.

There are full listening scripts at the back of the Student's Book. All Student's Book class audio material is also available online, accessible to both students and teachers through the resource centres. These audio tracks can be downloaded as MP3 files and played on various devices, from CD players to smartphones and tablets. This allows students to listen again to all audio material in their own time, even when on-the-move, giving them the flexibility to listen and re-listen to the class audio as much as they want.

In addition, the Listening section of the Online Workbook provide further listening practice with new recordings that students will not yet have heard in class.

How can I exploit the dialogues further?

Play some of the dialogues a second time and:

- pause the CD after questions for students to recall or predict the response (if they write these down as they go, you can ask them to recall the questions as well at the end)
- pause the CD after responses to questions and ask students to think of other possible responses
- pause the CD in the middle of lexical chunks (collocations, fixed expressions) for students to complete them either orally or by writing them down
- ask students to speculate about the personalities of the speakers in the dialogue
- ask students if they have ever met / done business with anyone like the speakers
- ask students if they would have reacted differently to the speakers in the dialogue

Reading texts

The reading texts in in company 3.0 Upper Intermediate have been chosen to involve, entertain and provoke students into lively discussion, as well as to contextualize key target vocabulary. Squeezing a text completely dry of all useful language usually demotivates a class, but many of the longer texts in in company 3.0 Upper Intermediate are information- and lexically-rich and can usefully be revisited.

The reading section of the Online Workbook uses new reading texts to provide further reading practice in a different context.

How can I exploit the texts further?

Try some of the following:

- students set each other questions on a text
- students set you questions on a text, and vice versa

INTRODUCTION

- give students several figures from a text and ask them to recall the context in which they were mentioned
- read the text aloud but slur certain words/phrases and have students ask for repetition/clarification
- students read/listen to a text and complete sentences to reflect their own reaction to it, e.g. *I thought the point about ... was interesting; I'm surprised that ...; I'm not sure I agree with what it says about ...; I'm not convinced that ...; I completely disagree with the idea that ...*
- give students the first half of 8–16 collocations and a time limit in which to search for the collocates
- give students a set of miscollocates and ask them to correct them by referring to the text
- students find expressions which mean the same as, e.g. *incidentally = by the way; moreover = in addition; generally = by and large;* or the opposite of, e.g. *in practice / in theory; in general / in particular*
- give students a set of prepositions and ask them to scan the text for noun phrases / phrasal verbs / idioms which include those prepositions
- read out the text, pausing in the middle of collocations / fixed expressions / idioms for students to predict the completions either by shouting out or writing down the answer

Fluency work

Each unit culminates in at least one fluency activity which draws on both the specific language presented in the unit and the wider linguistic resources of the students. Activity types comprise:

1. **skills workouts**, where students practise a specific micro-skill (such as effective interruption or voice projection) in a semi-guided way
2. **roleplays and simulations**, where students are given a scenario and perhaps some kind of 'personal agenda'
3. **case studies**, where students are confronted with an authentic business problem and then compare their solution with that of the actual company concerned
4. **'framework' activities**, where the students decide on the content for a presentation, email or phone call and the Student's Book provides them with a linguistic framework to help deliver that information

Preparation is essential for types 2–4 and it may sometimes be advisable to carry out the actual fluency activity in a subsequent lesson, allowing plenty of time for feedback.

Care has been taken in the selection of fluency activities in **in company** 3.0 Upper Intermediate to keep interest levels and motivation high by including two quite different kinds of task.

The first kind is the 'high content reality' task – one which closely resembles the sort of thing students routinely have to do in their work (solve problems on the phone, , strike up a conversation with a fellow passenger on a plane, team present a new project). This kind of activity has the advantage of being immediately relevant to student's needs and can be further personalized and fine-tuned to even more closely match their real work situation. It is less roleplay than what Adrian Underhill has called 'realplay'.

The second kind of task is the 'low content reality' task – one which, though the scenario may be unfamiliar to the students (for example, performing a speech from a play, creating a new country, taking life-and-death decisions or negotiating a record deal for a rock band), nevertheless requires language and cognitive processing skills which are very much part of what they have to do in their work. The advantage of this kind of activity is that it encourages a greater degree of creativity and, being quite different from what students usually do, does not run the risk of being similar to a real work situation but not quite similar enough – a common problem when you attempt to simulate real life in the classroom.

Some students will have a definite preference for one kind of activity over the other, but, in general, a balance of the two will prove most effective. Many management training courses are programmed so that participants progress from low content reality activities in the early stages to high content reality simulations at the end. For those of you who wish to follow this pattern, a wide range of alternative fluency activities are included in the Teacher's Resource Centre.

Working with video

Here are some suggestions of different ways of working with video.

Video dictogloss

This gives the students practice in grammar and vocabulary, with emphasis on sentence building. Use a short part of a video. Tell the students to watch and listen carefully as you play the extract. Play it once and ask them to write down in any order any words they can remember from the conversation. Then, ask them to work first in pairs and then in small groups, and to use the words they have written to recreate as much of the dialogue as possible. This activity works better with practice!

Questions for answers

This activity gives the students practice in prediction skills and practices question formation. Find five or six examples of questions and answers in the video script. Write the answers on the board or on a sheet of paper. Ask the students to work in pairs and guess what the questions for these answers are. Listen to their ideas, but don't correct them. Play the video so they can check if their predictions were correct.

Multi-listening tasks

This activity practices taking notes while viewing. Divide students into three or four groups, and give each group a different listening task. At the end of the viewing, groups exchange papers with someone else from the same group. Show the video again. Have them check their partner's answers and add more information. Finally, students form groups of three: with one person from A, B and C, and discuss what they learned.

Subtitles off / subtitles on

This activity practices listening for detail. Write sentences from a section of the video, preferably a continuous conversation. Photocopy the sheet (one copy for every three students) and cut up the slips of paper. Put students into groups of three. Hand out a set of slips to each group, in the wrong order. As students listen to the video (subtitles off), they put the slips into order. Play the video again (subtitles on), so students can check their order. Finally, have them practise the dialogue in their groups.

Stop and predict

This activity motivates students and develops classroom discussion. Press 'Pause' at an appropriate moment and ask students to guess what is going to happen next. Alternatively, ask students what the speaker is going to say next. Elicit ideas from your class. Then watch the next part of the video and find out the answer. Who guessed correctly? This activity only works when students watch the video for the first time.

Shadow reading

This activity gives students practice in rhythm and intonation. After students have watched the video, give them a copy of a short section of the script, preferably a dialogue. Give them a few minutes to read it through silently. Get them to practise reading the text aloud in small groups. Then play the video again and ask students to read the script aloud in time with the video. This can be difficult for students at first but, with practice, it can really help with stress, weak forms and rhythm. Start by doing this with short sections and gradually increase their length.

Fast-forward viewing

This activity helps students to understand the main ideas. Write a few basic questions on the board relating to the video clip students are going to watch. Play the entire clip on fast-forward (no sound). Encourage students to guess the answers from the quick viewing. Elicit other details they learnt.

Teacher's Book

In this book, you'll find comprehensive teaching notes which give an overview of each unit, detailed procedural instructions for all the exercises, and full listening scripts and answer keys.

A recurring feature of the previous edition is the inclusion of **1:1** teaching tips found following every group-based or roleplay activity throughout the procedural notes. These have been updated and their number increased for this third edition. The aim of these notes is to offer tips on adapting the material to suit one-to-one classes, which are so common in in-company teaching. This allows the teacher to make better use of the material, in all teaching contexts.

The procedural notes also contain *Language link* highlights, which are reminders of exercises in the *Language link* pages where students can find grammar explanations or further practice in a particular grammar or vocabulary area. This allows the teacher to focus students' attention on particular areas of difficulty or interest.

We hope you enjoy working with **in company** 3.0.

Mark Powell and John Allison

September 2013

01 Business or pleasure?

Learning objectives
This unit is about corporate entertaining and making conversation. There is a strong focus on fluency and students practise the business skill of socializing.

Students first discuss building relationships with business clients and study two short texts on small talk and networking. They then get to know the other students in the group through a small talk activity.

Students discuss the pros and cons of spending a lot of money on corporate entertainment. They listen to a recording of a planning committee discussing a visit from Russian clients and then share information in order to select an appropriate event for this group of visitors.

Students listen to businesspeople socializing at corporate events and study the functional language from the recordings. They get fluency practice in the form of a game in which they have to avoid saying no. Another recording provides further listening practice. Students then practise giving and receiving compliments and, in a final fluency activity, use suitable small talk topics to start a conversation and keep it going.

The grammatical focus is on reviewing tenses, and the lexical focus is on small talk.

Digital resources: Unit 1
Online Workbook; Placement test; Extension worksheets; Glossary; Phrase bank; Student's Book answer key; Student's Book listening script; Fast-track map

In this first section, students discuss socializing in business and read two short extracts on networking. They take part in a speaking activity to practise small talk and to get to know others in the group.

Warm-up
If this is a new class, ask students to interview each other about their jobs and free time interests and to list three memorable facts. Students can then give a short presentation about their partner. This will act as an ice-breaker and help you to establish students' professional roles and interests.

As a lead-in to the unit, ask students to brainstorm what is important in establishing a business relationship. Pre-teach: *All things being equal*. Ask students to read the quotation by Mark McCormack. Ask if they agree that friendship is of vital importance in the commercial world.

1:1 If you are teaching one-to-one, you may want to do a full needs analysis and find out about your student's job, what topics they are interested in and which business skills they need to focus on. Find out in what situations your student needs to use English.

1 Use this question to find out a bit about who meets clients. Which countries are these clients from? What percentage of time do they spend doing business and what percentage is relationship building? Do students believe it is important to like your counterparts?

2 After reading the extracts, check student's reactions to the key message. Do they have examples of successful people who made it to the top with successful networking skills? Check expressions such as: *to have a bearing on*.

3 Find out who is good at making small talk and who finds it difficult. Encourage students to tell you why they think small talk is difficult. Is it just personality? Have they worked in cultures where small talk is not important?

a Tell students to write notes in the chart, not complete sentences.

b Help students to create the scene for their conversation. Then ask pairs to sit in different parts of the classroom.

c Monitor the conversations. Take language notes.

1:1 Use this exercise to find out your student's areas of interest, and what interests you have in common.

4 Check with students to see which topics had the most mileage. Did they find anything in common? Point out that good socializers have a knack of finding something in common, which can spark genuine conversation.

1:1 If possible, record your conversation. This will allow you to participate in the activity without the distraction of making a note of your student's mistakes. Afterwards, listen to the recording together, pausing as required to identify any important or common mistakes and work on reformulating them into good language.

Corporate entertainment

In this section, students first discuss the value of corporate entertainment. They then listen to a recording about a group of visiting businesspeople from Russia, and study information on four possible events they could organize for the visitors. In pairs, students discuss and choose their preferred options.

12 01 BUSINESS OR PLEASURE?

BUSINESS COMMUNICATION

1 Lead in to the discussion by finding out who organizes corporate entertainment in the students' companies. Elicit a list of typical ways in which business visitors are entertained at local and national level, e.g. lunch/dinner, theatre trips, sporting events. Ask students if they think it is worth spending this money.

2 Write the following words on the board: *service, environment*. Elicit some collocations, e.g. *first-class/valet service, high tech environment*. Remind students why collocation is important – it is a key feature of English and is essential in the development of fluency. It is an important part of the lexical content of this course. Point out that focusing on collocation will help with the gap-fill task.

Elicit *maintain relationships* as the answer for gap (a) and then ask students to complete the task. Check the answers with the whole class. Ask students if they would use this corporate entertainment company and, if so, which event they would choose.

ANSWERS

a relationships   b clients   c members   d team   e experience
f office   g seats   h box   i viewing   j cuisine   k setting
l service

3 🔘 **1.01** Check if any students organize/have organized corporate entertainment. If so, elicit what they need to think about first, e.g. budget, finding out about the likes and dislikes of the visitors in advance, organizing a guide/interpreter. Ask them which events they enjoyed and which were the most successful, and why.

Before playing the recording, tell students they will hear four speakers. The first time you play the recording, ask them to see if any of their ideas were mentioned.

Before playing the recording a second time, check any problematic vocabulary: *quintessentially, people-oriented*. Encourage students to take notes; pause between each speaker to allow students time to finish their note-taking.

🔘 **1.01**
Speaker 1
Okay, well, now, we don't know a lot about what the team might be interested in. And this is going to be a mixed group with their partners so it'll be difficult to choose something they'll all like. But, since this is the first visit to Britain for some of them, I suggest we go for something, you know, quintessentially British. The main thing is to make sure nothing can go wrong. Most important, let's plan on something weatherproof! And we definitely need to provide a bit more than just an expensive dinner. What about doing something cultural?

Speaker 2
Hmm, I think culture can be tricky. We don't want to drag the group somewhere, only for them to be bored out of their minds. We just need a pleasant setting to be able to socialize. Let's think of a good restaurant where we can relax, enjoy decent food and talk about business. Of course, we need to check if any of the team are vegetarians before we make any bookings.

Speaker 3
Hang on. We'll have plenty of time to talk business in the meetings. This is about making sure we show them a good time. Russians are very people-oriented. This is an opportunity for us to build a good working relationship with them, you know, a bit of team spirit. In some ways it could even be a team-building kind of thing. And, let me tell you, Russians certainly like fine dining!
So top-quality catering, sure, but let's offer them something a bit special as well. And keep business out of it!

Speaker 4
Well, I think the main thing is to make the visit as personal as possible. I mean, we could spend a fortune on attending some big event, but that's not very personal, is it? In fact, spending a little less on the event might mean you could afford to do something extra for the team members – I'm not necessarily talking gifts, but something. And, by the way, I happen to know that their project leader, Yuri, spent a year studying in London, so we might think about taking them somewhere else. That means travel expenses, of course, but I'm sure we can keep those within reason.

4 Find out which students have made business or holiday trips to the UK. Elicit what impressed them as visitors and where they were entertained. If no one has been to the UK, brainstorm some famous venues for leisure and sporting events. Include the following examples from the texts on pages 118 and 129, if students don't give them: Silverstone – venue of the world-famous racing car event the British Grand Prix; Britannia – the former royal yacht, now a tourist attraction in an Edinburgh dock; Wimbledon – home of the lawn tennis championships; the London Eye – a high tech ride which gives great views over London; and the Tate Modern – a modern art gallery on the South Bank in London.

Before setting up the jigsaw reading activity, point out that the reading material in the course contains a wide range of lexically-rich and challenging texts. Encourage students to decide which words/expressions from each reading text they want to use as part of their active vocabulary and to make a note of these.

Tell students not to expect to know every word when they read, but remind them of useful strategies such as predicting the content and vocabulary, reading the text quickly first for gist and deducing meaning from context. With weaker groups, check/pre-teach: *to descend on, to soak up* (the atmosphere), *glamorous, breathtaking, to roll out the red carpet* (give special treatment to a guest), *to clash, awesome, capsule, cutting-edge*.

Divide the class into AB groups. Ask students to read their texts and make notes on the key information about each of the events. Set a time limit to ensure students only focus on the main points.

01 BUSINESS OR PLEASURE? 13

BUSINESS COMMUNICATION

5 Set up new groups, mixing A and B students, and rearrange the classroom seating to facilitate the meetings. Write the following agenda on the board:

Aim: to choose corporate entertainment for different groups of visitors

1 Short presentations – four possible events
2 Discussion
3 Final choice

With weaker students, brainstorm the pros and cons of the four events before students start the meeting. Point out the factors which students will need to consider, e.g. cost, your current relationship with the clients, the value of potential business. Set a time limit for the meeting. Monitor and take notes for later feedback.

> **1:1** Ask your student to read about two corporate events (see Group A on page 118). Read about and be ready to present the other two corporate events to your student (see Group B on page 129). Hold the meeting and discuss the options between yourselves, following the same agenda as outlined in 5. Ask your student to present your recommendations.

Making conversation

In this section, students listen to two recordings of businesspeople socializing at two of the events discussed in the previous meeting – the Royal Yacht Britannia and a Wimbledon tennis match. They focus on and practise the functional language used in the recordings. Students then play a game in order to say avoid saying no. Next, students listen to two further recordings of businesspeople socializing at the Tate Modern and the British Grand Prix. They focus on some of the useful expressions used when making general conversation. They then practise giving and receiving compliments. The unit ends with a fluency activity in which students practise keeping up a conversation.

1 🔊 **1.02–1.03** Lead in to this section by asking students how they rate themselves as socializers on a scale of 1–5. Ask if they are generally relaxed at corporate parties and events, or tense and a bit insecure.

Conversation 1
Get students to read through the questions for conversation 1 first. With weaker students, ask the following gist questions and play the recording through once to check: *Where are the speakers?* (on the Royal Yacht Britannia), *How do they know each other?* (they met at a conference), *What is the tone of their conversation?* (friendly).

Play the recording and get students to note down their answers to a–e. If necessary, play the recording again, pausing to allow students to listen for anything they missed. Students check their answers in pairs and then as a whole class.

ANSWERS
a They were all at a dinner together at a conference in Riyadh.
b Not at all. Be my guest.
c She complains about the music.
d You're joking!, You're kidding!
e 1 Have we met …
   2 It's not like …
   3 I thought I …
   4 It's all coming …
   5 I seem to …

Conversation 2
Give students time to read through the questions for conversation 2. Check they can paraphrase *warm, amicable, cordial, cool, strained* and *frosty*. For weaker students, ask the following gist question and play the recording through once to check: *What is the main mistake made by Mr Thompson's marketing staff?* (they told him Mr Ishida likes tennis when he in fact never watches it). Repeat the same procedure as for conversation 1.

Focus student's attention on the listening scripts on page 139. Get students to practise some of this language by writing cues on the board and getting students to complete the expressions, e.g. *Have we …?, It's not like me to …, I thought I … / I hear …, I understand …, I see ….* Highlight the intonation by marking the correct intonation over the sentence.

ANSWERS
a strained
b to introduce a change of topic
c paying Mr Ishida a compliment
d 1 I hear you're quite a tennis fan.
   2 I understand the Japanese are world table tennis champions.
   3 I see the Nikkei's looking strong. That must be good news for you.
e No

🔊 **1.02**
Conversation 1
A: Hi, mind if I join you?
B: Er, not at all. Be my guest.
A: Only if I have to sit through 'Rule Britannia' by the Band of the Royal Scots Dragoon Guards once more, I think I'll scream.
B: And I thought you Americans were supposed to like all of that traditional British stuff.
A: Yeah, well, you can have too much of a good thing. Thought I'd come out here and enjoy the view. I must say, though, it was an excellent lunch. Fabulous ship too.
B: Yes, isn't it? I'm James McRae, by the way. BP, engineering division.
A: Hello, James. I'm …
B: Helen Keating. Exxon Mobil.
A: Yes, how did you … oh …? Have we met somewhere before?
B: We have indeed, but I obviously failed to make much of an impression.
A: Wait a minute. It's not like me to forget a face. I know – Riyadh. The Petrochemicals Conference. I thought I recognized you.

14 01 BUSINESS OR PLEASURE?

BUSINESS COMMUNICATION

B: As matter of fact, we had dinner together.
A: You're kidding! Now, I think I would have remembered that.
B: Well, there were rather a lot of us in the group. At least 40. I don't think we actually spoke.
A: Aha. Okay. Yes, it's all coming back to me now. I seem to remember spending most of the evening trying to avoid some annoying little guy called Alan.
B: Alan Sullivan. My boss.
A: Oops! I'm sorry. I didn't mean to …
B: No problem. He's not my favourite person either. Anyway, Helen, looks like we've got the best part of the Royal Yacht to ourselves this afternoon. How about another drink?
A: Okay. Why not?

🔘 1.03
Conversation 2
A: So, Mr Ishida, let me freshen your glass.
B: Thank you. I'm fine.
A: Some more strawberries, then, perhaps?
B: Er, not at the moment, thank you.
A: I am sorry about this weather. Typical English summer, I'm afraid. The forecast did say we might have showers. But I'm sure it'll blow over in half an hour or so. So, how are you enjoying the match?
B: Ah, very entertaining, I'm sure …
A: Good. Splendid … So, tell me, have you been to one of these big tournaments before? The American Open perhaps?
B: Ah, no, I haven't.
A: Ah. But I hear you're quite a tennis fan, though.
B: Er, not really. In fact, I never watch tennis normally.
A: Oh, … I see. My marketing people must have made a mistake.
B: Maybe they meant table tennis. I used to play for my university in Tokyo – many years ago.
A: Table tennis! Ah, yes. I understand the Japanese are world table tennis champions, isn't that right?
B: As a matter of fact, that's the Chinese.
A: Ah, yes, of course … Erm, so, do you still play?
B: Not any more. Much too old for running around now.
A: Oh, I'm sure that's not true.
B: I assure you it is true, Mr Thompson. Bad heart, you see. Doctor's orders.
A: Oh, right. Sorry. Erm, … I see the Nikkei's looking strong. That must be good news for you.
B: Not especially. It makes our exports more expensive.
A: The world economy is still really unpredictable, don't you think?
B: It may seem that way for now, but I'm still hoping for some stability in the markets.
A: Ah, well, I suppose, er … Oh, look, the rain's stopped! Yes, the players are coming back on. Excellent. So, shall we return to our seats?
C: Quiet, please. Nadal to serve. Nadal leads by three games to two and by two sets to love.

> **Language links**
>
> Direct students to the *Phrase bank* in the *Language links* section on page 12 for more practice of useful expressions for making conversation, together with some small talk tips.

2 Ask the following questions as a lead-in: *What effect does saying 'no' have in your language? Is it acceptable, or considered over-direct? What is your experience of the way native speakers use 'no'? Have you noticed a difference between UK and US speakers?* Point out that when you do not know someone well, 'no' is too direct in British English, whereas this can be less of a problem in American English.

Before playing the game, give students a few minutes to write down their six sentences. Monitor and be ready to help weaker students with examples/ideas. Focus students' attention on the useful expressions in the box. Explain that these are all alternatives to saying no. Model the intonation of each of the expressions and get students to repeat, checking they don't sound flat/uncommunicative.

Demonstrate the game with a confident student first. Divide the class into pairs and get them to swap their lists of statements. Students play the game, working with a new partner when someone loses. Monitor and take feedback notes.

Get students to give their feedback on the task. Ask how successful they were in avoiding saying no and how they felt, e.g. awkward? quite confident? Then give feedback on overall fluency before highlighting any important or common errors.

> **1:1** Before the lesson, write down six false statements about yourself in order to play the no-no game with your student.

3 🔘 1.04–1.05 Before playing the recording, remind students of the other two corporate events – the Grand Prix and a visit to the Tate Modern – and explain that these are the contexts for the following two recordings.

Conversation 1
Check that students know what the Turner prize is. (The controversial prize awarded in the field of modern/contemporary art. Radical prize winners have included a sculpture which was a pile of bricks! Many people are not convinced this is art.) Check/Pre-teach: *laundry, heap, dying to do something*.

Use the first question as a pre-listening question. Play the recording once and let students compare their answers. Elicit the difference in attitude between Fiona and Alistair (neither of them is enjoying the exhibition but Fiona says what she thinks and is somewhat sarcastic; Alistair wants to give a good impression and is more tolerant).

Ask students to read questions b–e and answer them as far as they can from memory. Play the recording again and allow students to complete their answers. Ask students to check their answers in pairs before checking answers with the class. Now ask students to work in pairs to discuss their answers to question f.

01 BUSINESS OR PLEASURE? 15

BUSINESS COMMUNICATION

SUGGESTED ANSWERS

a posh, irritating, she's fussy, he's long-suffering
b 1 Please call me Dan.
  2 A pleasure to meet you both at last.
  3 Julian's mentioned your name, of course.
  4 You don't mind me calling you Fiona, do you?
c 1 saying   2 discussing
  3 talking   4 wondering
  5 trying
d He wants to speak to him in private.
e Don't go away.
  Would you excuse me a moment?
  I'll be right back.
  I'll catch you later.

Conversation 2

Again, use the first question as a pre-listening question. Play the recording once and elicit the answer. Ask students to read questions b–d and answer them from memory. Play the recording a second time and allow students to complete their answers. Allow students to check in pairs and then check answers with the whole class.

As a follow-up activity, refer students to the listening scripts of conversations 1 and 2 on pages 139–140. Play the recording again while students listen and follow the listening scripts. Get them to focus in particular on the stress and intonation of the language. Write some of the expressions on the board and have students mark in the stress and intonation.

ANSWERS

a No
b Talking of races, how's the South African bid going?
c 1 Glad you could make it.
  2 I wouldn't have missed it for the world.
  3 There's someone I'd like you to meet.
  4 Can't have you standing there with an empty glass.
  5 So, who's this person you wanted me to meet?
  6 I see you two know each other already.
  7 I'll leave you two to chat. See you later.
d They used to have a close friendship.

1.04
Conversation 1

A: Alistair, we've been here nearly three hours! Can't we just make our excuses and go? You know how I hate these things.
B: Look, Fiona, I'm not enjoying myself any more than you are, but this is business. Besides, I need to speak to Julian about this Internet advertising idea of his.
A: Oh, all right. Where is Julian, anyway? We haven't seen him all evening …
C: Hello! You must be Julian's guests. I don't think we've met. I'm Dan Wilson, Creative Director at JJK Advertising. I work with Julian.
B: Ah, pleased to meet you, Mr Wilson. No, we've not met. Julian's mentioned your name, of course. Alistair Hamilton. And this is my wife, Fiona.
C: A pleasure to meet you both at last. And please call me Dan.
A: We were just wondering what this pile of dirty laundry was doing in the middle of an art gallery.
B: Fiona!
C: So, you're not a fan of contemporary art then, Fiona – you don't mind me calling you Fiona, do you? Actually, this, er, 'dirty laundry', as you call it, came second in this year's Turner Prize, believe it or not.
A: Doesn't surprise me in the least, but, er, still just looks like dirty laundry to me, I'm afraid.
C: Well, yes, but I don't think that's what the artist would call it.
A: What does he call it, then?
C: Erm, I'm not sure. I'll check the catalogue for you … Here we are – erm, exhibit 12, oh, 'Dirty Laundry'.
A: What did I tell you?
C: Yes, quite. Erm, Alistair, I wonder if we could have a word? Julian tells me you're not very happy with the new Internet campaign.
B: Er, yes. Would you excuse us a moment, Fiona? Dan and I need to talk.
A: Oh, don't mind me. There's a heap of broken glass in the room next door I'm just dying to see.
B: Er, right. Well, I'll catch you later, then … Now, look, Dan, the thing is …

1.05
Conversation 2

A: Ricardo! Glad you could make it.
B: Hello, Tom. I wouldn't have missed it for the world. It's not every day I get invited to something like this. I hear Webber's out, so it should be a good race.
A: Yes, it certainly evens things up a bit with Red Bull down to one car. Talking of races, how's the South African bid going? I heard it was just between you and Swedish Steel now.
B: Hm, yes, the negotiations are still going on, but we're hopeful. I don't think the Swedes can beat us on price.
A: Well, let me know how it goes. We'd be happy to organize the transportation if you need it. We'd do you a good deal.
B: Sure, I'll certainly keep you in mind if we win the contract.
A: Great … Ricardo, there's someone I'd like you to meet.
B: Oh, really?
A: Yes, but first let me get you something to drink. Can't have you standing there with an empty glass. What can I get you?
B: Just mineral water for now, thanks.
A: Oh, all right … Here you go.
B: Thanks. So, who's this person you wanted me to meet?
A: Ah, yes … Oh, here she is now. Élise, this is Ricardo Piquet. Ricardo, Élise de Cadenet. Élise is …
C: Hello, Ricardo. Long time no see. What is it, five years?
B: Hello, Élise. Must be five at least. You haven't changed a bit.
C: Neither have you!
A: Ah, I see you two know each other already.

16 01 BUSINESS OR PLEASURE?

BUSINESS COMMUNICATION

C: Ricardo and I go back a long way, Tom.
B: Yes, actually, we first met in Monaco – at the Grand Prix, funnily enough … So, Élise, last I heard you got married.
C: That's right. In fact we only just got back from our honeymoon last month. But now it's back to work. It's been really hectic setting up this new business in Biarritz.
A: Er, well, I'll leave you two to chat. See you later. Don't forget the race starts at three.
B: Yes, see you later, Tom. So, Élise, how about something to drink?
C: Mm, sounds good. I'll have whatever you're having.

Language links

Direct students to the *Language links* section on pages 11–12 for more on making conversation.

4 Tell students they are going to play a light-hearted game, practising giving and receiving compliments. Give students time to think of compliments they could pay their partner. With weaker students, brainstorm ideas, e.g. colours/style of clothes/hair, personality traits, attractive belongings, abilities/skills, and elicit relevant examples.

Focus attention on the useful expressions in the box and check stress and intonation. Ask two confident students to demonstrate the game first. Then divide the class into pairs, getting students to work with a new partner if appropriate. Set a time limit of about two minutes and ask students to play the game. Elicit examples of some of the compliments students gave or received.

1:1 Before the lesson, prepare a list of compliments that you can pay your student in order to play the mutual appreciation game with them.

5 Check/Pre-teach *flattery* and get students to read the questions. Do the activity as a whole-class discussion or, with larger classes, divide students into groups. If appropriate, ask follow-up questions, e.g. *How genuine do you think compliments are when given at work? Would you compliment your boss? What 'rules' on giving compliments would you give to a visitor to your country?* Point out that in Britain, it is not acceptable for a man to compliment a woman on what she is wearing unless they are close friends or longstanding colleagues. It is fine for a woman to compliment another woman on the way she looks, or to comment in a neutral way on a man's appearance.

6 Ask students if they have heard of Dale Carnegie's famous book *How to win friends and influence people*. Carnegie's advice is to make people feel important and appreciated. (The implication for business is that financial success has as much to do with these people skills as with professional knowledge.) Elicit students' reaction to the statement from the book.

Divide the class into AB pairs. Ask them to select their three 'hot buttons'. Check with the A students that they understand that they have to initiate the questions and

with the B students that they have to appear unenthusiastic apart from when talking about their 'hot buttons'.

Focus attention on the conversation starters and give the A students a short time to formulate some ideas. With weaker students, check they know how they can continue each question by eliciting examples as a whole class.

Ask students to play the game. Monitor and take feedback notes, but don't give feedback at this point. Ask students to evaluate how successful they were at keeping the conversation going. Ask which topics students found easiest to talk about and why.

Give feedback on overall fluency and how successful students were at keeping the conversation going. Then give feedback on any important or common errors.

1:1 If possible, record your conversation. This will allow you to participate in the activity without the distraction of recording your student's mistakes. Afterwards, listen to the recording together, pausing to identify any mistakes and work on reformulating them into good language.

Language links

Direct students to the *Language links* section on pages 11–12 for further explanation of the use of tenses, and exercises to practise them.

Language links

ANSWERS

Vocabulary
Small talk
1 a, d, c, e, g, j, i, k, f, b, m, h, l
2 a Incidentally, … b Talking of … c By the way, …
  d Before I forget, … e That reminds me, …
  f On the subject of …
3 a Not yet, no. b No problem. c No, me neither. d Pity.
  e Me too. f Are you kidding?

Grammar
Tense review
1 1b 2c 3c 4a 5b 6a 7a 8b 9b 10a
2 1 know 2 is fast approaching 3 have not made
  4 have already come forward 5 are currently being considered 6 will have to 7 want 8 had 9 meant
  10 were walking 11 was 12 were still complaining
  13 had planned 14 I've been wondering 15 doesn't seem 16 do think 17 makes 18 think 19 I've scheduled 20 I'll speak

Phrase bank
Making conversation
1 start a, e 2 bring b, k 3 compliment f, g
4 contradict i, l 5 change h, j 6 break c, d

01 BUSINESS OR PLEASURE? 17

02 Information exchange

Learning objectives

This unit is the first to focus on the language of meetings. Many business English students will attend meetings in English with native and non-native speakers of English. Students may need to draw on a range of language and skills to ensure a successful meeting, so the sequence of units on meetings provides a wide range of language input and encourages students to develop key communication skills.

Students start with a discussion of their personal experiences of business meetings and read a joke which has been circulated on the web. They focus on buzzwords and play a language game to practise these. They then study common business collocations.

Students consider how direct and indirect different cultures are. They do an exercise matching vague language extracts from a meeting with their blunt equivalents. They then listen to and summarize the meeting, and do fluency practice paraphrasing some indirect statements.

In the next section, students do a listening task in which they try and spot discrepancies, followed by a fluency task with the same aim. Students do a further listening task and practise rephrasing statements. They do an exercise to practise opposites, and then focus on conditionals.

In the next section, students study a number of extracts from meetings in order to identify the missing word in a number of key phrases, and then listen to a recording in order to check their answers. They do further practice using meeting phrases.

In the final section, they participate in a fluency activity. Students read different sets of information, then introduce some radical proposals at a meeting. The lesson concludes with students completing a memo summarizing the conclusions of the meeting.

The grammatical focus is on conditional forms and the lexical focus is on the language of meetings.

Digital resources: Unit 2

Online Workbook; In company interviews Units 1–2 and worksheet; Extension worksheets; Glossary; Phrase bank; Student's Book answer key; Student's Book listening script; Fast-track map

---

1:1 This unit focuses on meetings. Before you begin, discuss with your student the kind of meetings they usually attend. Find out as much as you can about the meetings.

In this first section, students think about their own involvement in meetings. They read a joke which has been circulated on the web, and focus on a range of buzzwords. They do an exercise to practise some useful collocations.

Warm-up

Check that students understand the expression *Murphy's Law* (the principle that if something can possibly go wrong, it will). Find out reactions to the quotation.

1 Ask: *What exactly is a meeting?* and elicit ideas from students, e.g. some people feel that informal discussions with colleagues count as meetings; others think that meetings should always have an agenda and finish with an action plan.

2 Find out if anyone has seen this joke circulated on the web. You may need to look at some of the vocabulary, such as: *to gossip, to flirt, a nap, offload*.

3 Be ready to provide some examples of buzzwords in business, such as: *credit crunch, mindset*. Ask students to tell you what the buzzwords are in their field.

4 Do the first word with all students as an example. Then, students can work in pairs to complete the task.

ANSWERS
1 mindset   2 core competencies   3 paradigm shift
4 proactive   5 synergize   6 outside the box   7 drill down
8 buy-in   9 the next level   10 reality check   11 the bottom line
12 the big picture   13 benchmark   14 ramp up
15 empowerment

5 1.06 Ask students to select their bingo card from page 119 ready for the game.

1.06

A: Okay, people. Let's get the ball rolling. Well, you've all seen the latest figures and I don't need to tell you they're not good. It's clearly time for a reality check, ladies and gentlemen. This division is about to go under if we don't change our attitude and fast. What we need is a complete change of mindset. We need to synergize and take a much more proactive approach to product development. The same tired old ideas simply won't work any more. If we always do what we've always done, then we'll always get what we've always got. And what got us where we are won't get us where we're going.

B: I'm sorry?

---

18   02 INFORMATION EXCHANGE

BUSINESS COMMUNICATION

A: What I mean is we need to be thinking outside the box, maximizing our creativity. Yes, that's right. I'm talking about nothing less than a complete paradigm shift in the management of this company.
B: What's he talking about?
C: I don't know.
A: Okay, the bottom line is: if we don't figure out how to turn this operation around, we have no future in this business. So, let's look at the big picture and then see if we can drill down to the details.
D: Can I just say something, Daryl?
A: Fire away, Kelly.
D: Erm, I don't think we're quite with you.
A: I'm trying to say that it's very important I get your buy-in on this. What we have to do is establish what our core competencies are and then benchmark ourselves against the current market leader. Right now we're struggling just to compete. If we can only learn from our competitors, then we'll be able to upskill our own people, ramp up product development, and start to take this company to the next level.
C: Erm, and you really want our input on this?
A: Yes, Nigel. Change begins at the grassroots in an organization. Empowerment – that's what this is all about.
D: Daryl?
A: Yes, Kelly.
D: Have you ever played buzzword bingo?

6 Write *production margins* and *profit methods* on the board. Ask students to say what is wrong with the expressions and to give the correct collocations. Ask students to continue finding the correct collocations. Then check answers with the class.

Tell students that many of these collocations constitute core business language and they need to ensure they can use them. Check pronunciation of the compounds, highlighting difficult words like: *campaign, budget* and *recruitment*. Get students to mark the correct stress.

> **1:1** Put the words in each column onto different colour cards. This will allow your student to experiment with the collocations by moving the cards around.

ANSWERS
a 1 production methods 2 balance sheets 3 market trends
  4 staff appraisals 5 profit margins 6 distribution channels
b 1 quality control 2 sales projections 3 advertising campaigns
  4 cost cutting 5 supply chains 6 product development
c 1 customer relations 2 recruitment procedures 3 salary reviews
  4 training budgets 5 price setting 6 IT support

7 Ask students to work in pairs. Tell them that they should not use the actual words in the collocations, or any derivatives (for example, they cannot say *supplier* when explaining *supply*) but can use any other words they like.

At the end of the exercise, ask students which collocations are the most important for them to use in their fields.

> **1:1** Take turns with your student to explain these terms. Alternatively, prepare a few examples to go through with your student first, then hand over to the student to create explanations from the remaining collocations.

Making things clear

In this section, students first think about how direct various nationalities are. They then match a set of indirect statements with their more direct equivalents. They listen to an extract from a meeting in order to check their answers and then summarize the meeting. Finally, they paraphrase indirect statements in a more direct way.

1 Give examples of statements in a direct and indirect culture, e.g. *Shut the window./It's a bit cold in here.* Find out what kind of culture students are from. Ask them to do the exercise and then ask if they agree with the suggested answers on page 137.

2 Write these two sentences on the board: *We will be looking at the possibility of downsizing* and *People may lose their jobs*. Ask what the sentences have in common (they both state that people may be made redundant, but the first is indirect and the second is more direct). Ask students which style of expression is preferred in the culture/company where they work and if they have experienced any difficulties in interpreting 'vague' language. Ask students to match the lists of statements. Don't check the answers at this stage.

3 1.07 With weaker groups, check/pre-teach: *dismally, to overreact, innovative, clone, outsourcing*. Tell students they are going to listen to an extract from a meeting to check their answers in 2. Play the recording.

ANSWERS
a 4 b 6 c 2 d 8 e 7 f 3 g 1 h 5

> **1.07**
> A: Right. That brings us on to our main business this morning – the new Quasar Online Gaming System. As you already know, the news is not particularly good. In spite of a considerable investment in design and marketing, I'm sorry to report that the project has not been a complete success.
> B: Not a complete success? What you mean is it's failed – dismally!
> A: Now let's not overreact, Alan. Certainly, it's failed to meet our original expectations. And, yes, technically speaking, we have run into negative profit ...
> B: Negative profit! What do you mean negative profit? You mean we've made a loss – an enormous loss if these figures are anything to go by!

02 INFORMATION EXCHANGE   19

BUSINESS COMMUNICATION

C: Can we come back to the figures later, Alan, if that's okay? First, let's consider why sales are so disappointing. Now, in my view, it's not the product, but the market. I think there's a general lack of consumer confidence.

B: In other words, sales are falling. Look, I'm sorry, Hannah, but you're just looking for excuses. It's obvious that Quasar is simply not innovative enough for today's market.

A: Alan, we leave innovation to companies like Sony and Nintendo. What we do is clone the technology and do it cheaper.

C: Alan, you know we've always been a market-driven organization …

B: Market-driven? What you really mean is we've never had an original idea. I say we need to be developing an innovative new product line …

A: What, when the market's so massively oversupplied? I don't think so. Now is not the time to expand, but to consolidate.

B: So what you're saying is, let's do nothing.

A: No, I'm saying let's consolidate.

B: I see. And what will this 'consolidation' mean in terms of our staff? Redundancies, I suppose.

C: Well, obviously, there will have to be some restructuring of the department.

B: You mean people are going to lose their jobs.

C: It's a possibility, yes. And we may also have to consider outsourcing production to cut costs.

B: In other words, our assembly plant may be closed down too. I can't believe I'm hearing this!

A: Of course, we won't be able to finalise anything today.

B: You mean we'll have to hold another meeting! If we've all still got a job by then, that is.

A: Yes, well, I'm glad you raised that point, Alan.

B: What do you mean?

4 Ask if students wish to hear the recording again before they summarize the meeting. Students can work in pairs to summarize the meeting.

5 Write the four expressions in the box on the board and ask students to mark the main stress. Divide the class into pairs and ask students to read and respond to the vague statements.

> **1:1** Ask your student to read out sentences a–c, and paraphrase each of them in a more direct way. Then, exchange roles for sentences d–f. When you have finished, ask your student to comment on whether he or she is from a direct or a more indirect culture.

Queries and comments

In this section, students get practice in listening for discrepancies and do a roleplay in which they point out information which does not make sense. They listen to another meeting in which a CEO breaks bad news to the board; students formulate the board members' queries and comments from given prompts. They complete exercises on opposites and work on conditional forms.

1 1.08 Write the word *discrepancy* on the board and give these examples to clarify the meaning: *a discrepancy between estimated and actual spending; there was some discrepancy in the statement he gave to the police.*

Check/Pre-teach: *appraisal, to go on about, overspend, confidential.* Note that there is a short pause in each extract to give students the time to discuss the discrepancy. With stronger groups, play the first extract, pausing at the beep, and elicit the discrepancy as a class example. Then play the rest of the recording, pausing at each beep, and ask students to complete the task. Check answers with the class. With weaker groups, play the five extracts through once and ask students to list the main topic of each discussion but do not mention the discrepancy at this stage (a appraisals; b salary increases; c project budget and schedule; d main markets; e bringing in an outside consultant). Then play the recording again, pausing to allow students to point out the discrepancies.

ANSWERS
1 The meeting is an hour and a half long, not an hour.
2 The company pays employees twice as much as its competitors, not three times.
3 The project was supposed to take 16 weeks, not three months.
4 He said the company isn't doing well in the Far East, yet China is its biggest market.
5 He said he doesn't want to bring in people from outside the company but is thinking of bringing in his golf partner to help.

1.08
Meeting 1
A: Right, I'm allowing an hour and a half for this meeting. Kate is going to fill us in on how the appraisals went. That'll take about a quarter of an hour or so. So that only gives us 45 minutes to deal with everything else. We'd better get started.
B: Sorry, I thought we had an hour and a half.
A: What? Oh, yeah, sorry. We've got 75 minutes, haven't we? Still, there's a lot to get through.

Meeting 2
A: Look, it's no good going on about pay rises. We pay nearly twice what most of our competitors do. And I really don't see how people can expect another salary increase this year, when they're already earning three times the average rate.
B: Hang on a second. You said we pay twice as much, not three times.
A: Hmm? Oh, all right, twice as much, then. It's still a lot more than everybody else.

Meeting 3
A: You know as well as I do that this project was supposed to take sixteen weeks. And this isn't the first time we've run over budget, is it? I mean a 20% overspend is pretty serious. And surely three months was sufficient time to complete the project.

BUSINESS COMMUNICATION

B: Just a minute. I thought you said 16 weeks, not three months.
A: Okay, okay, that's four months, then. But you've taken nearly six.

Meeting 4

A: Frankly, with the Asian economic situation the way it is and both the euro and the dollar going up and down, we're not doing well in the Far East. South America is where we should be concentrating our efforts. As a matter of fact, Brazil is now our second biggest market after China.
B: Hold on. Didn't you just say we're not doing well in the Far East?
A: Well, I meant apart from China, obviously! China's always been a huge market for tobacco products.

Meeting 5

A: I'm sorry, but I don't want us bringing in people from outside the company to sort this problem out. There's a lot of highly confidential information on our intranet. And we should really be able to deal with this ourselves. There's a guy I play golf with who runs his own consultancy. He's offered to help us out.
B: Wait a moment. You just said you didn't want to bring in people from outside the company.
A: Erm, well, what I mean is I don't want just anybody. This guy's different. I've known him for years.

2 Some students are quite reticent to point out discrepancies to other speakers, so review polite ways of doing this: *Sorry, I thought you said …, Hold on a second, didn't you just say …?, Wait a minute. You just said …, didn't you?*

Divide the class into AB pairs. Refer the A students to page 119 and the B students to page 128. Give students time to read their reports. Help as necessary.

Model the activity by asking one student to read the first few lines of their report and getting the class to highlight the discrepancy. Refer students to the *Useful language* boxes after each role card.

Monitor and take feedback notes. If students fail to spot all seven discrepancies, ask them to repeat the task. Give feedback on how well students handled the interruptions and on overall fluency, before highlighting any important or common language errors.

1:1 Put the useful language for pointing out discrepancies on cards (*Sorry, I thought you said … etc*). Ask your student to read out these expressions in order to practise the intonation and stress. Then ask your student to turn to page 119 and read Speaker A's text aloud – you should interrupt whenever there is a discrepancy in order to model the activity. Then, turn to page 128 and read out Speaker B's text. This time, your student should try to point out the seven discrepancies.

3 1.09 To lead in to the activity, ask students to brainstorm the type of news the CEO could be about to give. With weaker classes, ask students to skim the extract and elicit examples of the bad news given by the CEO, e.g. disappointing sales figures, high production costs, inefficient distributors. With weaker groups, check/pre-teach: *projection, quarter (three months), in a row, to pick up, to break even, to phase out, drastic, layoff, to slide (into debt), to implement, a volatile market*.

Focus attention on the key words and the example and establish the kind of changes students need to make – tense, question word order, adding prepositions and pronouns, etc. Point out that there are both questions and comments and that students need to pay attention to the punctuation given with the key words. Then play the extract for students to compare their answers.

ANSWERS

b Are you suggesting we introduce price cuts?
c Surely you're not saying it's time to phase them out!
d Does this mean we should be investing more in new technology?
e Are you telling us there could be lay-offs?
f You mean some kind of job-share scheme?
g So you're saying we should be spending more on R&D.
h Does this mean you're thinking of centralizing distribution?
i I hope you're not suggesting the situation is hopeless.

1.09

A: Okay, everyone. It's bad news, I'm afraid. As you may have heard, the latest European sales figures are looking extremely disappointing.
B: Are you saying they've fallen short of projections again?
A: I'm afraid so. In fact, we may be 30% down. Now, this will be the third quarter in a row we've missed our targets and, frankly, unless things pick up considerably next quarter, we may have to rethink our whole pricing strategy.
C: Are you suggesting we introduce price cuts?
A: If we still can, Anna. Certainly if we'd done that a year ago, it might have stimulated demand. But do it now and we may end up running at a loss. As you know, we're barely breaking even on some of our product lines as it is.
D: Surely you're not saying it's time to phase them out!
A: No, no, of course not. At least, not yet. But what I am saying is that we need to keep production costs down somehow if we want to remain competitive.
B: Does this mean we should be investing more in new technology?
A: If only it was that simple, Erik. But right now we're not really in a position to invest in anything, even if we wanted to. No, I'm afraid the situation calls for more drastic action. It's clearly time for a major restructuring.
D: Are you telling us there could be lay-offs?
A: I don't see how we can avoid it, James – unless, of course, we can get some of our people to accept reduced hours.
C: You mean some kind of job-share scheme?

02 INFORMATION EXCHANGE   21

BUSINESS COMMUNICATION

A: Yes, either that or introduce a four-day week – providing the unions don't oppose it. Of course, it's not just a question of costs. It's also a question of product. The fact is, better products are coming onto the market all the time.

D: So you're saying we should be spending more on R&D.

A: As I've said, capital investment is no longer an option for us. Pour any more money into R&D and we'll simply slide further into debt. And then there are all the problems we've been having with our overseas distributors.

B: Does this mean you're thinking of centralising distribution?

A: Well, that's one option, yes. But even if we decided to do that, and it's a big if, it would take time to implement – time we simply don't have. As you know, our share price has fallen to an all-time low of just 85 cents. And I wouldn't be surprised if, by our next meeting, it's fallen even further. The fact is, we're selling old products at inflated prices in a volatile market through inefficient distributors.

D: I hope you're not suggesting the situation is hopeless.

A: Well, let's put it this way: we've cancelled the summer party!

4 Students can work in pairs or individually to discuss these opposites. Check answers with the class.

SUGGESTED ANSWERS

a encouraging figures   b exceed projections   c reach our targets
d run at a profit   e phase them in   f the unions approve it
g crawl out of debt   h domestic distributors   i reduced prices
j stable markets

5 With weaker classes, do a short review of the forms used in each clause with present and past conditionals. Students often make mistakes with the tense in the *if*-clause. Students re-read the extract and answer questions a–f. Ask students to compare their answers before checking with the whole class. Note that in addition to the conditional sentences, there are two examples of phrases in which one speaker answers the previous speaker's question conditionally: *If we still can, Anna* and *If only it was that simple, Erik*. As a follow-up task, ask students to ask and answer questions with a partner using the cues: *What would you do if ...?* and *What would you have done if ...?*

ANSWERS

a nine   b unless, and, providing   c If we'd done that a year ago, it might have stimulated demand.   d It shows that the decision is unlikely.   e I wish it was that simple.   f We don't want to invest in anything.

Language links

Direct students to the *Language links* section on pages 18–19 for further explanation of the use of conditionals, and an exercise to practise them.

The language of meetings

In this section, students do a vocabulary exercise and listen to meeting extracts, focusing on the expressions used. They then do a further vocabulary exercise.

1 Before students start the exercise, write the word *meeting* on the board and ask students to brainstorm types of meeting. Ask students to check how many examples they were able to predict from the meetings listed in 1. Students then complete the extracts a–h with the missing word. Don't check answers at this stage.

Language links

Direct students to the *Language links* section on page 18 for more on the language of meetings and, in particular, metaphorical language and idiomatic expressions.

2 1.10 Play the recording for students to check their answers. Focus attention on the short introductory words *Look, ..., Well, ..., Right ..., Now, ...* and ask what effect they have (they can make what the speaker is saying more forceful or show that what follows is a serious point).

ANSWERS

a position   b question   c option   d answer   e problem
f point   g situation   h fact

1.10

a
A: Right. Basically, the position is this: the contract is ours if we want it.
B: But we're not in a position to take on another project right now, are we?
A: I know. Jan, what's your position on this?

b
A: Look, it's not just a question of software, Alessandro.
B: Of course not. It's also a question of hardware. The entire system needs upgrading.
A: But that's out of the question. We can't afford that kind of capital outlay.

c
A: Sales are down. One option would obviously be to cut our prices.
B: That's no longer an option for us. We're barely breaking even as it is.
A: Well, then we've no option but to rethink our whole marketing strategy.

d
A: Well, there's no easy answer to this, but how about voluntary redundancy?
B: I don't think that's the answer, but maybe we could reduce people's hours.
A: That might have been the answer if we didn't already have a strike on our hands!

e
A: Now, let's not make a problem out of this. What if we just pulled out of Sudan?

B: Well, I've no problem with that, but our partners won't be happy.
A: No, but that's not our problem, is it? The political situation is just too unstable.

f
A: I'll get straight to the point. We're getting too many customer complaints.
B: I agree with you. But the point is we don't have the staff to deal with them.
A: That's beside the point. We shouldn't be getting them in the first place!

g
A: I'm afraid the situation is serious. And if the press get hold of the story, …
B: Look, we'll deal with that situation if and when it arises. Let's not panic just yet.
A: You're right. What this situation calls for is calm and careful planning.

h
A: The fact is, we're simply not spending enough on R&D.
B: As a matter of fact, we've doubled our R&D budget this year.
C: That may be so, but the fact remains we're losing our technological lead.

3 Students complete this activity individually or in pairs.

ANSWERS	
a opinion – I disagree!	b question – That's irrelevant!
c view – What about me?	d point – Good point!
e option – That's unimportant!	f idea – You're wrong!

> **Language links**
>
> Direct students to the *Phrase bank* in the *Language links* section on page 19 for more on useful expressions for debating issues in meetings and discussions.

Breaking the bad news

In this final section, students take part in a fluency activity by roleplaying an interdepartmental meeting.

1 Introduce the topic by asking students to define a 'hostile' takeover (one in which the company that is taken over is not happy about the acquisition). Set the scene by telling students that their company has been taken over by a competitor and everyone is waiting to find out what changes will be implemented by the new board. Tell students that they will be expected to support changes that the board would like to implement and to present them in a positive way. Pre-teach: *feng shui*.

Divide the class into ABCs. Tell students to study the proposals on the following pages: As on page 118, Bs on page 128 and Cs on page 133 and prepare for the meeting.

2 Remind students that they will need to present the proposals in a positive way and that they should discuss potential objections and decide how best to counter them. Give students time to discuss each aspect of the proposals.

Explain that while each group presents their proposals, the rest of the class should take the part of the company staff and raise queries and objections. It is the job of the presenters to deal with these as positively as possible and also to note comments and suggestions for the follow-up report. Review the useful language in the box.

Set a 30-minute time limit for the meeting. Draw up an agenda, so students know the order of the proposals. Appoint one student as the chairperson. Monitor and take notes.

3 After the meeting, give adequate time for students to complete the memos.

> **1:1** Ask your student to choose which topic they would like to present: work environment, travel budget or language training, and focus them on that information at the back of the book (Speaker A, page 118; Speaker B, page 128; or Speaker C, page 133). Give your student time to prepare. When your student is ready, ask them to announce the bad news in a mini-presentation. Set an approximate time for the activity, such as 10–15 minutes.

> **Language links**
>
> **ANSWERS**
> **Vocabulary**
> **Meetings**
> Metaphor: discussion is a journey
> 1 nearer, getting there, on the right track, a long way to go, going round in circles, making good progress, got sidetracked, returning to, go back to, getting ahead of, got as far as, getting very far, drifted, away, heading, wandered away from, coming to, covered a lot of ground, as far as we can go, come this far
>
> Idiomatic expressions
> 2 deleted words – a guess b much c sit d speaking
>   e each f so g responses h view i couldn't j No and yes k can't l spare m on n taken o for
>   p meaning q a point
> 3 1 a, c, g, l 2 d, h, p 3 e, k, n 4 o 5 f, i, m 6 b, j, q
>
> **Grammar**
> **Conditionals**
> b 3 c 3 d 2 e 1 f 3 g 2 h 3 i 3
>
> **Phrase bank**
> **Debating issues**
> a point b question c position d fact e option f time

03 Rapport

Learning objectives

This unit is about rapport in business and how it can be used.

Students begin by considering the strategies or techniques they can use to build rapport with the people they do business with. They then read and discuss an article outlining five top tips for building rapport.

Students look at two photographs and analyse the body language of the people. They then listen to a conversation between a director from a head office in the US and an HR manager of a subsidiary in southern Europe about a new teleworking policy, and consider why the two fail to establish rapport.

Students read a checklist from a training manual and complete the gaps. They then listen to a second conversation, which features the same people as the first, only this time there is a successful outcome. Students consider the differences between the two conversations and how rapport is established. Finally, students take part in two roleplays to practise establishing rapport.

Digital resources: Unit 3

Online Workbook; Extension worksheets; Glossary; Student's Book answer key; Student's Book listening script; Fast-track map

Warm-up

Write the word *rapport* on the board and ask students if they know how to pronounce it. Ask students if they can think of any useful collocations, such as: *to create/establish rapport with someone*; *have a good/poor rapport with someone*.

1 Focus students' attention on the cartoon and ask them to consider their answers to the questions. Elicit ideas.

ANSWER
He is trying to build rapport by looking, speaking and behaving like a teenager. He has gone too far and become so ridiculous that he is likely to alienate the teenager.

2 Put students in groups in order to brainstorm a list of answers to the question.

3 Ask students to read the web article and decide on a one-word title for each tip. When students have finished reading, elicit some suggested titles for each paragraph. Ask students to explain their choices and, if possible, agree as a class on each title.

Explain any challenging vocabulary, such as: *to set (something) aside, emotional intelligence, empathy, accentuate, in the long run, synchronize*. Then ask students to check the list of ideas they produced in 2 and read the article again carefully to see if they predicted any of the techniques.

SAMPLE ANSWERS
1 Basics   2 Appearance   3 Empathy (or Awareness)
4 Connection   5 Mirroring (or Matching)

4 Ask students to work with a partner and describe the body language in the photographs. Elicit which of the five techniques in 3 are being used.

ANSWER
Techniques 1, 2 and 5

5 🔘 **1.11** Explain to students that they will hear a conversation between a director from a head office in the US and an HR manager of a subsidiary in southern Europe about a new teleworking policy. Ask students to read the questions. Encourage them to take notes during the listening, and then discuss their answers with a partner.

SUGGESTED ANSWERS
a Jacob speaks loudly and aggressively in quick bursts. His voice is low and husky. Helena speaks quietly and hesitantly. Her voice is soft and high.
b Jacob is an older man, probably conservatively dressed. He is tense and unsmiling, and does not make much eye contact. His body language is closed or aggressive, with crossed arms. Helena is a younger woman, perhaps more informally dressed. She is intimidated by Jacob so her body language is closed, nervous and restricted, hands and feet together.

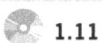

🔘 1.11

A: Come in, sit down. It's, um, Helena, isn't it? Jacob Sanders. I think we already met.
B: Erm, thank you. Yes, in Chicago, but it was, erm, several years ago. Did you erm, did you have a good flight?
A: Yeah. Well, Helena, you know why I'm here. We want to get this teleworking policy implemented as soon as possible.
B: Yes, well … would you like some coffee or tea?
A: No, I'm good to go.
B: Erm … well, as you know I, erm, I spoke to Harry Stross about the special circumstances here, and …
A: Harry's just transferred to South America, actually. Look, Ellen, um, Helena, I won't beat about the bush, this is a global policy. Head Office don't like exceptions, and it's my job to make sure that we don't have any.
B: I understand. Erm, it's just that people here don't really like the idea of working from home. And erm, not having their own office any more. It's quite upsetting for people who've been working here for years and years.

PEOPLE SKILLS

A: So which part of the policy is it they don't understand? I mean, it's not as if they were losing their jobs! We just want them to work from home three days a week. Most folks in the States are really happy with it.
B: It's just that …
A: I'm sorry?
B: Oh, erm, nothing.

6 🔘 **1.11** Ask students to read the questions, which focus on the content of the conversation. Play the recording a second time. Check students' answers. Then ask students to comment on the discussion.

ANSWERS
a Jacob is keen to implement the new policy without question. He feels Helena is not important enough to need to remember her name. Helena feels the new policy does not take her staff's special circumstances into account. She feels Jacob is unsympathetic and impatient.
b They fail to build rapport because neither of them is willing or able to make concessions and move towards the other's communication style.

7 Write *matching and mirroring* on the board and check that students know what this rapport-building technique is. (Students read about it in the article in 3.) Tell students that they are going to read a checklist from a training manual. Before reading, ask them if they can predict any points that the checklist may contain. Check also that students know the following words: *husky, staccato, gesture, expansive, pace, lead, posture*. Ask students to read the checklist and check their predictions. Students then read it again and insert the missing words.

ANSWERS
1 small 2 restricted 3 crossed 4 subtle 5 deep 6 husky
7 staccato 8 compromise 9 mirroring 10 outcome

1:1 As an alternative, before doing the gap-fill, write the ten vocabulary items in the box on small cards. Ask your student to divide the cards into three groups: words they know, words they think they know and words they don't know. Then ask your student to define the words they think they know. Confirm or assist them with the meaning. Then teach the words they don't know.

8 Give students a few moments to read the tips and techniques in 3 and 7 again, and decide how easy it is to use them, and which they might use themselves. Hold a class discussion and ask students to report on which techniques they might find easy or difficult to use, and if they find any of them insincere or manipulative.

9 🔘 **1.12** Tell students they will hear another recording, a second version of the meeting in 6. Ask them to note down any changes in the way Jacob and Helena communicate, and what they imagine their body language is like this time. Check students' answers. Ask students what they think about this meeting, and Jacob and Helena's behaviour, compared to the first one.

ANSWERS
- Jacob is less aggressive, his voice is progressively less deep and less loud as he starts to mirror Helena.
- Helena is less hesitant, she speaks less quietly, lowers her pitch and speeds up delivery to mirror Jacob.
- Sample answer: Their body language is probably more open, more relaxed and more in sync with each other; there is more eye contact, more facial expression and more smiling.

🔘 **1.12**
A: Hi Helena, Jacob Sanders.
B: Hello.
A: I don't know if you remember me, we met in Chicago.
B: Yes, of course I remember you! It was the conference with that awful team-building day, wasn't it?
A: Yeah; what a disaster that was!
B: Anyway, how are you? Did you have a good flight?
A: Not too bad, thank you. But I have to say, the Atlantic seems to get wider every time I cross it!
B: Yes, it's a long flight, isn't it? Maybe you should consider teleworking!
A: Aha, touché! But you know why I'm here, Helena. We want to get this policy implemented as soon as possible.
B: Yes. Erm, would you like some coffee or tea?
A: Yeah. A cup of coffee would be nice, thank you.
B: So, did Harry Stross fill you in on our special circumstances here?
A: Yeah. But you know Harry's just transferred to South America, don't you? So I'm taking over where he left off. I won't beat about the bush, Helena; this is a global policy. Head Office don't like exceptions, and it's my job to make sure that we don't have any.
B: I understand. And let me reassure you on that point, I'm confident that we can bring people round to the idea. It's just that we're going to need a little more time …

10 Explain to students that this roleplay will allow them to practise establishing rapport with a business consultant by trying out some of the techniques in the unit. Student A turns to page 138, and student B turns to page 129 and they read the information for Situation 1. When they are ready, give students about five minutes to perform the roleplay. Monitor and take notes. Repeat these steps for Situation 2. When students have finished the roleplays, ask them to say how well they managed to establish rapport in each case. Finish the lesson by providing language feedback.

1:1 Proceed with your student taking the role of Speaker A for both Situations 1 and 2, and you taking the role of Speaker B.

03 RAPPORT 25

MANAGEMENT SCENARIO A

Culture clash

Learning objectives

This scenario is based on the issue of cultural differences between colleagues in different companies.

Students do pre-viewing tasks, while-viewing tasks and then a post-viewing roleplay.

Students begin by describing their own experience of company culture. They then read a memo about a merger between two companies: Blue Rock and GWA (Global Water Aid). They watch a video in which two employees from these companies – Ed Ryan from Blue Rock and Jack Wright from GWA – meet for the first time. Students consider the differences between the company cultures from different perspectives, such as attitudes to time and dress code. They discuss how the two people in the video might become more 'culturally sensitive' in order to avoid a culture clash.

Students watch a second video and compare how these two employees' attitudes have changed. Finally, students hold a committee meeting to discuss how to help staff adapt to a merger, and evaluate their own performances.

Digital resources: Management Scenario A

In company in action A1–A2 and worksheet; Extension worksheets; Glossary; Student's Book answer key; Student's Book listening script; Fast-track map

Warm-up

Ask students to think about a company they worked for previously, or which they know well. Ask them to describe to their partner something they particularly liked about working there, and something they didn't like at all.

1:1 Ask your student to talk about their experience of travelling abroad and their exposure to different cultures. Find out if they have ever experienced culture shock. If so, where was it? Be prepared to describe experiences of your own to help the conversation along.

1 The first pre-viewing task asks students to consider the area of corporate culture. Go through the questions with the class. Write *relationships*, *attitudes* and *communication styles* on the board and encourage students to focus on company culture in these three areas. Put them in pairs for the discussion. After about five minutes, elicit students' ideas and collate them on the board. Looking at the range of different corporate cultures in the list, ask students which company or type of company they would prefer to work for.

2 Tell students they are going to read a memo from the CEO of Blue Rock about the merger with GWA. Before asking students to read the memo, check/pre-teach: *synergy, sanitation, sustainable, hygiene, to lobby, expertise*. Give students time to read the memo, make notes on their answers and then discuss them with a partner. Go through the answers with the whole class.

ANSWERS

a NGOs (non-governmental organizations) working to develop sustainable solutions to water, sanitation and hygiene problems in the developing world
b to achieve synergies and build a stronger organization with more resources, more expertise and more diverse talents
c to ask everybody to cooperate and make the move go smoothly
d differences in customs and attitudes, for example, relating to time, dress code, power distance, communication style, working methods and administrative procedures, and use of space and resources

3 **A1** Tell students they are going to watch a video of a first meeting between Ed Ryan from Blue Rock and Jack Wright from GWA. Give students time to read the list of cultural differences and check they understand each of them. You may need to give an example of power distance (the number of levels of hierarchy found in an organization. So, for example, a company with 'high' power distance has many levels of staff in the organization). Personal space is the amount of space you need around you to make you feel comfortable; in some cultures, it is normal to stand very close to other people, and even touching them is acceptable.

Play the video. As an introduction to the video, and to illustrate the differences in dress code, you could pause it at the opening scene and elicit a description of how Ed and Jack are dressed. When students have finished the pre-set question, ask them to compare their answers with a partner. Play the video again. Check students know the phrases: *don't stand on ceremony, to uphold, to fit in*.

ANSWER

All are illustrated or referred to except personal space.

A1

Ed: Hi there! I'm Ed Ryan. Welcome to Blue Rock!
Jack: Pleased to meet you, Mr Ryan. I'm Jack Wright, East Africa Operations.
Ed: Good to meet you, Jack. And please, call me Ed. We don't stand on ceremony around here!
Jack: Okay then, Ed.
Ed: I thought we should get to know each other. I'm a program analyst too, so I guess we'll be working together. Join me for a coffee?
Jack: Well, actually it's a bit early. Um, our coffee break is not till 11, and I really need to sort these files out.

26   A CULTURE CLASH

MANAGEMENT SCENARIO

Ed: Oh, I see.
Emma: Morning!
Jack: Morning, Ms Lambert. Er, Mr Ryan.
Ed: Ed.
Emma: Emma Lambert. Pleased to meet you, Mr Ryan.
Ed: That's one very busy woman! Your assistant?
Jack: My boss.
Ed: Oh. So you meeting the Minister today then?
Jack: I'm sorry?
Ed: Relax, I'm only joking! But you don't always dress like that, do you? I mean, we're not-for-profit, we're not selling anything!
Jack: Oh. Well, um, Ms Lambert likes us to dress smartly.
Ed: Huh, well that's management for you. I mean, they may look good but they haven't got a clue, have they?
Jack: Well, I don't know about Blue Rock but I think our management do an excellent job.
Ed: And you wouldn't want to upset management, would you? Anyway, listen, Jack. There's a few of us at Blue Rock go for a working lunch in a restaurant on Fridays. It's sort of half work, half pleasure, so we get back a little late, usually around three. But it's a good chance to exchange ideas and brainstorm problems. We thought you might like to join us?
Jack: Oh, I don't know, I'm supposed to be back at my desk for one forty-five. I don't think Ms Lambert will like the idea.
Ed: Oh, bring her along too. The more, the merrier!
Jack: No, I don't think so. We don't socialize much at GWA.
Ed: Oh dear, oh dear. Not a very happy little organization, then, are we?
Jack: What do you mean? What makes you think you have the right to judge us? You're worried that we take our work more seriously than you do, is that it? Well, at GWA we have a reputation to uphold, and now I have important work to do.
Ed: I was only trying to be friendly. Look, if that's the way you want to play it then fine, don't say I didn't try. If everyone at GWA is like you and your boss, you're going to find it hard to fit in here!

4 Ask students to put the words in the correct order. When they have finished, ask students at random to read out each of the sentences as a quick check. Then, ask them to match each of the phrases with one of the cultural differences in 3. Check answers with the class.

ANSWERS

a	We don't stand on ceremony around here.	power distance
b	That's one very busy woman! Your assistant?	gender roles
c	So, you meeting the Minister today?	dress code
d	Relax, I'm only joking!	attitudes to humour
e	I'm supposed to be back at my desk by one forty-five.	attitudes to time
f	Why don't you bring her along too? The more, the merrier!	attitudes to socializing

5 Ask students to study the slide on cultural sensitivity. The students should then work with a partner to match the beginnings and endings of the phrases on the slide. You may need to clarify the idea of making converts (getting people to agree with you in an 'us against them' situation). Check students' answers by asking individual students to read out each complete phrase.

SUGGESTED ANSWERS
1c   2a   3b   4f   5d   6e

6 Ask students to study the cultural sensitivity checklist on page 123. Put them in pairs to discuss what mistakes Ed and Jack made in this area. Elicit students' ideas.

SAMPLE ANSWERS
- Ed does not seem to understand GWA's culture. In fact, he is not really aware of potential differences with Blue Rock.
- Ed and Jack do not suspend judgement of the other culture. They are quick to judge. For example, Ed says: 'Not a very happy little organization, then, are we?'; Jack says: 'You're worried that we take our work more seriously than you do, is that it?'
- Both Ed and Jack do a similar job. It is likely that they share a strong desire to help people. However, they do not identify common goals and attitudes.
- Ed cannot resist the temptation to make converts. He suggests that GWA have to adapt to Blue Rock, not Blue Rock to GWA: 'I'll tell you this, if everybody at GWA is like you and your boss, you're going find it hard to fit in here!'
- At the end of the scene, Ed and Jack's language becomes insensitive; they use 'I' and 'you', rather than trying to be inclusive by using 'we'. They both give up trying to be objective and positive. For example, Jack says: 'What makes you think you have the right to judge us?'; Ed says: 'if that's how you want to play it, don't say I didn't try.'
- Neither Ed nor Jack were objective or positive.

7 🎥 **A2** Go through the instructions with the class and establish that in the second video clip, students will see how Ed and Jack's attitudes have changed. While they watch, ask students to note down how Ed and Jack changed, as well as their decision at the end. Be ready to explain phrases, such as: *to wind someone up, when the cat's away, to take the initiative*. Elicit students' summaries and collate a list of comments on the board.

SUGGESTED ANSWERS
a They are more conscious of their differences and both more prepared to make concessions and find satisfactory compromises.
b They decide to suggest drawing up some cultural guidelines.

🎥 **A2**
Ed: Yeah, well we originally said the eighteenth, didn't we? I'm sure it can move. Just hold on for me. Take a seat, Jack; I'll be with you in a minute. Sorry about that … Okay … Yep … Just give me their number again, will you? … Yep … Okay, well look, I'll give them a call and get back to you … You're welcome. Bye. Sorry about that Jack, what can I do for you?

A CULTURE CLASH

MANAGEMENT SCENARIO

Jack: Look, Ed, I want to apologize. I was a bit stressed out the other day, and …

Ed: Yeah, we got off on the wrong foot, didn't we? Look, I think I'm to blame as well. We like to wind each other up around here, and I should have realized that things might be different at GWA.

Jack: Yeah, I suppose we both overreacted. Anyway, what about that coffee you suggested?

Ed: Sure. But don't you guys take your coffee break at eleven?

Jack: Usually, yes. We find it's a good way to keep up to date with what's going on – a bit like your Friday lunches.

Ed: Right.

Jack: But since we're going to be working together, and my manager's in a meeting with your CEO – I think I can risk taking an extra break!

Ed: When the cat's away, eh? Come on, let's go!

Ed: There you go!

Jack: Cheers.

Ed: Mm. So no tie today then?

Jack: No, I thought I'd better try and blend in with the locals!

Ed: Actually, it wouldn't do us any harm to take a leaf out of your book. We had a Bolivian minister in a few weeks ago; she was shocked when she saw us all. Are you going to join us for lunch on Friday?

Jack: Well look, I'd love to. But I do need to be back for two o'clock.

Ed: Oh that's a pity. Still, if it can't be helped …

Jack: The thing is, we try to start and finish early, you know, beat the rush hour. I've noticed that Blue Rock people tend to work late …

Ed: Yeah – and your guys are always hard at work when we drag ourselves in in the morning!

Jack: But basically, as long as the job gets done, it doesn't matter when we do it, does it?

Ed: Exactly. I mean, after all, we're all in this together. But you know, I think it would be really useful to have some guidelines as to what's optional and what isn't.

Jack: Like what?

Ed: Well, take meetings, for example. Your guys are always ready to start on time, but some of our people are systematically ten to fifteen minutes late which is unacceptable! I think this merger could be a chance to really straighten things out.

Jack: I see what you mean. Maybe we should suggest something to management?

Ed: What? Staff taking the initiative? They won't like that!

8 A2 Before the second viewing, ask students if they can complete the missing words. Then play the video clip again and ask students to check their answers.

Ask students to match the completed phrases with the cultural tips a–f. Monitor and give help as required. Check answers with the class.

ANSWERS
1 foot e   2 away a   3 locals d   4 book f
5 helped b   6 together c

9 Tell students that they are going to take part in a roleplay. Their job is working on a committee to smooth over a merger between two companies.

Divide the class into small groups. Assign each student with a letter, A or B. Tell Student As to read the information on their company on page 118, and Student Bs to read the information on page 120.

Give students time to prepare. Student As prepare together in small groups; Student Bs work together to rank the agenda points and decide which aspects they would especially like to keep. Offer help with any vocabulary, such as: *innovation, conventional, discouraged, intern, chronic difficulty*. When they are ready, ask students to form small groups of Student As and Student Bs for the meeting. During the meeting, circulate and monitor, taking language notes.

When they have finished the meeting, ask students to complete the meetings checklist and the cultural sensitivity checklist on page 123. Then ask students to reflect on the meeting and say how successful it was.

Finish by providing language feedback as necessary.

> **1:1** In the roleplay, ask your student to take the role of Student A (page 118) and you take the role of Student B (page 120). Record the roleplays, if possible, and then listen to parts of the meeting together in order to complete the meetings and cultural sensitivity checklists (page 123). If recording is not possible, go through the checklists together, but encourage your student to lead the evaluation.

A CULTURE CLASH

04 Voice and visuals

Learning objectives

Giving competent and confident presentations is a vital skill for many business English students. There are two units on giving presentations and the language practised is useful for all students and for addressing both small and large audiences.

This unit has a specific focus on using voice techniques and visuals. Students start by doing a quiz to test their communicative awareness. They read two texts on the power of the voice and visuals in delivering a message. Students select some vocabulary they would like to remember from the texts. They then roleplay giving and receiving feedback on a presentation, and listen to a client giving feedback on the same presentation.

Students discuss the range of visuals available for presentations and practise useful language for referring to these. They draw a graph or chart and practise referring to it in a short presentation.

Students read what a communication expert has to say about the effective use of the pause. They hear a number of presenters speaking with varying degrees of confidence, and then work on the use of pause and stress to improve delivery.

Finally, students listen to a businessman talking about performance. They analyse and practise delivery techniques using a famous speech adapted from the film *Henry V* (based on Shakespeare's play of the same name). The unit concludes with students giving 90-second work-related presentations.

The grammatical focus is on modal verbs and the lexical focus is on the language of presentations.

Digital resources: Unit 4
Online Workbook; Extension worksheets; Glossary; Phrase bank; Student's Book answer key; Student's Book listening script; Fast-track map; Quick progress test 1

Warm-up
Ask students if they have to speak in public at all. Ask them: *How do you feel? What makes a good speaker?*

Ask students to tell you about the best presentation they have ever been to. If your students do not need to give formal presentations, tell them that this unit will be useful for attending business presentations and for overall language and fluency development.

Ask students to read the quotation from the British judge and tell you if they find it amusing. Ask students if they can explain what the judge is trying to say (that if a presentation is boring, to the audience it may seem to drag on). Ask students what this implies about judges' summing up and public speaking in general. Ask students if they have ever attended a dull presentation and, if so, what they did to get through it. This discussion will lead naturally into the first activity.

1 There are no correct answers to the questions, but students can give their own opinions about which aspect or aspects they consider most important in contributing to a successful presentation.

2 With weaker groups, before asking students to do the test, you may want to check some of the vocabulary in the quiz: *attention span* (1), *distracted* (2), *persuasive* (5), *authoritative* (9). Students do the quiz alone and then compare and discuss their answers. They will find the correct answers later in the texts in 3.

3 Divide the group into pairs and ask each student to read one of the articles on page 25. As a first reading task, set a time limit and ask students to scan their article for as many answers as they can find to the quiz. Ask students to share the information they read with their partner and check their answers to the quiz together. If you wish to exploit the text further, ask students to read it again, intensively. You may wish to work on some of the vocabulary such as: *orator, charismatic* (Voice lessons); *cliché, ditching* (Visual impact).

4 Gather reactions to the articles. There are no correct answers to the second question, but students might comment that the implications for a business presenter are: think about how to engage your audience; focus on speaking in a lower tone of voice; think about how to deliver information using your voice (by emphasizing, pausing, etc); think about your body language; select impactful visual aids; and present all your information in as dramatic a way as possible.

5 Ask students to go back through the text they read and highlight the words and phrases they would like to remember. Check which items students chose. Ask them if the vocabulary is just for recognition, or production.

1:1 This is the first of the units which focus specifically on giving presentations, and will be of special interest to those students who need to present in English. Before starting, ask your student about the type of talks they need to give at work, e.g. formal and/or informal; to what kind of audience – native speakers/non-native speakers/specialists; etc.

In the first section, students give their views on what keeps an audience interested in a presentation. They do a quiz to check their communicative competence. They then read two articles, one on voice and the other on visuals.

BUSINESS COMMUNICATION

Giving feedback

In this section, students consider how presentations might be received in different cultures. Students roleplay a post-presentation feedback session between a presenter and his manager. Then they listen to a recording of feedback from a member of the audience, which throws a different light on the presentation.

1 As a lead-in, get students to brainstorm what can go wrong during a presentation, e.g. the power fails, you lose the thread of your talk, people switch off, etc. If appropriate, give a personal example from a lesson that went wrong and/or elicit examples from the class.

Check/Pre-teach: *to force a smile, insulted, illegible, to crack a joke, to handle, to break the ice, amplifier*. Divide the students into AB pairs. Refer the A students to page 120 and the B students to page 138. Ask students to read the role cards and focus attention on the *Useful language* boxes on the students' respective pages. Elicit sample language to complete each phrase and check stress and intonation. Highlight the pronunciation of contracted forms in past modals.

Give students time to prepare for the roleplay, noting down key words/phrases. With weaker students, suggest that they note down the main points they want to make along with the key language. If appropriate, arrange the seating so that the B students need to go to A's 'office' for the meeting. Remind the A students they need to be direct but also make some suggestions for future presentations; B students should be clear about the reasons they had problems and also convince A that they won't happen again.

Monitor and take feedback notes. When students have finished, ask the A students how successful they think they were in delivering negative feedback and the B students if they were able to justify what happened. If giving feedback is important for your students, ask them to list techniques which make for effective feedback, e.g. summarizing the main points, sandwiching a negative message between two positive points.

1:1 Do the lead-in and pre-teaching of vocabulary as outlined above. Then, decide which role is more appropriate for your student to play – the presenter (Speaker B) who has had a difficult experience, or the boss (Speaker A). Put the useful language on cards beforehand, so that your student can practise saying these, and has access to them during the roleplay. Tell your student that the roleplay will take about ten minutes. Record the roleplay, if possible, so you can play it back in order to do language feedback.

Language links

Direct students to the *Language links* section on pages 29–30 for further explanation of the meaning and use of modal verbs, and exercises to practise them.

2 1.13 Check/Pre-teach: *low-budget, unappreciative, at the expense of*. Ask students to predict what the client will say and then play the recording through once. Check students understand the client's reaction (he was very positive about the presentation). Divide the class into pairs and ask follow-up questions, e.g. *Were you surprised at the voicemail message? Would you have changed your feedback to the manager if you had heard the voicemail earlier? Would you now tell the manager about the positive feedback?*

> **1.13**
> Hello, this is Cheng Jing from Nanogen Taiwan. I just wanted to let you know that your presentation this morning was a tremendous success with everyone here. What a brilliant idea to do the whole thing in such a casual, low-budget and alternative way! Very clever. The board certainly got the message.
> Our executives really liked your calm, quiet approach. So please pass on my congratulations to your excellent presenter.
> Oh, by the way, the joke about Beijing was greatly enjoyed – even in translation. So, see you at the next strategy meeting. Goodbye now.

Visuals

In this section, students focus on the equipment and visuals involved in giving a presentation and discuss the possible pitfalls of using PowerPoint. They focus on the language of referring to visuals and finally practise this language by giving a short presentation themselves, using a graph or chart.

1 Students give examples of the visual aids they use. Encourage them to justify their choice, giving the pros and cons of using the various types of resources and equipment, e.g. PowerPoint/DVDs have visual impact but can be affected by technical problems.

Language links

Direct students to the *Phrase bank* in the *Language links* section on page 30 for more on describing and commenting on visuals.

2 Focus attention on the title of the article and elicit the likely tone of the text. Students read the text quickly to check (the tone is humorous and irreverent). Check comprehension of: *to inflict, cumulatively, numbing, beware of* and then elicit other language which indicates the writer's tone, e.g. *death, defenceless, endless*. Ask follow-up questions, e.g. *Have you ever been bored in a PowerPoint presentation? What techniques has a presenter used to avoid such a reaction?*

3 Remind students that collocations form word 'units', e.g. *to put (something) in perspective*, and identifying these units will help them complete the phrases. When students have finished, check the answers and pronunciation of each expression. Write problematic examples on the board and mark the stress and intonation.

ANSWERS

Introduction
Have a look at this. As you can **see**, …
Highlights
One thing you'll immediately **notice** is that …
I'd particularly like to **draw** your attention to …

04 VOICE AND VISUALS

I'd also like to **point** out …
And perhaps I should **mention** …
Context
Just to **give** you some of the background to this, …
To **put** this into some kind of perspective, …
Conclusions
Clearly then, what these figures **show** is …
The lesson we can **learn** from this is …

4 Give students time to produce their graph/chart. Encourage them to use any available equipment to display their visuals. If you have sets of blank cards, ask students to transfer the expressions they would like to use from 3 onto individual cards. Many students like using these cards as prompts and writing key words stops students from reading a presentation aloud.

Divide the students into groups to give their presentations. Monitor and take notes and then give language feedback on important or common errors.

> **Language links**
>
> Direct students to the *Language links* section on page 29 for more practice of vocabulary for commenting on statistics and describing trends and developments in presentations.

Voice

Students start by reading a short text on the power of the pause. They then listen to six extracts from presentations to decide if the speakers have a positive or negative delivery. They analyse the speakers' delivery and then practise saying sentences in a fluent and confident way.

1 Ask students if there are any powerful speeches they remember from films or by politicians. Elicit the aspects of delivery that made them so powerful and memorable, e.g. repeating phrases, pauses at key moments, etc.

Draw students' attention to the title of the book by Courtland L. Bovée. Ask them to think why a pause may be used for effect. Students read the text quickly to confirm their predictions. Check comprehension of *shift* and *anticipation*. Elicit the four main points Bovée makes (emphasis, thinking time, moving on, heighten anticipation).

2 1.14 Ask students to read sentences a–f through quickly and deal with any vocabulary queries. Tell students they are going to hear the six sentences delivered in different ways and that they should write down the appropriate number 1–3 next to each one, depending on the speaker's delivery. Play the recording and get students to record their answers. Check the answers with the class.

ANSWERS
a 1 (fluent and confident)   b 2 (fluent but boring)
c 3 (hesitant)   d 1 (fluent and confident)
e 2 (fluent but boring)   f 3 (hesitant)

1.14
a There's a whole market in Eastern Europe just there for the taking.
b Quite frankly, the results we've been getting are absolutely incredible.
c Now, I'm sure I don't need to tell you just how crucial this is.
d Net profits are up 97% – yes, 97%.
e Would you believe that so far we've not been able to sell a single unit?
f Miss this deadline and we'll lose the biggest client this company's ever had.

3 Play sentences b and e again and elicit the answer.

ANSWER
He doesn't pause and fails to stress important words.

4 Play sentences c and f again and check the answer. Emphasize the fact that pausing in the wrong place will make a speech sound stilted and give the impression that the speaker is lacking in confidence.

ANSWER
She is pausing and stressing in the wrong place.

5 1.15 Divide the class into AB pairs – student A marks the pauses and student B underlines the stressed words. Play the recording and elicit the connection between stresses and pauses. Point out that the more pauses a speaker uses, the more stressed syllables there will be and the more dramatic it will sound.

ANSWERS
We tend to pause after stressed words.
a There's a whole <u>market</u> | in Eastern <u>Europe</u> | just <u>there</u> for the <u>taking</u>.
d <u>Net</u> <u>profits</u> | are up <u>ninety</u>-<u>seven</u> per <u>cent</u> | – <u>yes</u>, | <u>ninety</u>- | <u>seven</u> | per <u>cent</u>.

> **1:1** Before starting, listen to the first sentence (a) with your student and decide together which words are stressed and where there is a pause. Mark this onto the transcript. Let your student do the same with the second sentence (d). When your student has correctly described the connection between where we pause and where we put the stress, ask them to experiment with reading the sentences aloud.

1.15
a There's a whole <u>market</u> | in Eastern <u>Europe</u> | just <u>there</u> for the <u>taking</u>.
d <u>Net</u> <u>profits</u> | are up <u>ninety</u>-<u>seven</u> per <u>cent</u> | - <u>yes</u>, | <u>ninety</u> - | <u>seven</u> | per <u>cent</u>.

6 1.16 With weaker classes, demonstrate a fluent and confident delivery of the sentences first. Get students to repeat the phrases in a quick drill if necessary. Ask students to read sentences a–f out loud. Encourage them

BUSINESS COMMUNICATION

to have fun experimenting with the delivery. Play the recording to allow the students to compare their version.

1.16

a There's a whole market | in Eastern Europe | just there for the taking.
b Quite frankly, | the results we've been getting | are absolutely | incredible.
c Now, I'm sure | I don't need to tell you | just how crucial | this is.
d Net profits | are up ninety-seven per cent | – yes, | ninety- | seven | per cent.
e Would you believe | that so far | we've not been able to sell | a single unit?
f Miss | this | deadline | and we'll lose the biggest client | this company's ever had.

7 **1.17** Read out the quotation from Jan Carlzon and ask students to say what they think he means (that business involves an element of performance). Check/Pre-teach: *to make a debut, to take a deep breath, to act the part, classically trained actor, platform speaker, to pitch a client, to fake, paradoxically, to brush up*. Ask students to brainstorm the pros and cons of using drama techniques in business training, e.g. it can improve confidence / help with delivery; people may not take it seriously / it may not be relevant, etc. Tell students to see how many of their ideas are mentioned in the extract. Play the recording through once and check the answers.

Before playing the recording again, get students to read the questions a–d. Play the extract again, pausing after each speaker to let the students note down their answers. Students discuss the questions in pairs/small groups. Hold a short class feedback session to check the responses and elicit students' opinions.

ANSWERS
b how to speak effectively and relate to an audience
c self-belief

1.17

A: Welcome back to CBN Business. To be or not to be? That is the question for an increasing number of companies putting their staff through drama courses in an attempt to turn them into better public speakers. Jon Heller meets a group of British managers making their theatrical debut.

B: 'Next time you are about to make a presentation, take a deep breath and imagine yourself walking on stage – about to give the performance of your life.' That's the advice of William Freeman of Cambridge Associates, one of a new wave of management trainers who believe that presenting is less about PowerPoint and more about acting the part.
At Prospero, a company with a similar aims, Tina Packer and Michael Lame have taken the idea one step further and put Shakespeare on the programme. After all, who better to teach managers how to speak effectively and relate to an audience than classically trained actors?

Whether you're a platform speaker at the annual conference, a salesperson pitching to a client or just chairing your weekly staff meeting, actors have powerful communication techniques you can learn from. Prospero is certainly in demand, regularly running courses at Columbia Business School, Harvard and MIT.
So what is it that makes someone a brilliant speaker? Richard Olivier, Royal Shakespeare Company director, creative management consultant and son of acting legend Sir Laurence Olivier, thinks it's 'self-belief'. According to Olivier, 'Much of leadership is acting. Not faking it, but taking on a role. Paradoxically, the acting makes it real.'
But what do the trainees think? We questioned a few who'd taken a course in acting like leaders.

C: I thought my boss had gone mad at first. I mean, Shakespeare? No way! But, in fact, it's been really inspiring. And a lot of fun!
D: Frankly, I was terrified. Me, acting on stage? I don't think so. But I've learned a lot of stuff I never got on those boring presentation courses.
E: Well, the actors have been fun to work with. We've had a lot of laughs. I'm not so sure how useful it all is – you know, in a business context. But, hey, it got us out of the office for a couple of days, so I'm not complaining.
F: Well, this really isn't my thing at all. I mean, public speaking just frightens the life out of me, without getting up and acting in front of an audience. Frankly, it was hell. Never again!
G: Best course I've ever done – by far. Just totally brilliant. I never realized the true power of the voice and the confidence it gives you when you can make it work for you. I'd definitely recommend this kind of training.
B: So, there we have it. Time to shut down your laptop, brush up your Shakespeare and learn how to wow an audience with the professionals

8 Ask students if they have seen any Shakespeare plays being performed. If so, ask them what impressed them. Give students a few minutes to read the background to *Henry V*.

Work on the first few lines of the extract with the whole class to mark in the pauses, stressed words and parts of the text for special delivery. Work with a few confident students to get them to deliver the lines dramatically.

Divide the class into pairs. Give students time to study the text, write in the pauses and stresses and highlight key parts. Remind students that speaking quietly can arouse audience interest and that pausing creates dramatic effect. Encourage students to practise the speech more than once and get them to switch roles when they have finished. Monitor and help as necessary, but avoid directing the students yourself unless they find the task very difficult.

When the students have practised, get one or two students to come out and perform their speech. Allow students to have several 'takes' if they need them. If your students prefer not to perform in front of the class, get them to make an audio recording and play these at the end of the lesson. Get the students to light-heartedly suggest a best actor award!

BUSINESS COMMUNICATION

1:1 First, introduce the topic of Shakespeare, as outlined in 8. Then, work together with your student on the first few lines of the speech. Encourage your student to experiment with how to sound more dramatic. If possible, record your student's performance, either using a video camera or a mobile phone, or an audio recording device. When you play it back, decide with your student which parts of the recording they might like to try again. Your student could practise in their own time, and do the recording at the start of the next class. After the re-recording, listen again to identify any areas of improvement.

9 1.18 Play the recording so that students can compare their performance with the recorded version. (Point out that the recording is of an actor speaking in the style of the original performer, not the film actor himself.)

1.18

If we are going to die, we are enough
To cause our country loss; and if to live,
The fewer men, the greater share of honour.
This day is called the Feast of Crispian.
He who survives this day, comes safely home,
Will hold his head high when this day is named
And stand up at the name of Crispian.
He that shall live today and see old age
Will celebrate it yearly with his neighbours
And say: 'Tomorrow is Saint Crispian'.
Then he'll roll up his sleeve and show his scars
And say: 'These wounds I got on Crispian's Day'.
Old men forget; yes, all will be forgotten;
But he'll remember all too well
What he achieved that day. Then will our names:
Harry the king, Bedford and Exeter,
Warwick and Talbot, Salisbury and Gloucester,
Be between cups of wine newly remembered.
This story will the good man teach his son;
And Crispian will never go by,
From this day to the ending of the world,
But we shall be remembered for it –
We few, we fortunate few, we band of brothers;
For he today who sheds his blood with me
Will be my brother. However poor and humble,
This day will make of him a gentleman.
And gentlemen in England, now in bed,
Will curse the fact they were not here,
And question whether they are really men,
While anyone speaks who fought with us
Upon Saint Crispian's Day!

10 Students choose a title for a 90-second presentation, e.g. *motivating people*. With weaker groups, provide a template to help structure the presentation, e.g. name / job / an opening 'hook' such as a rhetorical question / main point(s) / closing statement. Remind students to concentrate on getting their message across confidently and to try to use delivery techniques from this unit.

Keep to the 90-second time limit for each presentation. Ask the class to give constructive feedback on each student's performance. Be ready to give your own feedback.

Language links

ANSWERS

Vocabulary
Presentations
Commenting on statistics
1 a increased tenfold   b quadrupled
  c more than tripled   d nearly doubled
  e plateau'd   f almost halved
Which of the above means the same as *a fourfold increase*? b
2 a huge/massive
  b significant/considerable
  c moderate/reasonable
  d slight/modest
3 a phenomenal/spectacular
  b encouraging/promising
  c disappointing/unimpressive
  d disastrous/miserable

Metaphor: trends and developments
4 + 5 And on the stock market today …

mountaineering equipment	peaked	↗
military hardware	boomed	↗
lifts	were up and down	∧
kitchen knives	went up sharply	↗
but the housing market	totally collapsed	↘

After a nervous start …

rubber	bounced back	∨
medical supplies	quickly recovered	∨
the automotive industry	rallied	↗
rifles	shot up	↗
and vacuum cleaners also	picked up after lunch	↗

In some of the fiercest trading seen in the City …

swimwear	plunged	↘
mining equipment	hit rock bottom	↘
ice skates	slipped a little	↘
and the market for raisins	completely dried up	↘

By close of trade …

fireworks	skyrocketed	↗
but paper products	were stationary	→
men's socks	remained unchanged	→
and theatre curtains	fell dramatically	↘

Grammar
Modal verbs
1 deleted verbs – a mustn't pay   b needn't take, needn't have taken   c didn't need to wait, mustn't wait   d would have studied   e would be, must have been   f could
2 1 shouldn't   2 must have   3 wouldn't   4 would have
  5 needn't have   6 can't   7 could have   8 'll   9 can't
  10 could have   11 must   12 won't   13 might   14 'll

Phrase bank
Describing and commenting on visuals
Introduction: d, l, o, p   Context: f, h, i, m
Highlights: a, c, e, g   Conclusions: b, j, k, n

04 VOICE AND VISUALS 33

05 Problems on the phone

Learning objectives

This unit is about the skill of telephoning in English. Many business English students find making and receiving calls in English challenging. This is because phone calls not only demand a good level of listening but also because students have to function without the help of paralinguistic features which normally aid communication, such as eye contact and gestures. Less fluent students may find speaking on the phone very difficult.

Students complete a text about chatterboxes on the phone. They listen to a recording of someone trying to get rid of an unwanted caller and then practise this in a roleplay. Students then focus on handling customer complaints and the appropriate language to use. They focus on the problem of angry or insulting emails, roleplay how to deal with them and rewrite two emails to make them more polite.

Students do a series of activities based on telephone conversations between two people who are trying to solve a problem. They then focus on idioms and useful expressions from the conversations. Fluency practice is provided by a final problem-solving exercise.

The grammatical focus is on complex question formation and the lexical focus is on phone, tablet and email.

Digital resources: Unit 5
Online Workbook; Extension worksheets; Glossary; Phrase bank; Student's Book answer key; Student's Book listening script; Fast-track map

In this first section, students discuss problems that other people phone them about. They read a text about how to deal with chatterboxes on the phone and delete the incorrect words in the text. They then listen to someone trying to end a phone conversation and use key expressions in a phone roleplay.

1:1 Due to the increase in the use of mobile phones, the possibilities for using real phones for telephone lessons in class have increased enormously; this has benefitted one-to-one teaching especially. Whether you use a landline or a mobile, check that you and your student can phone each other during a lesson, going into different rooms to increase the realism of the situation.

Warm-up

As a lead-in to this unit, elicit pros and cons of using the phone, e.g. pros: it can save time, it can help to solve immediate problems, you can do other things while you're on the phone; cons: there is no support from eye contact or body language, there can be technical and reception problems (especially mobiles). Ask students how they feel about using English on the phone. Ask: *Do you feel confident? Do you feel scared?*

Ask students to read the quotation from Henry Ford. Find out how students prefer to deal with problems – by phone, by letter, by email, or face-to-face – and ask them to give reasons for their answers.

1 Focus attention on the *Glossary* to check/pre-teach: *chatterbox*. Divide students into groups and get them to list the problems they have to deal with by phone at work. Ask the students to categorize the problems, e.g. internal calls with employees/management, external calls with clients, etc. Ask each group to report back to the class.

2 Check that students know how to say the term *24/7* (i.e. *twenty-four/seven*), which is in the *Glossary*. Write the main and sub-headings from the text on the board and ask students to tell you what techniques they have used to 'get rid of chatterboxes'. Students skim the text to see if any of their ideas are included.

With weaker classes, check/pre-teach: *telephony, tactful, abrupt, subtle, harsh, drastic*. Ask students to read the text again and select the correct alternatives. To check the answers, call out the letters and elicit the answers. Check that students understand the tone of the article (gently humorous). Ask them to give examples from the text which highlight this, e.g. *deadly game, genuine emergency*.

ANSWERS
a touch b point c in d time e latest f rumour g day
h can i expect j cut k something l keep m get n go
o listen p get q thing r stepped s off t in u there

3 Encourage students to also consider any reasons why social chat on the phone might be a good thing, such as building a relationship with a client.

4 1.19 Tell students they will hear a phone conversation between two men – Dan and George. Ask the students to note down who the chatterbox is, who is trying to get rid of him, and what the purpose of the call is. Play the recording through once and ask students to raise their hand whenever they hear any of the expressions in 2.

1.19
B: Hello?
A: Dan?

B: Speaking.
A: It's George. George Chatterton.
B: Ah, George … How are you?
A: Couldn't be better, mate, couldn't be better! Someone happened to mention they'd bumped into you the other day. So I just thought I'd give you a call. See how you're doing.
B: Oh, right. … yes … er, George …
A: So how's it going, mate? Just been promoted, so I hear.
B: Er, yes, that's right.
A: Glad to see they've finally started appreciating you.
B: Er, yes, thanks. So, George, what can I do for you?
A: Bit more money too, I imagine.
B: Hmm? Oh, a bit, yeah. Well, George, I expect you're calling about that project …
A: And how are your parents? Is the family doing well?
B: They're all fine. Thanks for asking. Look, George, I am rather busy right now. I've just got back from holiday, actually, and you know what it's like. Was there something you wanted to talk to me about?
A: Of course, how silly of me! You've just been on that safari you were planning last time we spoke, haven't you?
B: Yes, and what with the new job and everything, there's a bit of catching up …
A: Kenya, wasn't it?
B: What?
A: The holiday – Kenya.
B: Yes. Listen. George …
A: You know, I've always wanted to go to Kenya …
B: Well, now, George, I mustn't keep you.
A: What's that?
B: I'll let you get on. I'm sure you've got things to do, busy guy like you. It's been great talking to you, though.
A: Yeah, likewise.
B: We must get together soon.
A: Yeah, yeah. As a matter of fact, I'm going to be in London for a few days next month.
B: Oh, no!
A: Sorry?
B: I said 'Oh, nice.' Perhaps we can meet up for lunch or dinner.
A: Yeah, that'd be great.
B: But, erm, I'll have to let you go now, George. Someone just this minute stepped into the office.
A: Oh, right, I see.
B: And it looks like I've got an international call just come in on the other line as well. Yes.
A: No worries. I'll call you back in half an hour, then. I haven't told you my good news yet. Wait till you hear it!
B: What? Er, no. Erm, George? George?

5 Ask students to look at the listening script on page 143 and make a note of any key expressions they wish to use. If appropriate, get students to transfer the language onto cards to use as prompts during the roleplay. Check pronunciation and intonation of the key expressions.

Divide students into AB pairs. Refer the A students to page 120 and the B students to page 128. Have students read their role card and deal with any vocabulary queries. Check they know who is going to start the phone conversation. If possible, use internal telephones for the roleplay or ask students to sit back to back.

Monitor and take feedback notes. When the students have finished, ask one student from each pair to summarize the outcome of the conversation and to say if they did any business. Give feedback on overall fluency before highlighting any important or common errors.

1:1 Before you set up this activity, transfer key expressions onto cards so that your student has access to them during the roleplay. Before the activity, ask your student to read the expressions aloud in order to practise the intonation and stress. Set up the roleplay. Your student can choose the role of the chatterbox (Speaker A, page 120) or the person dealing with a chatterbox (Speaker B, page 128). Before the roleplay, remember to exchange personal information, as outlined in the bullet points on each role card. If possible, record the roleplay and listen to some or all of it afterwards in order to provide feedback on language.

Dealing with complaints

In this section, students discuss formal complaints they have made and then study a model of how to deal with customer complaints. They focus on the appropriate language to use when dealing with a phone complaint, comparing their choices with a recorded conversation. They read through two emails written in anger and then take part in a telephone roleplay with a partner to respond to the emails. They rewrite the angry emails to make them more polite and then repeat the follow-up phone roleplays to assess the difference.

1 Let students read the story and ask them to describe their reaction. Find out if students have ever been similarly harassed about the time they have spent on time-wasting.

2 Give an example of a formal complaint that you made and then ask students to discuss the questions in pairs.

3 Check/Pre-teach: *to reassure, to empathize*. After the students have put the stages in order, ask them to compare their answers with a partner.

SUGGESTED ANSWER
1 greet and reassure the caller   2 get the details   3 listen and empathize   4 suggest possible solutions   5 agree on a course of action   6 end on a positive note

4 When choosing the inappropriate expressions, encourage students to read the sentences aloud to highlight how they would come across to the person complaining. When the students have completed the

BUSINESS COMMUNICATION

task, check the answers and elicit what is wrong with the inappropriate expressions, e.g. over-familiar, over-direct.

ANSWERS

Stage 1 c What's the matter, then?
Stage 2 b What exactly is your problem?
Stage 3 a Tell me about it! I know just how you feel.
Stage 4 a Well, I suppose I could send you a new one, but I can't give you a refund. Sorry.
Stage 5 b Are you satisfied now?
Stage 6 c Good. Anything else or is that it?

5 🔘 **1.20** Check/Pre-teach: *to ring off, frustrating, to sort out, to wipe (data) off, to retrieve, refund, compensation.* Ask students to listen and note down: the problem; the outcome; the tone of the caller and of the customer services adviser. Play the recording through once and check the answers: the problem is with the hard drive and the caller has lost a lot of data; the company will send an engineer to sort out the problem or replace the faulty computer; the tone of the caller changes from anger to being pacified and the tone of the adviser is polite and helpful.

Play the recording again and get students to compare the phrases they chose in 4 with what the customer services adviser said. Check which expressions she used: stage 1 a, stage 2 c, stage 3 c, stage 4 c, stage 5 a, stage 6 b. Find out if students chose the same options. Point out that both sets of options are equally valid.

🔘 **1.20**

A: Hello. Thank you for calling the iDeals customer service line. All our customer service advisers are busy right now. Please hold and your enquiry will be dealt with shortly ... This is the iDeals customer service line. Thank you for holding. All our customer service advisers are busy right now. Please hold and your enquiry will be dealt with shortly ...

B: Oh, come on, come on!

C: Good morning. Lisa speaking. How can I help you?

B: Oh, hello. At last! I was just about to ring off.

C: I am sorry about that. The waiting system is a bit frustrating, isn't it? It's the only way we can offer our 24-hour service, you see.

B: Yeah, yeah. Look, it's about the computer I bought off you two weeks ago ...

C: Yes? What seems to be the problem?

B: Well, I was transferring my files to it from my flash drive and it's lost the lot. Everything!

C: Okay, now don't worry. I'm sure we can sort something out. First, can you give me a few details? The computer has lost all your data, you say?

B: Yes. But, you don't understand. It's wiped everything off the flash drive as well! My whole life, my whole life was in those files.

C: Oh, my goodness! Are you sure? Sounds like the problem's with your flash drive.

B: Of course I'm sure! And there's nothing wrong with my flash drive. I've had it years!

C: Okay. I can understand how upset you must be. Now, I don't think we can deal with this on the phone, so I'm going to send a service engineer to see if they can retrieve your data. Can you give me your product reference number?

B: Hmm? Er, yes. It's ... here it is ... it's SF11–003.

C: Thank you.

B: I'll be expecting a total refund and compensation if this can't be fixed!

C: Unfortunately, we're not authorized to give refunds, but what I can do is send you a brand-new computer. How would that be?

B: This is supposed to be a brand-new computer. You think I want another one of these, after what the last one did to my files?

C: Well, let's see what our engineer can do. Hopefully, it's not quite as bad as you think. Now, I've got your address here in your customer file. Oxford OX2 6BJ, right?

B: Yeah, right.

C: And it's Mr Harris, isn't it?

B: Yes.

C: Right, Mr Harris. We'll have an engineer with you this afternoon. And I'll ask him to bring a new hard disk with him. Is that all okay for you?

B: Er, well, I suppose ...

C: Good. Glad to be of assistance. Is there anything else I can help you with?

B: Hmm? Oh, no, no.

C: Well, best of luck this afternoon. I hope we can solve the problem for you.

B: Well, thanks. Erm, goodbye.

C: Goodbye, Mr Harris.

---

6 Check that students know the word *flame*. Discuss the question with the class and their experiences of receiving flames. Do they have a technique if they want to flame but know it is wrong, such as writing and saving, then going back when they are calm to make the email polite?

7 Check/Pre-teach: *to bother, to get round to, to foul things up, disgrace, pathetic.* Divide the class into AB pairs. Get students to read their email. Ask students what makes these emails inappropriate, e.g. use of direct questions, blunt/sarcastic tone, direct threats, use of capitals.

Tell students that they will now act out the telephone conversations which might have taken place after sending the emails. If possible, use internal telephones for this exercise or ask students to sit back to back. Give students a few minutes to prepare their calls. Remind the caller to be direct and the receiver to calm him/her down and deal with the complaint as successfully as possible.

With weaker classes, model the roleplay with two stronger students first. Monitor and take feedback notes. Get students to swap roles when they have finished the first call. Hold a short feedback session and ask the students about the outcome of the calls and if they dealt with the complaint well. Give feedback on overall fluency before highlighting important or common errors.

> **1:1** In the first call, take the role of the angry caller and ask your student to pacify you. In the second call, reverse the roles. Record both calls, if possible, and then go back and listen to them together. Go over the language, pausing and reformulating where necessary.

8 Point out that the mark // indicates that students should start a new sentence. Ask the A and B students to rewrite their respective emails using the prompts. With weaker students, elicit the opening lines of each email with the whole class first. Check possible answers with the class, accepting any appropriate alternatives.

SUGGESTED ANSWERS

a
Unfortunately I've been unable to reach you on the phone. Can you tell me if you're managing to make any progress on the Samsung report? If you're having problems, please let me know as soon as possible. I understand you've been preoccupied with other matters and may not even have made a start yet, although I hope this is not the case.
I did ask you some time ago for this report and, as you know, I do need it urgently for Thursday's meeting with the people from head office.
This is not the first time you've let me down and consequently I shall have to discuss the matter with you when your probationary period ends.
I really must know today how much longer it's going to take.

b
I am again writing to you with regard to our order, reference no 099X.
Our records show that our order of $15,000 shirts was placed three months ago but so far we have not received anything. Nor have you sent us an email explaining the reason for the delay. I am afraid this is quite unacceptable.
You advertise yourselves as the world's leading promotional products company. I therefore find your inability to take care of a simple order like this both surprising and disappointing. I did notice, however, that you were more efficient in debiting our account for the sum of $15,000.
I should like the delivery within 48 hours together with an apology. Otherwise I have no alternative but to hand the matter over to our legal department. I hope I have made myself clear.

9 Students exchange and read their rewritten emails. Set up the same roleplay as in 7 but, this time, tell the students to base the conversation on the rewritten emails. When students have finished, ask them to compare the two sets of calls.

> **Language links**
>
> Direct students to the *Language links* section on page 35 for more practice of prepositions in the context of vocabulary relating to phone, tablet and email.

Tackling problems

In this final section, the students listen to one side of a telephone conversation and guess the problem that is being discussed. They focus on idioms used in the conversation and then discuss how they would solve the problem described in the first recording. They go on to compare their solutions with those given in a second recording. Finally, they focus on useful expressions taken from the listening tasks and take part in a problem-solving exercise on the telephone.

1 **1.21** Check/Pre-teach: *trade fair, stand* (at an exhibition), *carriers*. Tell students that they are going to hear one side of a telephone conversation and they need to take notes and then work out what the problem is. Play the recording through once. Elicit and write key words as headings on the board, i.e. *stand, CDs, CD player, carriers, brochures*. Ask students to write what they think the problem might be under each heading. Focus attention on the phrases and check pronunciation. Elicit the type of language which can follow each phrase. Divide the class into pairs and have them discuss what they think the problems are.

> **1.21**
> B: Hello?
> A:
> B: Yeah, speaking. Is that you, Piotr? Aren't you supposed to be at the Trade Fair in Krakow?
> A:
> B: What?
> A:
> B: You haven't got a stand? Well, how did that happen?
> A:
> B: Maybe it's the laptop you're using.
> A:
> B: Well, what happened to our laptop?
> A:
> B: Those carriers! They're unbelievable! That's the last time we use them! I'll give them a piece of my mind when I speak to them.
> A:
> B: Where's Liesl?
> A:
> B: This just gets worse, doesn't it?
> A:
> B: What's gone wrong with the brochures?
> A:
> B: Portuguese! Oh, no ...
> A:
> B: That may be because I forgot to phone Tony. You remember we were going to attend the Lisbon Trade Fair originally.
> A:
> B: It completely slipped my mind. Oh, I'm really sorry, Piotr.
> A:

05 PROBLEMS ON THE PHONE 37

BUSINESS COMMUNICATION

B: Well, we're snowed under at the moment trying to get things ready for the Midas launch, but, look, don't worry. I'll sort something out. Can I call you back in an hour?

A:

2 🔘 **1.22** Play the recording and get students to compare their guesses with what really happened.

1.22

B: Hello?
A: Graham?
B: Yeah, speaking. Is that you, Piotr? Aren't you supposed to be at the Trade Fair in Krakow?
A: I am at the Trade Fair in Krakow, Graham. I'm just about the only thing that arrived here in one piece!
B: What?
A: Well, the stand got badly damaged in transit, so I've basically just got a table here, a few chairs and a couple of posters with nothing to attach them to! It's a complete disaster!
B: You haven't got a stand? Well, how did that happen?
A: Don't ask. Look, it's not just that. I've just tried out three of the promotional DVDs and two were defective – wouldn't play at all. I don't know how many more are like that.
B: Maybe it's the laptop you're using.
A: Wouldn't surprise me. I had to borrow it from another exhibitor.
B: Well, what happened to our laptop?
A: I'll give you three guesses.
B: Those carriers! They're unbelievable! That's the last time we use them! I'll give them a piece of my mind when I speak to them.
A: Yes, well, never mind that now. You've got to do something, Graham. I'm working flat out on my own here.
B: Where's Liesl?
A: She's come down with some sort of virus. I left her at the hotel.
B: This just gets worse, doesn't it?
A: Wait till you hear about the brochures …
B: What's gone wrong with the brochures?
A: The English ones are okay. The others are all in Portuguese.
B: Portuguese! Oh, no …
A: What?
B: That may be because I forgot to phone Tony. You remember we were going to attend the Lisbon Trade Fair originally.
A: And you didn't tell Tony about the change of plan?
B: It completely slipped my mind. Oh, I'm really sorry, Piotr.
A: Graham, you've got to get me out of this mess.
B: Well, we're snowed under at the moment trying to get things ready for the Midas launch, but, look, don't worry. I'll sort something out. Can I call you back in an hour?
A: Okay, I'll be waiting to hear from you.

3 Ask students to complete the gaps from memory and then check answers with the class.

ANSWERS
a flat   b slipped   c snowed

4 Elicit from the class the five problems and write them on the board. Ask students what they would do in each of these situations.

5 🔘 **1.23** Play the recording through once and elicit the solutions Graham and Piotr come up with. Let students compare their own solutions with those in the recording.

1.23

A: Hello?
B: Hello, Piotr.
A: Graham! You said an hour.
B: Sorry. I got held up.
A: What's happening, then?
B: Right. I've been on to the carriers and they're sending a new stand out on the next plane. You should have that by tomorrow morning.
A: Well, at least that's something.
B: Can you get hold of the organizers and tell them we'll set up tomorrow at seven?
A: Yeah, sure. I don't suppose you remembered to put another laptop in with the stand?
B: I've sent two – just in case.
A: Oh, right. Good. Thanks.
B: And do you happen to have a phone number for the promotions people? Because if those DVDs are defective, I'll get them to send more by courier.
A: I've got it somewhere. Graham, is there any chance of sending someone else out here? Kim, for instance.
B: Piotr, you know how short-staffed we are here right now.
A: What's this exhibition costing us, Graham? $18,000?
B: You're right. I'll check with Liz and see if she can spare Kim for a few days.
A: Thanks. It's murder here.
B: Well, I'll see what I can do, but I can't promise anything.
A: Hmm. And would you mind getting some brochures to me in Polish, seeing as I'm in Poland?
B: Yes, we're having a few problems with that – seem to have run out. Is there any point in sending the ones we've got in Russian?
A: No, Graham, not a great idea. Send the German ones, if that's all we've got. But are you absolutely sure we didn't order a reprint of the Polish ones?
B: I'll look into it the minute I get off the phone.

05 PROBLEMS ON THE PHONE

BUSINESS COMMUNICATION

A: Okay, but could I ask you to hurry that up a bit, please? It is pretty important.
B: I know, I know. Would it help if we got a local Polish interpreter in? I know you speak Polish, but it might help you out a bit.
A: Well, I wouldn't have much time to brief them on the product, but yeah, anything's better than nothing.
B: Okay, I'll get on to that right away. Leave it to me.
A: I did leave it to you and look what happened!
B: Yeah, well. You're doing a great job Piotr. I owe you one!

6 Students match the sentence halves. To check the answers, ask individual students to read out the complete sentences.

ANSWERS
a 4 b 7 c 2 d 1 e 6 f 5 g 3 h 11 i 14 j 8
k 13 l 9 m 12 n 10

Language links
Direct students to the *Language links* section on page 35 for a further explanation of complex question formation, and an exercise to practise it.

7 Divide the class into AB pairs. Refer the A students to page 120 and the B students to page 130. Tell students to note down the key information for each call and keep it to hand for use in the roleplay. Monitor the roleplays. Use internal telephones for this exercise if possible, or ask students to sit back to back. Monitor and take feedback notes. Hold a short feedback session. Find out if the scoring made students change their approach in the conversations. Finally, give feedback on overall fluency before highlighting any important or common language errors.

1:1 Decide how many of the four roleplays you would like to do with your student. Allow sufficient time between each roleplay for you and your student to study the information and prepare. Ask your student to study the information on page 120; you look at the information on page 130. Record some or all of the conversations, if possible. Listen to them with your student afterwards in order to identify any language problems, reformulating the language where necessary.

8 Put students in pairs in order to discuss if they would follow up the phone calls they had in 7 with emails or meetings. Elicit feedback. Encourage students to give reasons for their answers.

Language links
Direct students to the *Phrase bank* in the *Language links* section on page 36 for more useful expressions for use on the phone.

Language links
ANSWERS
Vocabulary
Phone, tablet and email
1 up 2 in 3 on 4 out 5 up 6 down 7 off 8 around
9 out 10 off 11 as 12 under 13 back 14 up
15 by 16 on 17 down 18 up 19 on 20 on
21 out 22 on 23 off 24 for 25 on

Grammar
Complex question formation
Polite question forms
b I wonder if you could help me?
c Could I ask you not to mention this to anyone else?
d Do you think I could ask you to do some overtime next week?
e Would you like me to put in a good word for you?
f Would you mind not whistling while I'm trying to concentrate?
g Do you mind if I leave early today?
h Would it help if I gave you a few days to think about it?
i Would you mind if I asked you a personal question?
j Do you happen to know when Mr Alvarez is coming back?
k I don't suppose you could lend me €50 until Friday, could you?

Phrase bank
Small talk on the phone
1 a How's   b How are you
  c Congratulations on   d I heard you're
  e Have you just   f Have you heard
  g Good

Getting down to business on the phone
2 a Anyway, …
  b So, what can I do for you?
  c I expect you're calling about …
  d Was there something you wanted to talk to me about?

Requesting assistance on the phone
3 a Would you mind
  b Can you get hold of
  c Could I ask you to
  d Is there any chance of
  e I don't suppose you could
  f Do you happen to have
  g Are you absolutely sure you can't

Offering assistance on the phone
4 a see + promise   b check + see
  c worry + get   d look + Give
  e help + give   f leave + get

Ending a call
5 a I mustn't keep you.
  b I'll let you get on.
  c Someone's just stepped into the office.
  d We must get together soon.
  e It's been great talking to you.
  f I'll have to let you go now.
  g I've got a call just come in on the other line.
  h Listen, I'm running a bit late.

05 PROBLEMS ON THE PHONE

06 Leading meetings

Learning objectives

This unit provides useful language for participating in and chairing meetings. The business skills, strategies and functional language covered will be especially useful for those students who need to chair meetings.

Students discuss features of meetings and focus on common problems encountered in meetings. They work on collocations for talking about these problems and look at some radical and surprising solutions, which includes listening to an extract from a business news programme. They focus on the skills involved in chairing meetings, at the specific language used and then study a text which presents an interesting alternative approach to running meetings.

Strategies for handling disagreement in meetings are studied. A recording presents the language used to control a meeting. Students then study useful expressions for chairing meetings. Students play the chairperson's game and finally participate in three meeting simulations.

The grammatical focus is on linking and contrasting ideas, and the lexical focus is on the language of companies and capital.

Digital resources: Unit 6
Online Workbook; In company interviews Units 4–6 and worksheet; Extension worksheets; Glossary; Phrase bank; Student's Book answer key; Student's Book listening script; Fast-track map

---

In this first section, students discuss their own meetings, exchanging ideas on aspects like hierarchy and layout. They focus on useful collocations for describing typical problems in meetings and then read a suggestion for dealing with some of these problems. A recording provides examples of radical approaches to running meetings. Students discuss if any of these solutions could be applied in their own companies/places of work.

1:1 Meetings are challenging to roleplay in one-to-one situations, since they usually involve more than two people. More formal meetings usually have someone in the chair, and involve taking a vote on issues. Some things that you can do in one-to-one are: have a discussion with someone where you have opposing viewpoints; produce an agenda of items to work through with your student; cover useful functions such as making proposals, agreeing and disagreeing, summarising, interrupting, etc. Your student can then produce a set of follow-up notes.

Warm-up
Lead in to the topic by asking focus questions, e.g. *Do the meetings you attend have a chairperson? Do you think it's better to have a chairperson? Do different meetings require different approaches? Why / Why not?*

1 Focus attention on the quotation which Ted Turner, the founder of CNN, has on his desk. Ask students to tell you what they understand by it. (It suggests that people need clear vision and that if you don't fall in line with whoever is in charge, you shouldn't obstruct him/her; if you don't have a clear view, you shouldn't interfere). Get the students to assess how much influence they have in meetings and to describe how they see their own role: leader, follower, or general observer.

2 If appropriate, give a brief description of a regular meeting that you attend, e.g. a staff or teacher development meeting. Use a diagram to highlight the layout/hierarchy if possible. Give students a few moments to think about the questions and draw a simple diagram if possible.

Divide the class into pairs or small groups. If students work in the same company, ask them to regroup so that people in different departments are sitting together. Students explain how their meetings work referring to their diagram if appropriate. Hold a short feedback session, eliciting anything interesting which arose in the discussion. If students have drawn diagrams, they can come out and draw them on the board so that students can discuss if there is an optimum layout/format.

3 As a lead-in, write the word *communication* on the board and brainstorm words and phrases which can form collocations, e.g. *communication breakdown, to break off communication*, etc. Divide the class into teams and set up the activity as a race with a time limit of two minutes. Check the answers.

ANSWERS
1 communication breakdowns   2 communication barriers
3 time wasting   4 point-scoring
5 hidden agendas   6 pulling rank
7 inadequate preparation   8 late starts
9 overruns   10 group-think

Get students to match seven of the collocations with their definitions and check the meanings with the class. Check pronunciation and get students to practise the language by asking questions across the class, e.g. *What do you do when someone pulls rank? By how much do your meetings overrun?*

ANSWERS
a 1   b 9   c 4   d 10   e 5   f 6   g 2

4 Ask students to read the short text and give their reactions. (The approach described in the text may help to alleviate communication breakdowns and overcome

BUSINESS COMMUNICATION

communication barriers. On the other hand, it would probably prolong meetings, as people may get too comfortable!)

5 Ask students to estimate how much time they spend in 'unofficial' meetings. Does business really get done in these kinds of informal gatherings? Get students to work in pairs and predict the key features of each type of meeting. Elicit some ideas for each example and write them on the board.

6 1.24 With weaker classes, check/pre-teach: *indispensable, to dispense with, twist, mingle, irrespective*. Before playing the recording, check pronunciation of the company names. Play the recording through once and ask students to match the approaches to the companies.

Let students listen to the recording again and note down the key features and any pros and cons mentioned for each approach. Play the recording, pausing after each example to give students time to take notes.

ANSWERS	
Ritz-Carlton:	short stand-up meeting
Yahoo:	informal drinks and snacks meeting
Michaelides & Bednash Media:	the non-stop meeting

1.24

A: Coming up on CBN Business: an interview with media king and head of News Corporation Rupert Murdoch, the stock market report and Katy Alexander with the week's business news round-up. But first, suffering from boardroom blues? Tired of taking minutes at meetings that take hours? Tess Liebowitz may have the solution …

B: According to diplomat and economist JK Galbraith, 'Meetings are indispensable when you don't want to do anything.' Therefore, logically, if you really do want to do something, it's the meetings you must dispense with. But can you dispense with meetings altogether? And what would take their place? At several well-known companies they think they've found the answer.

At leading hotel company, Ritz-Carlton, meetings have taken on a different twist. Hotel employees have short stand-up meetings styled much like the catering events they set up for their own guests. They stand, mingle and chat about the latest developments within the hotel. This stand and talk style provides high energy and motivation for the staff to keep maximizing hotel service.

Yahoo has gone one step further by holding regular Friday meetings in and around the work cubicles. Talk is casual and relaxed yet informative – centred around the snack and drink tables set up in the office area. This creates an inclusive communicative atmosphere that can't be replicated in any normal meeting room!

At media strategy company, Michaelides & Bednash they've come up with a different solution. All employees, irrespective of status, work around one enormous central table. Meetings become unnecessary when everyone in the company is sitting just across the table from you the whole time. The working day is a constant meeting!

7 Divide the class into groups and get them to discuss each of the ideas, referring to their notes from the recording, if necessary. Ask students to decide if any of the ideas would work in their own company. Hold a short class feedback session and elicit the students' reactions to each of the ideas. Ask them to vote for the one they think is most workable and then elicit other surprising or radical ways in which companies have approached the problem of ineffective meetings.

Chairing skills

In this section, students first discuss how to complete a phrase about chairing a meeting and then focus on collocations that express what the leader of a meeting might do. They read and discuss a text on the role of the chairperson in meetings and why meetings are often ineffective. They then focus on diplomatic disagreement strategies.

1 Get students to complete the phrase within a two-minute time limit and then compare their ideas. Possible answers include: *a chicken without a head / a country without a leader / a company without a director*.

2 Give students one minute to brainstorm typical things a chairperson does in meetings and write a list on the board, e.g. *welcome attendees, state aims*, etc. Students complete the collocations, using the nouns/noun phrases. Check the answers with the class, highlighting the word stress on compound nouns, e.g. *key issues*.

Students then categorize the skills as to whether they are managing content (C) or people (P). Check the answers and then give follow-up practice by asking questions using the collocations, e.g. *Is it always possible to anticipate areas of conflict? How can a chairperson discipline troublemakers at a meeting? How important is it to stick to the agenda?* etc. Finally, ask the students to highlight three skills that they themselves demonstrate in meetings.

ANSWERS	
a open/close the meeting	P
b welcome/introduce the participants	P
c set/stick to the agenda	C
d ask for/summarize points of view	P
e establish/define the main goals	C
f deliberate over/take the final decision	C
g bring in/shut out other speakers	P
h anticipate/avoid areas of conflict	C
i identify/discipline troublemakers	P
j work out/draw up an action plan	C
k prioritize/assign follow-up tasks	C/P
l explain/focus on the key issues	C

3 Ask students what they think is the most important task of a chairperson. Elicit possible answers and write them on the board, e.g. *keeping to the agenda, dealing with troublemakers, ensuring that an effective action plan is produced*.

Check/Pre-teach: *anthropologist* and refer students to the *Glossary* explanations of *tepee, tribe* and *blaring*. Explain the play on words in the title of the article. The usual

06 LEADING MEETINGS 41

BUSINESS COMMUNICATION

expression is "We have to/must stop meeting like this!" and you say it when you continue to accidentally bump into the same person over a period of time.

Students skim the article quickly to check for the general idea – what happens? where? Then, ask students to read the text intensively and compare their ideas on a chairperson's most important task with that of the author. (His view is that the most important task is to listen.) Elicit students' reaction to this view and to the description of the meeting from the film.

4 Divide students into groups and have them discuss what Begeman would consider the ideal meeting, referring back to the text as necessary to support their ideas. With weaker groups, elicit key language that students can use first and write it on the board, e.g. *For Begeman the ideal meeting is ... Everyone tries to be ... and not to ... The atmosphere promotes ... and discourages ...* etc. Check answers with the class.

As an optional follow-up activity, let students watch the meeting scene from the video/DVD *Dances with Wolves* and give their reactions.

SUGGESTED ANSWER
People listen to each other and have patience with each other, respect each other's views, try to reach a consensus before making decisions; they deal with disagreements diplomatically; people work as a team but respect each other's authority.

5 Check/Pre-teach: *to save face* (do/say something which will stop you feeling embarrassed or looking a fool). Focus attention on the questions and give students a minute to think about a time when they had to disagree strongly with someone without hurting their feelings. One piece of advice is to support the person, but 'attack' the problem, i.e. disagree with the idea expressed, but at the same time say something conciliatory. Elicit some examples and ask students what helped them manage the situation. Elicit how important 'saving face' is in the students' own culture.

6 Elicit ways of disagreeing diplomatically, e.g. *I see what you mean, I hear what you are saying,* etc. Have students read the list of disagreement strategies and match them to the examples a–j. Check the answers.

Point out that it is important to sound sincere when using these phrases. Check students' pronunciation and intonation, getting students to exaggerate their voice range if they sound rather 'flat'. Get students to practise the phrases by giving opinions on a range of topical subjects and eliciting appropriate disagreement, e.g. business practices, current news stories, etc. Students continue giving opinions and disagreeing diplomatically, working in pairs/small groups.

ANSWERS
1 e and i   2 a and g   3 c and h   4 d and j   5 b and f

Managing meetings

In this section, three recordings of a chairperson managing people in a meeting provide listening practice. Students then focus on the language used in the recordings, and then play the Chairperson's game.

1 1.25–1.27 Check/Pre-teach the usual meaning of *timeshare* (holiday accommodation bought by various groups of people so that they can each spend a different time of the year there). Tell students that the start-up company referred to in the recording has a different idea for timeshares.

Play extract 1 and ask students to say what this idea is and what examples are given (to let people buy the use of a luxury item for a short time, e.g. a Ferrari sportscar, a Rolex watch or an item of clothing by top fashion designer Jean-Paul Gaultier). Ask students to brainstorm the pros and cons of the company's idea and write their ideas on the board.

Check/Pre-teach: *to buy something outright, seed capital, to get side-tracked, procurement and delivery system, prohibitive*. Give students the names of the speakers in the extracts: Pieter, Ross, Jack, Tania and Lance. Ask students to listen to all three extracts and compare the pros and cons mentioned with the students' lists on the board. Play the extracts again and elicit further examples. Ask students to read through the questions and answer any that they can. Play the extracts again and get students to complete their answers. Check the answers with the whole class. As a follow-up, ask whether or not students would invest in dotcom companies.

ANSWERS
Extract 1
a Lance. His flight back from Chicago is delayed.
b to review last week's talks; to decide whether to take the proposal further
Extract 2
c The commercial viability of the dotcoms.
d Jack
e Pieter's
Extract 3
g Pieter to investigate logistics; Tania to find out about insurance
h the chair seems to be fairly effective

1.25
Extract 1
A: Okay, thanks for coming, everybody. Erm, has anybody seen Lance, by the way? He was supposed to be here.
B: Oh, yeah, he phoned to say his flight in from Chicago had a two-hour delay. He said to go ahead and start without him.
A: Oh, I wanted his input on this one. Okay, never mind, let's get started, then, shall we? Erm, so, as I said in my email, the purpose of this meeting is to review last week's talks with the people from timeofyourlife.com and, secondly, to decide if we're interested in taking things further. Pieter is going to fill us in on the background. Pieter?
C: Yeah, thanks, Ross. Well, now, timeofyourlife is a really exciting business proposition. Basically, the idea is that ordinary people can buy a kind of timeshare in various luxury goods that they could never afford to buy outright. What happens is you buy points online at the timeofyourlife website and you can use these

points to buy, like, a Ferrari for a day, a Rolex Oyster for a weekend or a Jean-Paul Gaultier original for an evening! Neat, huh? I just love this proposal …
D: Er, sorry to interrupt, but is this going to take long, Pieter? Only I have an appointment at eleven and we have all read the summary on this company already.
A: Jack, could Pieter just finish what he was saying? We're looking at $20 million in seed capital here. I don't want us rushing into anything. But perhaps we could speed things up a little, Pieter. We are short of time and by the end of this meeting I'd like some kind of decision on this.

🔘 1.26
Extract 2
C: So, as you can see, the advance publicity alone is attracting half a million visitors to the timeofyourlife website every day.
A: Sorry, Pieter, but we seem to be getting side-tracked here. This is all very interesting, but can we go back to what we were discussing earlier?
C: Oh, okay. Sure.
A: Perhaps we can come back to this later. Tell us about their logistics.
D: Can I just say something here?
A: Hold on a minute, Jack – you'll get your chance in a moment.
D: It's just that I thought we'd agreed we weren't investing in any more dotcoms.
B: No, Jack. That's what you wanted. But nobody actually agreed.
D: Tania, we've been through this.
B: Wait a minute. Who was it that said …?
A: Okay, okay! Let's all just calm down, shall we? We're here to talk about this proposal we have on the table. Tania, what's your position on this?
B: Well, I agree with Pieter that it's a great business plan. Like you, I'm a little concerned about the logistics, though. The procurement and delivery system for a business like this would be extremely complex. And the insurance costs could be prohibitive.
C: Now, hold on a second! This is all covered in the proposal, Tania. What are you saying? I thought you were with me on this one.
A: Pieter, I think what Tania is trying to say is she likes the idea but the figures don't quite add up.
B: Exactly.
A: Okay, maybe we should take a short break at this point, grab a coffee and meet back here in 15 minutes.

🔘 1.27
Extract 3
A: Okay, so just to summarize what we've said so far. Basically, we like the timeofyourlife idea. At least most of us do. We're aware of the risks involved in a major investment in an e-business, but we think the concept has great potential. We need to make another appointment with these people because we have some doubts about their logistics. Pieter, can I leave that one with you?
C: Sure. I'll get right on to it.
A: We're also a little concerned about the amount of insurance a business like this would need. Tania, can you get back to me on that?
B: No problem, Ross.
A: Great. I think that's about as far as we can go at this stage. Thanks, everybody.
E: Hi, guys. Sorry I'm late. Tania told you the story, right? Say, did I miss anything here?

2 Students focus on the idioms in the listening.

> **ANSWERS**
> a input   b further   c rushing   d through   e figures

3 Write the six categories for chairing language on the board. Elicit examples that students can recall from the recording without looking at the gapped expressions and write them on the board. Then ask students to work in pairs to complete the task.

Check the answers and students' pronunciation by asking them to read their answers aloud. Give initial practice by calling out different language functions and eliciting the correct expression(s), e.g. opening the meeting, moving the discussion on, coming back to the main point, asking someone to wait their turn etc.

> **ANSWERS**
> **Opening the meeting**
> a Okay, let's get started, then, shall we?
> b Thanks for coming, everybody.
> **Setting the agenda**
> c As I said in my email, the purpose of today's meeting is to …
> d By the end of this meeting I'd like some kind of decision on this.
> **Managing the discussion**
> e We seem to be getting side-tracked here.
> f Can we go back to what we were discussing earlier?
> g Okay, so just to summarize what we've said so far.
> **Managing other speakers**
> h Jack, could Pieter just finish what he was saying?
> i Okay, okay! Let's all just calm down, shall we?
> j Tania, what's your position on this?
> **Assigning follow-up tasks**
> k Pieter, can I leave that one with you?
> l Tania, can you get back to me on that?
> **Closing the meeting**
> m I think that's about as far as we can go at this stage.
> n I'm afraid we'll have to stop it there.

4 🔘 1.25–1.27 This is a good chance for students to hear the model sentences in context. Play the recording again and get students to tick off each expression as they hear them. With weaker classes, be prepared to pause the recording briefly as necessary. Elicit the expression which is not used.

> **ANSWER**
> n I'm afraid we'll have to stop it there.

BUSINESS COMMUNICATION

06 LEADING MEETINGS 43

BUSINESS COMMUNICATION

5 Divide the class into As and Bs to play the Chairperson's game. You will need a coin and a small playing piece to represent each student. Monitor the games and be ready to provide language feedback.

Language links
Direct students to the *Phrase bank* in the *Language links* section on page 43 for more on useful expressions for chairing meetings.

6 As a lead-in to the task, write the focus of each of the three meetings on the board and get students to brainstorm related issues and ideas. Check/Pre-teach relevant vocabulary (as shown in brackets below):

Meeting 1: Should genetic tests decide job prospects? (*psychometric tests, to undergo testing, vulnerability, stroke, to inherit, screening, (un)ethical, DNA*)

Meeting 2: Employers spy on workers (*to check up on, CCTV, computer surveillance, gaming websites, covert, phone taps/tapping, security measures, tagging devices, implants, to track, invasion of privacy, to eavesdrop, to trace*)

Meeting 3: Creative way to better management (*fad, weird, to build team spirit, to 'think outside the box', to put on a show, to think laterally*)

Divide the students into groups of three. With larger classes, or if you have an uneven number of students, ask two students to play the same role, but advise them to choose only one chairperson for each meeting. Refer the A students to pages 121 and 130, B to pages 121 and 136 and C to pages 121 and 134. Give students time to read their role card and the relevant article for each meeting. Deal with any vocabulary queries as necessary.

Set a time limit of 15 minutes for each meeting. Before students start the roleplays, check they are clear about their stance on the issue and get them to make notes on the key argument for or against each proposal. With weaker classes, allow students with the same role to work together in preparing for the roleplay. Remind the student who is chairing each meeting to listen to the other students first, to keep the meeting to time and to try to reach a decision on what recommendations to make. Monitor each of the roleplays and take feedback notes.

Ask students to assess how well they chaired their meeting and to say what decisions were reached. Give students feedback on the skill of chairing and on their overall fluency. Then give feedback on any important or common errors. You can choose one of the three meetings for the students to lead. If there is time, you can run all three meetings.

1:1 Do the lead-in as described above. When you have generated some ideas, discuss with your student which two meetings you wish to roleplay. For all the roleplays, it is necessary for both of you to read the background information (see above for page numbers). In the roleplays, you should take the opposite position to your student. If possible, record the meetings so you can play back some extracts later and listen for any language problems.

Language links
Direct students to the *Language links* section on page 42 for more practice of vocabulary relating to companies and capital, and the financial pages.

Language links
ANSWERS

Vocabulary
Companies and capital
1 set up = establish, found, start-up
    take over = acquire, buy into, buy up
    restructure = de-layer, rationalize, streamline
    develop = build up, expand, grow
    close down = liquidate, sell off, wind up
2 1 global 2 economy 3 customer 4 value 5 vision
    6 stakeholders 7 flatter 8 outsourced 9 functional
    10 layers 11 networked 12 flexibility 13 empowered
    14 learning 15 effectiveness 16 total

The financial pages
3 a 3 b 6 c 8 d 7 e 1 f 4 g 2 h 5
4 a takeover bid   b top
    c base rate   d tipped to
    e crackdown   f fourth-quarter
    g hit   h offshore investments
    i stock market flotation j dries up
5 a downturn in demand   ✗
    b sales boom   ✓
    c windfall profits   ✓
    d housing slump   ✗
    e upswing in the economy   ✓
    f economic recovery   ✓
    g rise in the cost of living ✗
    h rise in the standard of living ✓
    i stock market crash   ✗
    j credit crunch   ✗

Grammar
Linking and contrasting ideas
a A despite   b A owing to
   B in spite of the fact that   B consequently
   A Whilst   A although
   B all the same
c A seeing as   d A though   e A as a result of
   B though   A Nevertheless B whilst
   C and yet   A in order to
   A To   B in order that
                                   A seeing as

Phrase bank
Chairing meetings
a in on / to   b over / with
c back to / out   d Hold on
e off / for   f anything they want
g back to / on   h to
i up / up

44   06 LEADING MEETINGS

07 Coaching

Learning objectives

This unit is about coaching in the business world.

Students begin by considering when coaching can help businesspeople, and when it is not appropriate. Students then discuss a cartoon. After that, they decide on exactly what a coach does by selecting items from a list.

Students read an article entitled *The Coach Approach*. They study a model called the GROW model and complete a GROW chart with specific steps relating to this model. Students then examine some phrases used in a coaching session which follows the GROW model.

Students listen to a coaching session and do a note-taking task. Finally, students take part in a roleplay to practise their coaching skills.

Digital resources: Unit 7

Online Workbook; Extension worksheets; Glossary; Student's Book answer key; Student's Book listening script; Fast-track map

1:1 Find out whether your student is more likely to be a coachee in their job, or if they have a specific role in their organization to coach employees. Give your student frequent opportunities to relate the material in the unit to their own work situation.

Warm-up

Write the word *coach* on the board and tell students that coaching is one of the fastest growing areas in the business world. Ask them to discuss with a partner whether they think that coaches do a useful job, or whether they are unnecessary. Elicit students' responses. Finish off by asking students if they would consider hiring a coach themselves, if they haven't already done so.

1 Explain to students that there are areas in which business coaches may be helpful, and areas in which they cannot be effective. Elicit or provide an example of each and write them on the board, e.g. *a business coach could help with motivating someone, but not with relationship problems, as this has nothing to do with work*. Put students in small groups to make two lists: areas in which coaches can help, and areas in which they can't help. Then, ask one student from each group to present their ideas to another group. Finally, elicit students' ideas and collate them on the board.

SUGGESTED ANSWERS

- Coaching can help with things like day-to-day management issues (team-building, motivation, etc), communication skills (presenting, leading meetings, doing staff appraisals, etc), time- and workload-management, leadership, stress management, career development, building a professional network and moving to a new job.
- Coaching is less effective for dealing with personal problems, especially problems that are not work-related.

2 Ask students to study the cartoon and elicit their responses to the two questions.

SUGGESTED ANSWERS

The man in the cartoon is like a coach in the sense that he helps the other man to get where he wants to go when he seems to be stuck. On the other hand, coaches generally do not provide solutions. They try to get their client or coachee to discover the solutions for themselves.

3 Tell students they will now look in more detail at the kinds of things a coach actually does. Check that students know the words *to impart* (e.g. knowledge) and *intuition*. Ask students to work with a partner and read the list of things that may be done by coaches, management trainers and other professionals. Ask them to underline what they think a coach definitely does. They can also mark what the coach definitely shouldn't do (such as influence behaviour). Elicit students' answers and collate them on the board.

ANSWERS

asking questions, listening, supporting, giving feedback, clarifying goals, facilitating commitment to goals, building rapport, using intuition, establishing priorities, showing empathy, focusing on action

1:1 As an alternative, write the phrases in the box on small cards and give these to your student. Ask your student to sort them into two categories: what a coach does, what a coach shouldn't do.

4 Tell students they are going to read an article called *The Coach Approach* which focuses on some of the things a coach does. Ask students to scan the article and look for any information confirming what a coach does, and what a coach shouldn't do. Tell students to check their answers with their ideas from 3 on the board.

5 Focus students on the highlighted words in the text. Remind students that guessing words from context is a very useful skill. Do an example with the class. Give students time to check the meaning of the highlighted words. Monitor and help as necessary. Check answers with the class. Ask students if any of the words were new and, if so, how they worked out the meaning.

ANSWERS

guru = famous expert
expertise = expert knowledge
career-wise = concerning your career
soft skills = personal qualities and people skills
transitioning = changing

07 COACHING 45

PEOPLE SKILLS

personality clashes = disagreements or conflicts between people
burn-out = getting to a position where you have worked so hard you are exhausted
personal hang-ups = fears or anxieties
obstacles = things preventing you from doing what you want to do
hard-earned wisdom = knowledge you only gain by working for a long time in a job, facing challenges and making mistakes
paramount = of the greatest importance
hold-ups = delays

6 Explain to students that they will now look at a coaching technique called the GROW model (Goal, Reality, Options, Way forward). The steps can be outlined as follows:

G First, set the goal, or aims, of the coaching session.

R Second, ascertain the reality of the current situation – describe what is wrong with it and why it is problematic.

O Thirdly, draw up a list of the options available, and also why these options might prove difficult to implement.

W Finally, in the way forward, the coachee agrees on his or her future course of action, and sets a date to work towards.

Put students in pairs to transfer the eight phrases to the correct part of the diagram. Check answers with the class.

ANSWERS
GOAL: 1 decide on the conversation topic, 2 set objectives for the session
REALITY: 3 describe the current situation, 4 give examples of present challenges
OPTION: 5 discuss alternatives, 6 identify possible obstacles to those alternatives
WAY FORWARD: 7 commit to specific actions, 8 put a timeframe on those actions

7 Ask students to read the list of expressions, all of which the coach said during a coaching session. With reference to the GROW model, ask students to decide at what stage in the GROW process each expressions was said. Ask them to write the correct letter (G, R, O or W) next to each. Do not check students' answers at this stage.

8 2.01 Play the four extracts from a coaching session so students can check their answers to 7. Pause after each section. Check answers with the class.

ANSWERS
a O b W c G d R e O f G
g O h R i W j G k W l R

2.01
Step 1, Goal
A: … Well, that's great, Jim. I'm pleased for you. It sounds like all that work we did on your presentation really paid off.
B: It really did.
A: I knew you could do it … Okay, so what would you like us to work on today?
B: Well, there was one thing. Actually, it's to do with the presentation.
A: Uh huh.
B: I mean, as I said, the talk itself went really well.
A: Right.
B: But then afterwards there was this networking event.
A: Oh, yes?
B: Yeah, and, obviously, a lot of people came up to talk to me about my presentation. And this was my chance to make some useful contacts, but, you know, I didn't feel I really made the most of it.
A: Okay, and what makes you feel that?
B: Well, I didn't seem to get all that many appointments with people. You know, I came away with the usual mountain of business cards, but not that many firm commitments to meet.
A: Okay then, let's look at that, then, shall we? Now, what precisely would you like to get from this session?
B: Well, I suppose I'd just like to be better at going beyond the small talk and doing more real business at these networking events.
A: All right. And, on a scale from one to ten, how important would you say this issue is to you? Let's say one's not important at all and ten's extremely important.
B: Um, well, at least an eight. Maybe a nine. I mean there's no point attending these events if I don't bring home the business.
A: Right, so an eight or a nine. This is obviously a priority for you right now. Okay, so …

Step 2, Reality
A: … Okay, then. So what's the most challenging thing about this right now for you?
B: I think the most challenging thing is just making sure I don't end a conversation with a potential contact without trying to fix a definite appointment. But, you know, I don't want to look desperate or pushy. The problem is, once the event's over, it's much harder to follow up, you know?
A: I understand that. So, ideally, how would you like things to be?
B: Ideally, I'd like to be getting appointments with at least 60% of the people I'm meeting.
A: Okay, and, in comparison with the ideal situation, where are you at the moment with this?
B: Hmm, I'm getting maybe 30% – on a good day!
A: So you're looking to double your effectiveness?
B: Well, I know that sounds like a lot to ask, but yes, I suppose I am.
A: All right. And can you give me a few examples of what you're finding most challenging?
B: Well, I guess the trickiest thing is just making the switch, you know.
A: The switch?
B: Yeah, the switch from small talk to business.
A: Oh, okay.
B: It's like that awkward moment when you have to say: 'So, perhaps we could do some business together?' I mean, however you say it, it's difficult if they don't make the first move.
A: All right, let's explore some options here …

Step 3, Options

A: Okay, now we've talked around the issue a bit, Jim; looked at some of the problems you're having. So what alternatives do you think you have here?
B: Well, you know, as we've been talking, it's struck me that maybe I'm coming at this the wrong way.
A: Uh huh. Go on.
B: Well, maybe I'm focusing too much on what I'm getting out of these networking events, instead of focusing on the people I'm meeting.
A: Sounds interesting. Would you like to say a bit more about that?
B: Well, I could be spending more time thinking about what I can do for them rather than what they can do for me.
A: Okay. And is there anything else you could be doing?
B: I think maybe there is. I mean these events are hopeless for doing business, anyway. There's no privacy. Everyone's moving around, drink in one hand, food in the other. All I want is the chance to talk to them again after the event. So perhaps if I can do them a favour of some kind – send them some interesting data, introduce them to someone else – that's all the excuse I need to contact them again and start to build some kind of business relationship.
A: Sounds like another good idea. So what's stopping you from pursuing these options?
B: Well, nothing, I suppose – except that I'd need to know a lot more about the people I'll be meeting, before I meet them.
A: Good point. Okay, let's think about how you might manage that …

Step 4, Way forward

A: All right, Jim, I think we're making some progress here. We've looked at some of the options you have for improving your networking – in particular, how to turn things around and focus on your contacts a bit more. So what are the steps you need to take now?
B: Um, well, I obviously need to be doing a lot more research on the people I'm meeting at these events, so that I can have some ideas for ways in which I might be able to help them without actually having to talk business with them straightaway.
A: All right.
B: And I need to have a reason to contact them again at least once, maybe twice, before raising the subject of business. And, hopefully, I won't need to raise it at all, because they'll do it.
A: Okay. So build the relationship first?
B: Exactly. I think maybe I could also benefit from some kind of course on networking. Perhaps I could improve my communication skills there. You know, learn some tricks of the trade?
A: That could help too. So, what do you think is the first thing you need to do?
B: I'm not sure. I need to start getting my client research sorted out. That could take some time and I may need some assistance with it.

A: Do you have someone to help you with that?
B: Yes, I think so. And I should also find out about networking courses. Maybe that's my first step. I'd like to feel I'm taking some immediate action.
A: Okay, and when are you planning to take that first step? Shall we commit to a date by which that will be done?
B: Yes, I think that's something I can probably do by the next time we meet.
A: In two weeks?
B: In two weeks, yeah.
A: All right, so shall we discuss that next time?
B: Yes, let's do that. And in the meantime I'll also talk to my assistant about that client research.
A: Good idea …

9 2.01 Tell students that they will hear the recording again. This time, ask them to take notes on how Jim responds to each of the questions. Check answers with the class. Finally, ask students how successful they think this coaching session was.

ANSWERS

a He could focus more on what he can do for people, rather than what they can do for him.
b Do research on the people he's going to meet, and find a reason to contact them again.
c He'd like to work on his networking.
d Making sure he doesn't end a conversation without fixing an appointment.
e He could do them a favour, e.g. send them some information, and then he has an excuse to contact them again.
f Getting better at going beyond small talk and doing real business.
g Nothing – but he needs to know more about the people before he meets them.
h He's getting appointments with 30% of the people he's meeting.
i Get his client research sorted out.
j At least an eight, maybe a nine.
k By the next meeting, in two weeks' time.
l Making the switch from small talk to business.

10 Divide the class into groups of three, and assign the three roles: coach, coachee and observer. In cases where there is an extra student, there can be two observers in the group. Ask students to read their role card on page 124 and give them a few minutes to prepare their role. Remind the coach and the observer to review the GROW model.

When ready, give students about five minutes to perform the roleplay. Monitor and take notes on language and students' use of coaching skills. Allow five minutes for the observer feedback. Finish by providing feedback on coaching skills and language.

1:1 Proceed with your student taking the role of the coachee and you of the coach. If your student needs to coach others in their job, reverse the roles. Reflect together on the stages of the coaching meeting and see if your student can identify the extent to which it followed the steps of the GROW model.

MANAGEMENT SCENARIO B

Coach crash

Learning objectives
This scenario is based on the issue of giving supportive feedback on a presentation. Students begin by discussing their thoughts on how sports coaches provide feedback and how this differs from the business world. They read a memo asking an employee to give a presentation at short notice. They then watch a video in which the presenter receives feedback on her presentation. They consider ways in which the feedback could have been handled more sensitively. Students then watch a second video and compare the ways in which the coach has improved his feedback technique. Finally, as a post-viewing follow-up, students work in pairs in order to give their own presentation and give appropriate feedback on their partner's presentation.

Digital resources: Management Scenario B
In company in action B1–B3 and worksheet; Extension worksheets; Glossary; Student's Book answer key; Student's Book listening script; Fast-track map

Warm-up
Ask students to think about a presentation they have given which they were happy with and one which they felt unhappy with. Tell them to describe both presentations to their partner, giving reasons why they were pleased or disappointed.

1:1 Ask your student to talk about their experience of giving and attending presentations to discover if this is something they need to do professionally. Find out if they have ever received feedback on a presentation, or if they have given feedback to others. Ask your student if any of the feedback they have given or received was delivered skillfully, and why they think so.

1 Before starting, brainstorm the names of some famous football coaches that students are likely to know, such as Sir Alex Ferguson (previously with Manchester United); José Mourinho (previously with Chelsea), and Pep Guardiola (previously with Barcelona); or other well-known sports coaches, including a national coach. Invite students to discuss the two questions with each other, and then elicit students' ideas. Collate these on the board.

SAMPLE ANSWERS
- Most sports coaches use a 'carrot and stick' approach, motivating and encouraging the sportsperson to perform, but sometimes shouting at them so that they get angry and want to win.
- Business coaches usually encourage people to build on their successes. They identify weaknesses more sensitively. They certainly would not bully someone, as a sports coach might.

2 In this task, students read an email to Cassie from Peter Neubauer in which he asks her to prepare a presentation. Students will answer true or false comprehension questions. Give students time to read the email. You may need to pre-teach or check that students know the phrases *expenditure, a dry-run, to iron out (a problem)*. Go through the answers with the whole class and ask students to justify why they have chosen a particular answer.

ANSWERS
a T to increase their contribution
b F it's short notice
c F he won't be back in London until Friday morning
d F it's short notice, he puts pressure on her (it's top priority), he's not available to help her

3 🎥 **B1** Tell students they will now watch the first of two videos. In the first one, they watch Peter Neubauer giving feedback to Cassie on her presentation. Give students time to read the list and check they understand each of the items. Tell them they should put a tick next to the correct person. Play the video and then ask students to compare their answers. Check answers with the class by asking students to tell you who does what. Ask the students what they think about the feedback Peter gives. Ask them to describe how they think Cassie, Peter and Sue feel.

ANSWERS
Cassie	feels nervous, makes excuses
Peter	is insincere, criticizes personal behaviour, refuses to share responsibility, makes judgements
Sue	is diplomatic, makes constructive suggestions

🎥 **B1**
Cassie: So, um, as I said before, um, although we've had very successful fund-raising campaigns this year, our costs have risen, um, a lot. And, er, we expect them to continue to increase, um – unlike two years ago when they actually fell. Er, oh I forgot to mention the tax changes last year which means we'll have even less money available – sorry about that. Um, and, oh um, yes, er, the other big problem we're facing is, um, foreign exchange. If the pound continues to weaken, um, our project costs will increase. Er, but I don't want to go into detail on that now. Um, so, um, basically, that's, that's about it. Er, that's the situation we're facing. Um, yeah, er …

Peter: All right, Cassie, let's leave it there. Um, we'll take the questions as read. Um, good job … basically.

Cassie: Oh, er, thanks. Did you think it was all right?

Peter: Well, er, yeah, not too bad. The, er, the new logo looked good.

MANAGEMENT SCENARIO

Cassie: Yeah, it's nice, isn't it?

Peter: But for goodness sake, Cassie, a presentation has to have a structure! I mean, that was a complete mess! Has no-one ever told you that a presentation should have a beginning, a middle and an end?

Cassie: I'm sorry Peter, I just didn't have enough time …

Peter: Look, I'm not asking for perfection, just an introduction at the beginning, and a conclusion at the end. I mean, your presentation just … kind of fizzled out. You have to have a strong finish, leave your audience with the key take-home message … and at least invite them to ask questions!

Cassie: Well I wasn't really sure … I didn't know how long you wanted it …

Peter: Come on, Cassie, don't make excuses! I told you to ask if you needed help. You didn't ask, so I thought everything was okay.

Cassie: Yes, but you were in Stuttgart …

Peter: So why didn't you just call me? If I'd known there was a problem I could've done something about it! Oh, I hate it when this happens! Look, Cassie, crying won't getting us anywhere; pull yourself together and … be professional.

Cassie: It's okay, I'll, I'll work on the structure …

Peter: Yes, but it's not just the structure. The whole thing was a disaster from start to finish! I mean, your body language, your voice, your slides … You mustn't look nervous, you have to sound confident, otherwise you make your audience feel uncomfortable! And why did you speak in that funny little voice?

Cassie: I don't know, I just don't know!

Peter: It's not good enough, Cassie, do you hear me? We'll have to do this again on Monday morning.

Sue: Feedback on her presentation, right?

Peter: You heard it?

Sue: I was in the office next door. These walls are thin.

Peter: Sorry. Honestly Sue, I didn't mean to upset her. If I'd known this was going to happen I'd have done the presentation myself.

Sue: Don't you think you're being a little hard on her?

Peter: I tried to be positive, but … it was just such a mess!

Sue: I see. Well, I got this at a management training session last year. You might want to look through it over the weekend. I found it very helpful.

Peter: Oh. Okay, er, thanks, Sue, I'll do that.

4 ▶ **B1** Check and clarify some of the tricky or new expressions in the video such as: *a mess, to fizzle out, to pull yourself together*. Ask students to read through the questions. In the second viewing, pause the video from time to time in order for the students to write down their answers. Check answers with the class.

ANSWERS

a He likes the logo. He is trying to find something positive to say.
b lack of structure, weak ending, no invitation to ask questions, body language, voice, slides
c not enough time, Peter didn't give enough guidance and wasn't available to help
d 'These walls are thin.' i.e. very diplomatically
e 1 Peter refuses to share responsibility by putting the emphasis on Cassie not coming to him for help.
  2 Peter makes negative judgements about Cassie's personal qualities. Peter is insensitive.
  3 Sue uses an indirect question to be diplomatic.
  4 Sue makes a constructive suggestion.

5 Ask students to work in pairs to consider their own personal experience as a presenter who has had a disastrous experience; someone who has given feedback to others on a presentation; or someone who has, like Sue, coached an employee on how to provide feedback. Give students a few minutes to discuss their response with a partner. Then elicit some students' answers. Encourage other students in the class to ask probing questions for more details.

6 Students have a chance to discuss good techniques for giving feedback to someone. Put students in pairs in order to discuss ways in which Peter can improve. Tell them to make notes under the heading *dos and don'ts of coaching*. Elicit students' ideas and collate them on the board.

7 Divide students into As and Bs. Tell As to look at page 122 and Bs to look at page 129. Monitor and help with any vocabulary as necessary, e.g. *to extrapolate*. Put students together for the information exchange. Ask students to look at the list of dos and don'ts on the board and compare these with the information at the back of the book. Ask students to comment on how easy or difficult they think the skill of providing feedback is.

8 ▶ **B2** Tell students that they will now watch a second video clip in which they will see Peter and Cassie working on the presentation again. As a way in, watch the first section showing Cassie's presentation with the sound down. Focus the students on her body language and ask them to speculate on how well the presentation went. Then, ask students to watch the video and tick the points on the list of dos on page 122 that Peter implements. Check answers with the class.

ANSWER

Peter implements all points on the list.

▶ **B2**

Cassie: So in conclusion, let me just summarize the main points. Over the last two years our costs have increased significantly. Unfortunately we expect them to continue to increase. Despite successful fundraising campaigns this year, our overall level of funding continues to fall. In addition, tax changes and the weakening pound have reduced our capacity to fund overseas projects. The bottom line is this: unless we can find additional sources of funding, our ability to fight water-related disease will decrease – and that means more children in East Africa will be at risk. Ladies and gentlemen, I hope I've convinced you that the lottery should increase its grant to Blue Rock. I'll be happy to answer your questions.

MANAGEMENT SCENARIO

Peter: Cassie, that was excellent! Really, really good!
Cassie: Thank you. Well, to tell the truth, Sue gave me some help over the weekend.
Peter: Did she now? That was kind of her. She gave me some help too, actually. Look, I owe you an apology, Cassie. I was much too hard on you on Friday.
Cassie: No, it's all right. I know you just wanted to improve the presentation. And I have to admit, it was rubbish!
Peter: No, it just needed a bit of polishing, that's all. But I shouldn't have been so aggressive. I'm sorry about that. Anyway, you've made a huge improvement.
Cassie: Really? Did you think it was all right?
Peter: Definitely. Have you got a few minutes to talk about it now?
Cassie: Yeah, sure.
Peter: All right. Um, you go first – how did you feel about it?
Cassie: Well, overall much better. I think the structure was a lot clearer. Um, but maybe it was a bit too long?
Peter: No, not at all. It was just the right length.
Cassie: Oh, right. Well what did you think?
Peter: Well there were lots of really good points. The structure was fine, like you said. You were confident, you looked comfortable – having the pointer in your hand was a really good idea – and your voice was better, much more authoritative, more in control. That'll make a really good impression.
Cassie: Thanks, Peter.
Peter: And the ending was really clear; you did a good job there.
Cassie: Oh, thank you for being so positive. What about the negatives, what didn't you like?
Peter: Actually there's only really one question in my mind. I just wonder whether we still have too many slides?
Cassie: Yeah, I thought about that too. I wanted to cut two or three, but I wasn't sure which ones.
Peter: Maybe there's a couple of places we can condense two slides into one; shall we have a look through them together?
Cassie: Yeah.

9 **B2** Check that students know the words *authoritative* and *to condense*. Ask students to read the phrases and see if they can decide which coaching tips each one represents. Then play the video again. Ask students to listen out for the five phrases, and to check and confirm their answers. Elicit students' answers.

> **ANSWERS**
> a Get permission to give feedback.
> b Invite the presenter to give feedback first.
> c Start with the positives.
> d Use questions and indirect language.
> e Try to agree on a specific action plan.

10 In this task, students will give a short, 'past-present-future' presentation, asking for money. Put them in small groups to discuss what investments they could ask for. Check that all students have decided on one before they start preparing their presentation. Ask students to work alone to prepare their presentation. They could do this for homework. Students can use any tools available to them, such as PowerPoint or overhead transparencies.

Divide the group into pairs. Each student gives their presentation to small groups (or to the class) while their partner takes notes using the checklists on page 133. After the presentations, students give their partner feedback. When they have finished the feedback, encourage each presenter to tell their 'coach' how useful the feedback was. Finish the lesson with language feedback.

1:1 Decide whether it is more useful for your student to take the role of the presenter or the coach. If you are the presenter, give a fairly basic presentation which is not too polished, so that there is scope for your student to genuinely offer help using the checklists on page 133. Record the session and then play it back in order to prepare language feedback for your student. Alternatively, listen to the recording together and deal with feedback on performance and language as you listen. If it is not possible to record the presentation, ask your student to reflect on their performance as either presenter or coach and to say what went well and how they could improve.

08 Promoting your ideas

Learning objectives

This unit is about how best to promote your ideas, taking your own feelings, style and abilities into account, as well as those of your audience. It will be of particular interest to students involved in giving sales or product presentations.

Students discuss how important it is to present ideas professionally in their business. They listen to five business presenters talking about what makes them nervous and focus on useful language from the recording. They then brainstorm ways to keep a presentation short and simple.

Students discuss cross-cultural aspects of giving presentations based on recordings about audience expectations in different countries. This is followed by a language focus on phrasal verbs and idiomatic expressions. They read a short text on intrapreneurs – creative minds within an organization – and study useful expressions from the text. A second recording of two managers presenting a new product idea provides a detailed model for students to prepare their own sales presentation in a final fluency activity.

The grammatical focus is on the passive and the lexical focus is on phrasal verbs.

Digital resources: Unit 8

Online Workbook; Extension worksheets; Glossary; Phrase bank; Student's Book answer key; Student's Book listening script; Fast-track map

---

In this first section, students focus on the importance of presenting ideas professionally and discuss how they themselves feel about giving presentations. They listen to a recording of five business presenters explaining why they get nervous. They then focus on useful expressions for saying what went wrong and practise phrasal verbs taken from the recording. A short text containing a radical idea for keeping presentations brief and clear provides stimulus for discussion.

1:1 This unit is ideal for any student who needs to give a presentation. The language covered involves 'pitching' an idea. Before starting, find out as much as possible about situations in which your student needs to present, so you can customise the unit. For example, when your student decides on a product for their pitch in 'Pitching your idea' (on page 52), they can select a product from their own industry, if possible.

Warm-up

Ask students if they have ever heard a speech which went wrong, e.g. an after-dinner speech that went on too long, or if they have ever given a disastrous speech themselves. Ask students to read the quotation from Forbes and ask if anyone shares the same fear of public speaking.

1 Ask students if they need to put forward ideas in formal presentations as part of their job. Do a quick show of hands on who is keen on giving presentations and who tries to avoid them. Elicit exactly what students enjoy/dislike about giving presentations.

2 2.02 Get students to brainstorm a list of what they think the five speakers will mention, based on the students' own examples in 1. Collate the ideas on the board. With weaker groups, check/pre-teach: *to sweat, nightmare, to stare at, not to have a clue, to ruin, to rush, distracting, tense*. Play the recording through once and get students to check their predictions. Then ask students to summarize the problem for each speaker, and discuss any worries they share with the speaker.

2.02

1 Erm, well, to tell you the truth, there's a part of me that's still scared I might just dry up completely. I mean, you know, your mind goes completely blank? Makes me sweat just thinking about it. I have this nightmare where the audience has gone deadly quiet, and everybody in the room's just staring at me and I haven't got a clue what to say next! It's only ever happened to me once, thank goodness, but I still lose sleep over it in case it ever happens again.

2 Technology. Well, if anything can go wrong, it will. About a year ago, I had not one, but two projectors break down on me. And then my mike went funny as well. I sounded like Darth Vader out of *Star Wars* for about half an hour until they fixed it. Completely ruined my whole presentation, obviously. I went mad with the technicians afterwards. But what can you do?

3 I always seem to run out of time and then have to rush the end of the talk or, even worse, run over schedule. Audiences hate that. I've had people tell me I overprepare, but it doesn't seem to matter what I do, I always have at least 20 minutes too much material. So, for me, every talk's a race against the clock!

4 Well, some people, older people especially, have told me that I move around too much when I speak in public – you know, that I pace up and down and wave my arms about. They say it's distracting. They can't concentrate on what I'm saying. But for me, as an Italian, you know, it's quite normal for us to jump around, be rather dramatic. So, now I worry about trying to stand still. And that just makes me feel tense and uncomfortable.

BUSINESS COMMUNICATION

5 What was it Franklin D. Roosevelt said? The only thing to fear is fear itself? That's the thing I'm afraid of, still, after all these years in business – fear. Ridiculous, isn't it? But fear's an absolute killer in a presentation. Your mouth goes dry. Your heart speeds up. Your legs turn to jelly. In my experience, the first two minutes are usually the worst. Survive those and you're in with a chance.

3 Students guess the word. Point out they can use any tense of the verb *go* to complete the expressions.

ANSWER
goes

4 Give students a few seconds to identify the two phrases and elicit the answers.

ANSWERS
you can't think of anything = a (your mind goes blank)
your microphone doesn't work properly = c (your mike goes funny)

5 Students complete the task and then compare their answers with a partner. Check answers with the class by calling out each letter and inviting individual students to read out their answers.

For further practice, get the students to ask questions across the class using the expressions in 4 and 5, e.g. *Has your mind ever gone blank? Have you been involved in a project which has run over schedule?*

ANSWERS
a You dry up completely.	b Your equipment breaks down.
c You run out of time.	d You run over schedule.
e You pace up and down.	f Your wave your arms about.
g Your heart speeds up.	h Your legs turn to jelly.

6 Ask students to guess what the acronym K.I.S.S. stands for. (It is from training in writing skills and other areas and is the title of the short text in this exercise.) Ask students to read the text and elicit their reaction. Students then brainstorm other ways of keeping a presentation short, e.g. using a friend in the audience as a timekeeper.

Audience analysis

In this section, the students listen to a series of recordings on audience expectations in different countries and discuss cross-cultural aspects and stereotypes. Students then focus on phrasal verbs and idioms from the recordings.

1 2.03–2.08 As a lead-in to the listening task, ask students if they have ever given a presentation to an audience from another country or culture. Ask focus questions, e.g. *Did you change the content or the way you delivered the presentation to suit that audience? If so, how?* For example, including more technical data to justify their argument, or omitting jokes they would have otherwise included.

Check/Pre-teach: *to offend, eloquent, the hard sell, assertive, slick, gimmick, humour, wisecrack, to overwhelm, harmony, compatibility, commitment, anecdote, (jokes) at your own expense, to build rapport, to wow.*

To prepare students for the listening task, elicit what expectations they think the countries have and what adjectives they associate with each nation. Play the recording, pausing between each extract and give students time to record their answers. Play the recording again if necessary. Ask students to check the answers on page 122 and elicit their reactions. Check the key words students selected to justify their answers. Refer them to the listening script on pages 146–147 to see the full context if appropriate.

ANSWERS
USA	3	assertiveness, gimmicks, competitiveness, humour
Germany	1	expertise, technical information, PowerPoint, no jokes, detail
Japan	4	quiet confidence, thoroughness, formality, sense of harmony, long-term commitment
UK	5	sense of humour, knowledge, storytelling, not too technological
France	6	style, formality, logical organization, preparation, ability to deal with tough questions
Kuwait	2	personal touch, eloquence, enthusiasm, liveliness

2.03
Extract 1

Er, well, I think the most important thing to remember is that people expect you to be an expert in your field of business. I mean a real expert. That means you should have all the technical information at your fingertips. Which is not to say they won't want to see it all in print after the presentation as well. And if you don't cover every detail in your pitch – costings, cashflow projections, everything – believe me, they won't be slow to interrupt you to ask for it. People here seem to like PowerPoint, the whole technology thing, you know. A word of warning, though: forget the jokes. If you try to be a comedian, they just won't take you seriously.

2.04
Extract 2

Erm, I think the main thing here is to give your presentation the personal touch. That's what they value above everything else. You see, they're judging you as much as, if not more than, what you're actually talking about. But, erm, I think too many presenters worry about offending the local culture and then they end up sounding much too conservative. Don't. Be loud, be lively, be eloquent. They love all that. It's true that attention spans do tend to be a bit short sometimes and you'll get loads of interruptions, but just go with the flow. In any case, people will probably want to talk to you about everything all over again later.

2.05
Extract 3

Well, it's almost a cliché, but the hard sell does actually work here. And, believe me, you really can't be too assertive. In fact, they want you to impress them and expect you to work hard to maintain their interest. So, be fast, be slick, make sure you have a few gimmicks up your sleeve. They like all that stuff. And you can say as many nasty things about your competitors as you like – especially if they're funny. Humour's nearly always appreciated, and, er, you don't need to be too subtle with that. They don't want dark sarcasm, though – so nothing too negative. Wisecracks, clever remarks – that's what they tend to go for.

2.06
Extract 4

Erm, my main piece of advice here is: don't overwhelm them with your enthusiasm. Of course, they expect you to be highly competent and confident, but quietly confident. People will probably have read through all the paperwork beforehand, but they'll want you to go through all the main points again. For the sake of formality and politeness, they'll want to hear it directly from you. But don't get so carried away talking about your own ideas that you forget to point out why it's their company you especially want to do business with. That's very important – creating a sense of harmony and compatibility between you and them. Oh, and a long-term commitment for them, by the way, is 20 to 25 years, not three to five, as it is in the States.

2.07
Extract 5

I suppose having a sense of humour's the main thing. In fact, you can't do without it really. Certainly, if you haven't made them laugh even once within the first five minutes, you probably won't be very popular. People may even switch off altogether. Speakers are kind of expected to be fairly entertaining as well as knowledgeable about their product or service. You don't actually have to crack jokes the whole time, but anecdotes and amusing stories seem to go down well. Making jokes at your own expense, especially, seems to help build rapport with an audience that can otherwise seem a bit cold and unfriendly. And don't try to wow them too much with technology. Be too techie and people'll just think you're showing off.

2.08
Extract 6

Being stylish seems to be what matters here – both in terms of your personal appearance and how you actually come across as a person. It's true that you do have to keep up a certain formality and your talk should always be logical and well-organized, but within those constraints you can be as imaginative and innovative as you like. In fact, unless you are offering something pretty special, something attractive – something unique that they haven't seen before, you'll find them very difficult to persuade. Obviously, knowing exactly who you're presenting to is always important, but here it really is essential that you do your homework. And, er, don't be surprised if the questions you get asked seem quite hostile. Tough questioning is all part of the business culture here.

2 Ask students how far they agree with the profiles given by the speakers and if they see globalization as a way of eliminating stereotypes. Point out that while it may be useful to know common features about a cultural group, there is a negative side to stereotyping, which can be dangerous and harmful.

3 After the students have matched the phrasal verbs, check the answers and the word stress.

ANSWERS
a 4　b 5　c 1　d 8　e 7　f 2　g 6　h 3

4 Students match the phrasal verbs with the meanings. Check answers with the class. As a follow-up, divide the class into groups and get students to write questions using some of the phrasal verbs. Do an example with the whole class, e.g. *How do Americans come across?* and then get students to ask and answer their questions.

ANSWERS
a present yourself = come across　b lose interest = switch off
c be appreciated = go down well　d try to impress = show off
e like = go for　f repeat = go through
g maintain = keep up　h manage without = do without

Language links

Direct students to the *Language links* section on page 53 for more practice of phrasal verbs.

5 Tell students to imagine a visiting presenter has asked for tips on giving effective presentations in their own culture. With weaker groups, ask specific focus questions such as: *Should they use PowerPoint? Give a lot of technical data? Give a handout? Tell jokes?* etc. Students present their ideas to the class, using an OHT if appropriate. With monolingual groups, students can compare their advice across groups; with multilingual groups, ask students if the advice fits with their own expectations about the nations discussed.

6 Ask students to complete the idioms from memory if possible. Refer students to the listening script on pages 146–147 to check their answers.

ANSWERS
a You should have all the technical information at your **fingertips**.
b Give your presentation the personal **touch**.
c You'll get loads of interruptions, but just go with the **flow**.
d Don't get too carried **away**.
e Have a few gimmicks up your **sleeve**.
f It really is essential that you do your **homework**.

7 After the students have decided which piece of advice is most important, ask them to compare their ideas in small groups.

Innovation

In this section, students read a short text on *intrapreneurs* (a term derived from *entrepreneur* used to describe people who are the driving force behind ideas in companies). They

BUSINESS COMMUNICATION

listen to a four-part recording of two managers presenting an idea for a new product to their board of directors.

1 Elicit examples of companies that need to keep ahead of competitors by bringing out innovative products/ services, e.g. Google gives employees time to develop their ideas; Microsoft® creates products which customers then realize they need; pharmaceutical companies which invest huge amounts in R&D (research and development). Ask students how important innovation is in their company and elicit some examples.

2 Write the word *intrapreneur* on the board and ask students to guess the meaning. Students then read the text to check. Ask students to discuss this type of initiative-taking in relation to their own company.

3 Ask students to read the text again and look for the words and phrases. Remind students to look for a word in the same form as the definition and also to use the context to help them. Check the answers with the class and then get students to record any of the new words they want to use in their active vocabulary. Expand on these by eliciting other forms of the words or useful collocations, e.g. *persistence, to overcome an obstacle*, etc.

ANSWERS
a hands-on   b dedicated   c persisted   d obstacles
e common denominator   f champion

4 Find out if students have been involved in the development of new ideas in their company and ask them to give examples. If students haven't, ask if there is an R&D department which handles new ideas. Elicit ways in which the students' company keeps up with innovations in their industry, e.g. by attending international conferences.

5 Ask students to study the flow chart for a couple of minutes then add the stages of the presentation to the chart in the correct order. Check answers with the class.

ANSWERS
1 Open the presentation   2 Outline the objectives   3 Arouse interest   4 Quote some relevant statistics   5 Identify a gap in the market   6 Introduce the new product   7 Describe the main product features   8 Sum up the key message   9 Ask for project approval   10 Lead into the Q&A session

6 2.09–2.12 Lead in to the recording by asking students how important the fitness industry is in their country. Ask students to estimate what percentage of people regularly attend a fitness centre/gym and what form of exercise they themselves take, if any. Give students the names of the managers – Rachel Weissmuller and Brad Kennedy. With weaker groups, check/pre-teach: *couch, disgraceful, findings, respondents, to stretch (a brand), to complement, prototype, sleek, to disassemble, child's play, setting, bulky*.

Extract 1
Ask students to read the questions. Play the recording once and give students time to make notes. Then ask students to check their answers in pairs. Play the recording again if necessary. Check answers with the class.

Extract 2
Ask students to read the questions. Play the recording once and give students time to make notes. Then ask students to check their answers in pairs. Play the recording again if necessary. Check answers with the class. Elicit possible answers to d and write ideas on the board.

Extract 3
Play the recording as far as *the ultimate go anywhere exercise machine* to let students see if they predicted the product correctly. Before playing the complete recording, check/ review the vocabulary in the table in task c: *to fit into, to assemble*. Ask students to read questions b–d and play extract 3 through once. Play the extract again if necessary and then check the answers. Ask students to work in pairs to do question e, then elicit possible answers.

Extract 4
Point out that all the phrases in the box are passive forms. Ask students to read and complete the extract. Play the extract through and let students check/complete their answers. Elicit why the passive has been used in this part of the presentation (the focus is on aspects of the product, not on the people who performed any of the actions). Divide the class into groups to discuss the questions in task b. Hold a short feedback session, eliciting what other information is needed, e.g. more details on the exact timescale of the ROI (return on investment), more market research, etc.

ANSWERS
Extract 1
a Yes, because they built up anticipation before presenting the product.
Extract 2
a 1 a mere 13% = the number of Americans that are satisfied with their physical appearance
  2 a staggering 92% = the number of Americans that are dissatisfied with their level of fitness
b mere = surprisingly low; staggering = surprisingly high
c Nationwide survey: reasons given for not becoming a member of MaxOut Health Clubs
  too busy = 53%   too embarrassed = 32%
  too expensive = 15%
Extract 3
a a micro-gym
b 18 months
c Main product features
  • weighs just over **1lb/450 g**
  • fits easily into **a coat pocket**
  • assembles in **under 45 seconds**
  • offers 35 different **exercises**
d You can exercise anywhere.
Extract 4
1 has been fully costed   2 is included   3 is still being carried out
4 would probably be reasonably priced   5 has been suggested
6 could be recorded   7 are currently being considered

54   08 PROMOTING YOUR IDEAS

BUSINESS COMMUNICATION

2.09
Extract 1

A: Good morning, everybody. Thanks for coming. I'm Rachel White, area manager for the north-west division, and this is Brad Kennedy, head of our physiological research unit.

B: Hi.

A: As some of you already know, Brad and I have been working on a project of our own for some time now – a project, which we think you're going to be as excited about as we are. Brad?

B: Thanks, Rachel. Well, now, as the USA's leading chain of health clubs with over a thousand centres in 35 states, we pride ourselves on providing the best in fitness training programmes. And for us, staying in shape is not just a business. It's a way of life. According to the National Center for Health Statistics, 7 out of 10 of us don't take regular exercise. In fact, figures recently published by the Surgeon General show that 70% of Americans are now seriously overweight. That's an alarming statistic. But, you have to admit, a tremendous marketing opportunity! The question is, how do we reach that market with something totally new?

2.10
Extract 2

A: A recent report claims that a mere 13% of Americans are satisfied with their physical appearance. And a staggering 92% are dissatisfied with their current level of fitness. So, why aren't they doing something about it? We did a nationwide survey of people who had previously shown an interest in joining a MaxOut club and then changed their minds. Full details are in the report in front of you, but this chart highlights our main findings. As you can see, 15% of respondents said joining a gym was simply too expensive. 53% said they'd love to join if they weren't so busy. And, interestingly, 32%, almost a third, admitted they were just too embarrassed to join a health club in their present physical condition. They wanted to get fit first! So, what does all this mean? We think the implications are clear. There's obviously a huge market for an inexpensive alternative to going to the gym for people who are conscious of their appearance but short of time. And this represents a golden opportunity to stretch the MaxOut brand and develop a new product that perfectly complements our existing business.

2.11
Extract 3

B: And here it is! The MaxOut Micro-GYM! 40% of our project budget went into constructing the prototype, and it's taken 18 months to get this far with the design, but isn't this just the coolest thing? I'll pass it around in a moment. Ladies and gentlemen, what you're looking at is the world's smallest full-body workout system – ever. It's the ultimate go-anywhere exercise machine. And, we believe, it could be a significant part of this company's future. With its sleek, lightweight design, the Micro-GYM weighs just over a pound, or 450 grams. Disassembled, it fits easily into a coat pocket. The assembly itself is child's play. You can be ready to exercise in under 45 seconds. Now, I know what you're thinking. Can something so small possibly work? Yes, it can. The Micro-GYM offers 35 different exercises for upper body, lower body and mid-section. It can be adjusted from the five-kilo setting for gentle exercise right up to the 18-kilo setting for a real workout. In fact, it can do just about anything that much bulkier and more expensive equipment can. When you can't get to the gym, the Micro-GYM comes to you. You can get fit at home, on vacation, at the office, even in-flight!

2.12
Extract 4

A: You'll have to excuse Brad. He gets a little carried away sometimes. But we do think the Micro-GYM could be an enormously successful sideline to our main business. Okay, to wrap things up. The Micro-GYM has been fully costed – a complete breakdown is included in the report. Product testing is still being carried out, but we would obviously need the go-ahead from you before we proceed further with that. The Micro-GYM would probably be reasonably priced at around $35. It has been suggested that exercise demonstrations could be recorded on DVD and sold online. Both these suggestions would incur extra costs, but are currently being considered. The prospects for Micro-GYM are exciting. What we hope you'll give us today is the authorization to move on to the next stage. Thank you very much.

B: Thank you, Rachel. Okay, we'd like to throw this session open now for questions and suggestions. Feel free to try out the Micro-GYM for yourself. But, sorry, you can't take it home. It's the only one we have at the moment!

> **Language links**
>
> Direct students to the *Language links* section on pages 53–54 for further explanation of the use of the passive, and exercises to practise it.

Pitching your idea

In the final section, students have a chance to try out the techniques studied in the unit. Students prepare and deliver a team presentation on a new product/service.

> **Language links**
>
> Direct students to the *Phrase bank* in the *Language links* section on page 54 for more practice of language for pitching an idea.

Tell students they are going to try out their creativity and presentation skills. Give students a few moments to read through the steps to set the scene. Divide the class into two teams. Team 1 look at page 131 and Team 2 page 135. Tell students to choose their product.

08 PROMOTING YOUR IDEAS

BUSINESS COMMUNICATION

Step One: Prepare
Give students plenty of time for the preparation phase. Offer help where necessary. With weaker groups, write questions on the board to help students focus their ideas, e.g. *How is it different? Has it been done before? How will it fit in with your current product/service range? What are the key USPs/selling points?* Encourage students to invent the necessary data and prepare visual materials.

Step Two: Practice
Tell students to refer to the template of preparing a pitch in 6. Encourage them to incorporate any phrases from 7. Monitor the practice phase and help with vocabulary and pronunciation as necessary. If appropriate, hand out blank cards and get students to write out the key expressions they want to use. Get them to decide who will present each section and to make the handover between presenters as smooth as possible, using bridging expressions, e.g. *Thanks, … / As … was saying, … / As … has already pointed out, …*

Step Three: Perform
Reorganize the seating if necessary to simulate a typical presentation – a semi-circle or rows may be preferable to standard classroom layout. Check that the audience can see the presenters and any visuals they want to use.

Students give their team presentations to the rest of the class. Join in as part of the audience if you wish, but ensure you take feedback notes for each team. Let students conduct the question and answer session after each presentation but set a time limit for each one.

At the start of the feedback session, ask students what they thought went well and what they would change or avoid doing if they gave the presentation again. Give students general feedback on fluency and on their presenting skills before feeding back on important or common errors.

1:1 Before starting, discuss with your student which product would be best to present, or whether your student could use a product from their own company. Write the key expressions for giving a successful presentation on blank cards so that your student can refer to them if they wish during the presentation. Remember that your student can prepare and rehearse at home, use PowerPoint or other presentation software, and give the final presentation in the next class. Video or record the presentation, if possible, and watch/listen to it together, pausing to give language feedback.

Language links

ANSWERS
Vocabulary
Phrasal verbs
1 a We *took*
   on too much work.
   down a few details.
   out a bank loan.
   over the project.
  b They *came*
   through the recession.
   across an accounting error.
   into a lot of money.
   under pressure to resign.
  c She *went*
   on to talk about training.
   over the figures with us.
   off the idea.
   for option B.
  d We *got*
   around the problem in the end.
   into an argument.
   through a ton of paperwork.
   on well.
  e They *put*
   in hours of work on it.
   off the meeting.
   out a press release.
   up most of the cash.
2 a round to + on to
  c up with + up for
  e up against + round to
  g in for + down as
  b on about + on with
  d out of + ahead with
  f in for + back to

Grammar
The passive
1 b We've unofficially been given the go-ahead.
  c Several options are currently being considered.
  d It was generally felt that the project was taking too long.
  e It was unanimously agreed that the proposal required further discussion.
  f The new software has been thoroughly tested.
  g The plant closure will be formally announced next week.
  h The training budget has been provisionally okay'd.
  i It has been tentatively suggested that we could import the raw materials.
2 b It was assumed that this would be accepted.
  c It was stated quite clearly in the contract that payments must be made on the first of the month.
  d It was presumed that current health and safety regulations would be complied with.
3 I've decided to hold an interdepartmental meeting every month from now on. In this way, you'll be able to meet and bring each other up to speed on recent developments in other departments. You'll also get the chance to exchange views on various matters relating to overall corporate strategy. I've pencilled in next Thursday for the first meeting. Look forward to seeing you there.
Robert

Phrase bank
Pitching an idea

Down
1 players
2 competition
3 survey
4 breakdown
5 focus
6 light
9 benefits
10 feedback
12 potential
13 details
15 homework

Across
1 project
7 range
8 figures
11 need
14 advantage
16 brand
17 point
18 findings
19 session

09 Relationship-building

Learning objectives

This unit is about building successful client relationships. Socializing and networking are key business skills, and can be challenging for many students who are able to speak about their business, but find it difficult to converse on more general, everyday topics.

Students talk about first impressions and do a fun questionnaire on networking. They discuss aspects of networking and listen to businesspeople discussing the same points. A further recording provides listening practice and students practise their networking skills in a fluency activity.

The central part of the unit is based on three articles around the theme of getting out of the office. Students listen to a recording of businesspeople socializing before and during a round of golf. They take part in two roleplays, practising mixing sport with business. A second listening task set around a dinner invitation to a colleague's home continues the theme of socializing. There is a focus on the social language used during the evening. In the final section, students act out a similar social situation.

The grammatical focus is on multi-verb sentences and the lexical focus is on social English.

Digital resources: Unit 9

Online Workbook; Extension worksheets; Glossary; Phrase bank; Student's Book answer key; Student's Book listening script; Fast-track map; Quick progress test 2; Mid-course test

---

In this first section, students discuss first impressions. They do a questionnaire about networking. They discuss aspects of networking and then listen to businesspeople talking about the same points. Students consider phrases they could use in a number of situations, listen to three short conversations and act out the same situations.

1:1 Before starting this unit, find out how good your student feels they are at networking. If they do not feel they are especially good at making small talk or socialising successfully, this unit can help. Start each lesson with five minutes of small talk, such as discussing what's in the news.

Warm-up

Ask students how important personal relationships are for their own company/business sector. Let students read the quotation by Henry Quadracci. Ask if they agree, and if they can follow his rule in their business lives.

1 To generate interest in the text, tell students that it is possible to form a first impression in just five seconds and it might take another 20 meetings to change that impression. Check students can pronounce the word *rapport*. Students work in pairs to discuss the questions before reporting back with interesting examples/anecdotes. Draw students' attention to the expressions used in the questions: *to feel an instant rapport with, to take an immediate dislike to, to take too much notice of*. Encourage them to notice and record longer 'chunks' like these to help develop their own fluency.

2 Find out who thinks of themselves as a good networker and tell students they are going to do a questionnaire to find out who is most effective in this area. With weaker groups, check/pre-teach: *to hover, to break the ice, to talk shop* (to talk about your own job/profession), *to let your hair down, to mingle, to persevere, to slip away, to give someone a nod*.

Elicit the answer to 1a in the questionnaire as an example. Point out to students that identifying the fixed expressions/collocations, i.e. *look them in the eye, say hello*, will help them complete the exercise. Students work individually to complete the questionnaire. Check the answers with the class. Students then circle one answer for each question in the questionnaire. Refer students to page 122 to read the analysis of their answers.

ANSWERS

1 a look + say	b hover + wait	c crack + break
2 a talk + catch	b moan + complain	c relax + let
3 a stick + ignore	b try + draw	c feel + mingle
4 a persevere + find	b make + escape	c introduce + slip
5 a look + pretend	b go + make	c give + keep
6 a cut + get	b get + mention	c exchange + get

3 First check students know the word *cliché*. They then discuss statements a–d with a partner. Elicit whole-class feedback on anything interesting which came up, such as examples where humour has helped a situation, or where it has caused problems.

4 🔘 2.13 Tell students they will hear four extracts of businesspeople discussing the questions in 3. Pause after each extract to allow students to make notes.

🔘 **2.13**

Extract 1

Yes, well, it's easy to say don't judge by appearances, but, I mean, we all do it, don't we? You take one look at somebody and you're already weighing them up, deciding how friendly they are, how confident, how interesting … It's automatic. And then two minutes talking to them and you've got them labelled – successful, intelligent, pushy, funny, boring, potentially useful contact … or not.

09 RELATIONSHIP-BUILDING 57

BUSINESS COMMUNICATION

You know, I read somewhere that we actually evaluate people within 10 seconds of meeting them. And apparently that's it! It could then take 10 or 20 more meetings with that person to alter our first impression of them. I'm not so sure that's true, but I do think you can tell a lot about a person on first meeting them. It's the little things – a classy watch, a sharp suit, a nice smile, a nervous gesture, an ugly tie. Bitten fingernails are a no-no for me. Or a limp handshake. The wet fish! Absolute turn-off.

Actually, I think a good firm handshake is really important. I'm working in Germany at the moment. You know the Germans shake hands practically before every meeting? Even if they've already met you!

Extract 2

Actually, I think it's last impressions that we sometimes overlook. I mean, it's the impression you leave people with that counts. If you're meeting a lot of people all at the same event, it's easy just to drift around from group to group and never really make contact, like some kind of social butterfly.

I think you've got to be good at listening and drawing people out, investing some time in them and then making sure you close the conversation in a positive way. The old 'Oops, gotta go. Been great talking to you' thing is really bad. Or 'Here's my card. Give me a call.' Way too impersonal. You have to be careful how you end the conversation because that's what people are going to remember. And there's no point having the conversation in the first place if you're not going to try and make that person feel like it's been really worthwhile.

Extract 3

I think a good sense of humour is essential. At least, in Britain and America, it is. Humour's very much how we build relationships over here. On the other hand, have you ever done business in Finland? I have. Very different situation. You can forget the humour. They don't even really like small talk all that much. They'll lounge around with you in the sauna, no problem! But they don't give much away personally. Just not part of the business culture there.

Of course, it may be that they just don't understand our humour. I mean, humour's very cultural, isn't it? You watch a comedy on a foreign TV channel and it's hard to see what on earth they're laughing at. They probably think the same about our jokes.

But then I think jokes are usually a mistake, anyway, unless you know the other people very well. But you don't have to tell jokes to be humorous. Better just to make a few amusing observations. The worst thing is telling a long complicated joke and nobody laughs. Agony! Don't do it!

Extract 4

Of course, now that we live in the so-called 'network economy', everyone makes a big deal about networking. But it depends who you're networking with. Take the Russians. I mean, they'll have a serious conversation with you on any subject you care to name, but small talk is not really their thing. Same with the Germans, the Swiss, the Swedes – generally very good English, happy to talk about work, but not really keen on the social chit-chat.

But, go out with a group of Russians after work and they really let their hair down! In that sense they're a bit like the Chinese. They like a big sit-down meal with plenty to eat. What they don't like is the mingling, the wandering around chatting to people.

Basically, it's the British, the French, the Latins and the Americans who are into the schmoozing thing. Americans, especially, have made an art of it. I mean, they're always easy to talk to. It doesn't get very deep usually, but they'll come right up to you and start a conversation and, actually, I quite like that. Working the room, as they call it, and that's what it is for them – work.

5 2.13 Allow students to listen again to complete the phrases. Check answers with the class.

ANSWERS

a limp handshake   b social butterfly   c lounge around
d social chit-chat   e schmoozing   f working the room

6 Do the first situation with the class as an example, writing ideas on the board. Then give students time to make their lists in pairs. Monitor and help as necessary.

7 Ask each pair to join up with another pair to compare what they have written.

8 2.14–2.16 Play the conversations and ask students to match each conversation with the situations in 6.

ANSWERS

Conversation 1 – c   Conversation 2 – a   Conversation 3 – b

2.14

Conversation 1

A: Alessandro!
B: Hello, Janine! How are you? I didn't expect to see you here!
A: No, I don't normally come to these things. But a colleague couldn't make it, so I stepped in at the last minute.
B: How long has it been?
A: Oh, ages. A year, at least. You're looking very well.
B: Just got back from holiday. St. Lucia.
A: Lucky you! Look, Alessandro, I was just on my way to an appointment.
B: Oh, okay. No problem. Don't let me keep you. Perhaps I'll catch you later.
A: I hope so. As a matter of fact, I should be free in about an hour or so. Will you still be around then?
B: Oh, yes. It's just me on the stand this year, I'm afraid.
A: Oh, well, in that case, why don't I meet you back here when I'm done and perhaps we can go out for a drink – or grab a bite to eat if you're free. I've lots of news to tell you. And I want to find out all about your holiday!

BUSINESS COMMUNICATION

B: Great. No, I've no plans for this evening. See you later, then.

2.15
Conversation 2

A: Ms Mendoza?
B: Yes.
A: How do you do? I don't think we've been introduced. I'm Martin, Martin Shaw, the new assistant sales manager for our North American division. First week here, as a matter of fact.
B: Oh, pleased to meet you. Welcome to Mexico!
A: Thanks!
B: So you're working with Richard, no?
A: That's right.
B: I head up the biotech team at Zantis here in Tampico. Perhaps Richard has mentioned me.
A: Yes, of course. He told me all about your set-up here. Actually, Richard's just been detained for a moment. But I'm sure he'll be joining us shortly. Can I get you anything to drink, Ms Mendoza?
B: No, I'm fine, thanks. And please, call me Victoria.
A: Right, Victoria, well, you don't mind if I ...?
B: No, no, of course not! What are you going to try?
A: I'm not sure. Could you recommend something typically Mexican?

2.16
Conversation 3

A: Good morning. Ms Vatland?
B: That's right.
A: We haven't met. I'm Daniel Crane. Ana Lindstrom gave me your name. She might have mentioned me?
B: Ah, Mr Crane! Yes, Ana said you'd be stopping by. Can I offer you anything? A coffee, perhaps?
A: Thank you, that would be very nice.
B: Okay. ... There you go. So how are you enjoying the Fair?
A: Well, this is all new to me, but I'm hoping to make some useful contacts. It's certainly been an eye-opener so far. I'd no idea the industry was so developed here.
B: Oh, yes. There's a lot of interest right now. I understand from Ana that you're looking for agents in Scandinavia, is that right?
A: Yes, that's right. We're also looking for a good business lawyer with local knowledge to work with over here. I don't know if you happen to know of anybody?
B: Well, I can think of several people who might be able to help you there. And, as far as agents are concerned, I can certainly put you in touch with some very professional operations.
A: That would really be very helpful, Ms Vatland.
B: Please. Lena.
A: Lena. Ana said you were the person to talk to and I can see that she was right.

9 **2.14–2.16** Play the conversations again for students to compare the language with their lists in 6. Refer them to the listening scripts on page 148 in order to note down any phrases they wish to record.

10 Explain that students are going to do a roleplay which will allow them to try out their networking skills. Divide the group into pairs. Give students a few minutes to prepare and set the scene.

11 Monitor the roleplay and take language notes. When finished, ask each pair to report back on the outcome. Ask what went well and what they would do better/differently next time.

1:1 Before starting the roleplay, discuss the background details with your student, and establish who is who and where you are. Give your student some time to look at the expressions in the phrase bank on page 62. Write down, or encourage your student to write down, any key expressions onto cards. These can be accessed during the roleplay. To make the roleplays more real, prepare the room so that you simulate the three venues: the hotel bar, at a trade fair and at a conference. Record one or more of the conversations, if possible, so that you can listen to it with your student afterwards and give language feedback.

Language links

Direct students to the *Phrase bank* in the *Language links* section on page 62 for more on networking language.

Getting out of the office

In this section, students read three articles about sport/recreational activities and business. They discuss issues raised in the texts and then focus on the meaning of some of the expressions used. The students listen to a group of businesspeople socializing before and during a game of golf, and then practise some of the multi-verb phrases used in the recording.

1 Tell students they are going to read three articles. Let students read the titles and see if they can predict the key points. Students skim the texts first to check if their predictions were correct. Pre-teach the following: *ritual, expertise, scale back, seal a deal, a scratch golfer, humility, lapping, conducive, gaze*.

Focus students on the questions for each article and then allow them to discuss these with a partner. Monitor the speaking activity. Hold a whole-class feedback session, inviting pairs to give feedback on any interesting points which came up during their discussions.

2 **2.17–2.18** Tell students that the recording is divided into two extracts and there are four names to listen out for: Stella, Max, Craig and Karen. Check/Pre-teach: *to partner, to team up with, disposal operation, to dispose of, toxic substance, competitive spirit*. Ask students the following gist

09 RELATIONSHIP-BUILDING

BUSINESS COMMUNICATION

question and play the recording through once to check: *What are the characters talking about and what is the tone of their conversation?* (extract 1 – who will team up with who and the plans for the morning; friendly; extract 2 – how well they're playing; the disposal operation for some toxic waste; the candidates for an important job; more businesslike and slightly strained between Craig and Stella).

Ask students to read the questions for extracts 1 and 2. Play the recording again and let students complete their answers. Check the answers with the whole class. Ask students to give their reaction to each of the characters and how they handled the situation.

ANSWERS
Extract 1
a It's just the right thing on a chilly morning.
b They only want to play for a couple of hours, and they've booked a table for lunch.
c competitive

Extract 2
a badly
b the location of the oil platform disposal
c be more competitive

2.17
Extract 1
A: Stella! Max! You're just in time to join us for a little pre-match get together.
B: Hi, Craig. Hi, Karen. Mmm … is that coffee I can smell?
A: Sure is. They use Arabica beans here – it's just fantastic! Would you like a cup? It really hits the spot.
C: Oh go on then, I could do with warming up a bit.
A: There you go. Stella?
B: Yes, please. It is a little chilly this morning. Beautiful day, though.
A: Isn't it? Well, now, we should probably be thinking of making a move quite soon. Unfortunately, we can't count on the weather staying fine at this time of year. Max, you're partnering Karen. And Stella, you're stuck with me, I'm afraid. Now, I've arranged for us to have lunch at the clubhouse – they've got an excellent restaurant there. So I thought we'd start at the tenth and just play the last nine holes, if that's okay with you. That way we should be able to get round the course in a couple of hours or so.
B: Sounds perfect.
A: And, Max, I think you'll find my game's improved a little since we last played.
C: Splendid! I always like a challenge, Craig. You know that …

2.18
Extract 2
A: Oh, come on! I don't know what's the matter with my game today. I just can't seem to get the ball straight. Sorry, Stella. You must be wishing you'd teamed up with Max.
B: Well, you have been in two sand traps and a lake, Craig! And this is only our third hole!

A: I know, I know. Your shot, Max …
B: Craig, I've been meaning to have a word with you about this disposal operation of ours.
A: Ah, I was wondering when you'd get round to mentioning that. Look, Stella, you know my position on that …
B: Now, Craig, listen to me. You know I want that oil platform disposed of at sea. It's by far the most cost-effective method. Oh, sorry, Max. I'm not trying to put you off your game. Oh, great shot! Wow, that's almost all the way to the flag! Craig, you didn't tell me Max was such a fantastic player.
A: No, I, er, look, Stella, this oil platform – disposing of it at sea. Don't you think it's a bit risky? I know it's technically possible. But there must be 130 tonnes of highly toxic and radioactive substances on that platform!
B: Craig, you're starting to sound like a Greenpeace activist, for goodness' sake! … By the way, I understand you've applied for the top job here in Scotland.
A: Yeah, so?
B: So's Max.
A: What?
B: Yeah. And the way it's looking he may well get it. Seems the board like his competitive spirit.
A: I see.
B: Of course, I could probably put in a word for you. Let's talk later. For the time being, I'd like you to concentrate on your game! I'm not a good loser, Craig!

3 Point out that multi-verb sentences are complex because of the word order and range of structures that can follow different verbs, e.g. *-ing* form, infinitive with or without *to*, a preposition. Ask students to reorder the words in bold to make correct sentences. Refer students to the listening script on pages 148–149.

ANSWERS
a We **should probably be thinking of making** a move quite soon.
b We **can't count on the weather staying fine** at this time of year.
c I **have arranged for us to have lunch** at the clubhouse.
d We **should be able to get around** the course in a couple of hours or so.
e You **must be wishing you had been teamed up with** Max.
f I **have been meaning to have a word with you about** this disposal operation.
g I **was wondering when you would get round to mentioning** that.

Language links

Direct students to the *Language links* section on pages 61–62 for further explanation of the use of verbs in multi-verb sentences, and exercises to practise them.

4 Divide students into AB pairs. Tell Speaker A to turn to page 123 and Speaker B to turn to page 131. Give students time to prepare before each of the two roleplays.

Monitor the two roleplays. Debrief the roleplays: *Did you manage to mix sport and business successfully, or not?* Finally, provide language feedback.

> **1:1** Decide in advance if you are going to do one or both roleplays. In each roleplay, there is a boss and an employee. You will need plenty of time to prepare your role, which you can both do at the same time. Check your student is clear about the concept of a 'hidden agenda'.

Visiting someone's home

In this section, students listen to a couple entertaining a colleague at home. They practise expressions that both host and guest could use in this situation.

1 Ask students if it is common to invite business associates home. Elicit some of the advantages and disadvantages.

2 🔊 **2.19–2.21** Brainstorm typical gifts you could take to a business associate's home. Elicit examples from students' own experience of gift-giving in different countries.

Tell students they are going to hear a dialogue (in three parts) of a dinner at someone's home. Let the students read through the questions for extracts 1–3 and predict as many answers as possible. Play each of the extracts in turn and ask students to complete their answers. Check answers with the class.

ANSWERS
Extract 1
a Yes, she got a bit lost coming off the ring road.
b He's been in the kitchen for a long time, working hard.
c something to drink, or some dessert
Extract 2
a The house needed a lot of building work doing.
b It was almost ruined but now it's okay.
c a refill
Extract 3
a crispy, juicy
b Anne. She wants to know what's going on in Poland.
   I've been <u>meaning</u> to talk to you about this business in Poland.
c He says he'll go and see to the dessert.
d Two

🔊 **2.19**
Extract 1
A: Magda!
B: Hello, Anne. Brrr! It's a bit nasty out there tonight.
A: Horrible, isn't it? Come on in. Let me take your coat. You managed to find us okay, then?
B Well, I got a bit lost coming off the ring road, as usual. Sorry I'm a bit late.
A: Oh, don't worry. Martin's still slaving away in the kitchen. Actually, he had a bit of a crisis with the starter just half an hour ago. You should have heard the language! Probably just as well you weren't here.
B: Oh, right. So Martin's cooking, is he?

A: Mm. He's quite an expert in the kitchen – fortunately for me. I can't boil an egg myself!
B: Oh, I brought you this.
A: Oh, thanks, you shouldn't have. I'll put it in the fridge. Come on through.

🔊 **2.20**
Extract 2
B: Oh, what a fabulous apartment!
A: Thanks. We like it.
B: Have you been here long?
A: Um … about two years now. The whole place was an absolute wreck when we moved in. We had to do just about everything to it. Now, how about something to drink?
B: Whatever you're having is fine.
A: Okay. I'll be right back. Make yourself at home.
C: Hi, Magda. I'm Martin. I don't think we've met.
B: Hello, Martin. Pleased to meet you. You're the chef, I understand.
C: Oh, yes. Doing a good job of setting fire to the kitchen at the moment. I had to rescue the starter.
B: So I heard.
A: Ah, so you two have met. Good. There we are, Magda. Let me know if you want a refill.
B: Thanks.
A: Are we nearly ready, then, darling?
C: Er, yes, I'm just waiting for the sauce. In fact, I'd better go and check on it. I don't trust that new cooker.
A: Oh, okay.

🔊 **2.21**
Extract 3
C: Dinner's ready when you are.
C: Right, Magda, sit wherever you like. Now, we're having duck in a berry sauce.
B: Mm, smells delicious!
C: Now, there's more duck if you want it. And help yourself to vegetables.
B: Mm, this is absolutely delicious.
A: It's one of Martin's specialities.
B: Mm, it's really good. The duck's all crispy on the outside and juicy on the inside.
C: I'm glad you like it.
B: You must let me have the recipe.
C: Oh, it's very simple, really. You just need the right ingredients.
A: Magda, I've been meaning to talk to you about this business in Poland.
B: Oh, yes, that.
A: Do you know what's going on there? Because no-one seems to be able to tell me anything.
C: Right, well, excuse me a moment. If you two are going to talk business, I'll go and see to the dessert.
B: Well, I ought to be making a move soon. Early start tomorrow.
C: Oh, you don't have to rush off just yet, do you? How about some more coffee?

BUSINESS COMMUNICATION

> B: Okay, just half a cup. And then I really must be going.
> B: Well, thank you both for a lovely evening. Martin, you're a brilliant cook.
> C: Oh, I don't know about that.
> B: Next time you must come to my place, although I can't promise you such a fabulous meal.
> A: Bye, Magda. Take care now. See you tomorrow.

3 This exercise reviews the social language in the recording. Set a time limit and get students to work individually. Students check their answers in pairs. If students have not been able to complete any of the phrases, play the recording again. Then check the answers with the whole class. Students can refer to the target language in the listening script on page 149.

Activate some of the language by describing what happens in the dialogue and eliciting the key expressions, e.g. Anne asks if Magda had any problems finding the flat – *You managed to find us okay, then?* Magda indicates she wants to leave – *I ought to be making a move soon.*

ANSWERS

Arrival	Let, brought, have, through, what, something, yourself
The meal	ready, wherever, want, yourself, absolutely, glad, must
Farewells	ought, rush, about, just, going, both, place, Take

Language links

Direct students to the *Language links* section on page 61 for more on the language used in social English.

A dinner invitation

In this final section, students take part in a roleplay. One student plays the host and the other plays the guest, visiting the home of a colleague.

As a lead-in to the roleplay, elicit what is expected of a 'good' host and a 'good' guest. This may differ for different nationalities. Ask students if there is any special dynamic when the host is a guest's immediate boss.

Divide the students into 'guests' and 'hosts'. If you have an odd number of students, create a group of three with two students playing the role of guests. Ask each pair to decide on a name, location and business sector for their company and to specify their roles. Students also establish how business is going and specify current problems and opportunities. With students who are short of ideas, give them the following information as a framework:

> Company: Teleworld International
> Location: headquarters in Paris
> Sector: mobile phones
> Business: fantastic current sales, but no one can predict where the market is going

Tell students that they both have an ulterior motive for the dinner. Refer the guests to page 131 and the hosts to page 123. Give students time to read the information.

Focus attention on the photos and brainstorm/review useful vocabulary from the photos. Also refer students back to the useful expressions in 3 on page 59.

Monitor the roleplay, taking feedback notes. When students have finished, ask them how they think the evening went and how they handled their ulterior motive. Give feedback on students' overall fluency and performance in the roleplay.

1:1 Discuss and decide in advance with your student who will play the guest and who will play the host. Decide with your student your names, and the location and main business activity of your company. Establish your roles at work, especially the guest's job title. Establish how business is going and specify any current problems and opportunities. If possible, use your student's field of work to maximize the relevance of the roleplay. Tell your student that both the guest and the host have an ulterior motive for the dinner. If your student is the guest, ask them to study the information on page 131; if they are the host, they should go to page 123.

Language links

ANSWERS
Vocabulary
Social English
1 1 think + happen   2 tells + going   3 makes + think
   4 's + be   5 is + accept   6 reckon + is   7 mean + talking
   8 looking + ask   9 got + joking   10 see + doing
   11 suppose + heard   12 knew + coming   13 is + getting
   14 had + would   15 can't + say   16 's + help
   17 might + known   18 stop + get   19 hear + going
   20 shouldn't + saying

Grammar
Multi-verb sentences
1 to do – agree, aim, refuse, manage, hope, expect, promise, fail
   doing – admit, suggest, put off, carry on, enjoy, miss, avoid, dislike
   both – try, stop, remember, go on
2 1 to have   2 to send   3 asking   4 to fix   5 doing
   6 asking   7 to get
3 in making, on telling, about putting, about having, of being

Phrase bank
Networking
1 meeting   2 bumping   3 paying   4 asking   5 catching
6 raising   7 offering   8 referring   9 breaking   10 taking
11 looking   12 saying

1 d, t   2 h, o   3 b, k   4 a, v   5 f, q   6 j, x
7 g, p   8 m, s   9 e, r   10 i, u   11 l, w   12 c, n

10 Making decisions

Learning objectives

This unit is about decision-making in business, as well as in one's personal life.

Students start by discussing decision-making and what they would do in different life-or-death situations. They do a quiz on survival situations, and focus on the language of likelihood and giving advice. They then practise giving advice in a fluency-based task.

A recording offers insight into the decision-making process at three different meetings. Students study some of the idioms used in the recording and practise the language of decisions.

Students discuss crisis management in the workplace, and read and summarize two recent accounts of crisis situations at McDonald's and Mercedes. They focus on the use of definite and indefinite articles and practise key collocations for dealing with crises.

The unit concludes with a case study – a crisis at Coca-Cola – and students take part in a roleplay as a group of crisis management consultants to the company.

The grammatical focus is on articles and the lexical focus is on English for marketing.

Digital resources: Unit 10

Online Workbook; In company interviews Units 8–10 and worksheet; Extension worksheets; Glossary; Phrase bank; Student's Book answer key; Student's Book listening script; Fast-track map

In this first section, students discuss decision-making before reading a short text from a website on worst-case scenarios. They then do a quiz and discuss the choices they would make in eight life-or-death situations. A recording gives advice on how to survive these situations and allows students to assess their survival skills. Students focus on the language of likelihood and complete an exercise on giving advice. Finally, they decide on the advice they would give in worst-case scenarios and workplace dilemmas.

Warm-up

Ask students to brainstorm different ways of making decisions. Ask students to read and explain the quotation from Margaret Thatcher (she says it's dangerous not to say which side you support in an argument).

1 Ask students to think about the questions for a few moments and then compare their answers in pairs.

2 Focus attention on the photograph and on the title of the text and ask students to predict the content of the text. Check/Pre-teach: *to lurk, to pass out, shark fin*. Students read the text quickly and check their predictions.

Get students to read the text again and discuss the questions in pairs or small groups. Ask students to give feedback on anything interesting arising from their discussion. Point out that there is also a worst-case scenarios book, which may have been translated into the students' own language.

3 In order to generate interest in the quiz, elicit examples of life-or-death situations and ask students to assess their survival skills on a scale of one to ten. With weaker groups, check/pre-teach: *to roll, cliff edge, crash barrier, to play dead, to flap, to drown, to collapse, to touch down, insulation, to leap, obstruction, to skid, to plunge, to wind up/down, to trap, to free-fall, to snorkel, to punch, to splash about*.

Divide the class into two groups, A and B. A students stay on the page; B students turn to page 124. Ask students to read the quiz questions quickly, encouraging them to guess any new words from context before you answer vocabulary queries. Set a time limit of five minutes and ask students to hold their meetings. When they have finished, ask them to give their choice of answers.

> **1:1** Do the lead-in and vocabulary check as outlined above. Assign a certain number of worst-case scenarios to you and your student. Each of you should then explain and justify your choices, making comments and discussing each scenario as appropriate.

4 Put the students in pairs and ask them to report back on their quiz questions, the alternatives, and on the decisions they took.

5 2.22–2.29 Check/Pre-teach: *to resist, fierce, futile, to overshoot, to triple, to crawl, water pressure, to grab, in distress, vulnerable*. Play the recording, pausing after each extract so that the students can check their answers.

QUIZ ANSWERS
1 c 2 b 3 a 4 b 5 b 6 b 7 c 8 a

> **2.22**
> **1** Don't even think about jumping from a moving vehicle. At 70 miles per hour the chances of surviving are remote. And crashing into the mountainside at this speed will almost certainly send you straight through the windshield. So, even though you may be scared of going over the cliff, your best chance of slowing the car down is to repeatedly run it against the crash barriers. After all, that's what they're there for.

BUSINESS COMMUNICATION

🔘 **2.23**

2 Resist the temptation to run. You cannot outrun or outclimb a mountain lion. And put any ideas of playing dead out of your mind. While it may work with grizzly bears, to a mountain lion you'll just look like a free lunch. Your best bet is to shout and flap your coat at the animal to make yourself look bigger and fiercer than you really are. Mountain lions are not proud. If you look like more trouble than you're worth, there's a fifty-fifty chance they'll back away.

🔘 **2.24**

3 When landing a light aircraft, make sure that the nose of the plane is six inches below the horizon. As you approach the runway the plane should be flying at an altitude of about 100 feet. If you're higher, you'll overshoot the runway completely. The optimum speed on landing is about 60 miles per hour. Go faster and you may take off again. Go slower and you'll drop like a stone. Upon landing, it's a good idea to brake as soon as you've gained control of the steering. By reducing your groundspeed by 50% you triple your chances of survival.

🔘 **2.25**

4 Water transfers heat away from the body 25 times faster than air. So trying to keep warm is more or less futile. And while you're staying calm and conserving energy, the chances are you're dying. You have to get out. Turn in the direction you fell and use your elbows to lift yourself onto the edge of the ice. Reach forward as far as possible and kick your feet as if you were swimming. Once you are back on the ice, crawl to shore. Do not in any circumstances try to stand up.

🔘 **2.26**

5 The current world record for the long jump is just under nine metres, but most people can barely manage three or four. The chances are you can't either. To clear four and a half metres in conditions that are far from ideal you'd need a 20 to 30 metre run-up, perfect timing and a great deal of luck. Frankly, your chances are slim. The truck is a much better idea and it is quite possible to fall from the sixth floor and live. But don't jump out from the building unless there are balconies in the way. You'll be carried forward and miss the truck completely. Drop vertically and take care to land on your back to avoid breaking it.

🔘 **2.27**

6 The taxi could take anything from a few minutes to just a few seconds to sink. But there's not much point trying to force the door open because the water pressure will make this almost impossible. If the car does sink there'll be little or no air left anyway, so forget about trapping air inside. By far the most sensible thing to do is to open the window and actually let more water in. Even if you can't escape through the window, once the water pressure inside and outside the car are equalized, there's a fair chance you'll be able to open the door and save yourself – and maybe the driver too!

🔘 **2.28**

7 It's very unusual for both parachutes to fail, so by struggling with the emergency chute there's an outside chance you'll get it to work. But don't bet on it. You may just be wasting precious time. If you can share one of your friends' parachutes you're in with a chance, but just grabbing onto the nearest person is not a smart move. The G-force when the parachute opens will throw you apart. At 14,000 feet and falling at your terminal velocity of 120 miles per hour you've got about 75 seconds before your appointment with Mother Earth. So firmly attach yourself to the chest straps of another parachutist. You don't stand a chance unless you do.

🔘 **2.29**

8 You are 30 times more likely to be struck by lightning than to be attacked by a shark, but this is little comfort in your present position. Splashing around and making a noise will simply give the shark the idea you're in distress and easy meat. It's a common mistake to think the shark's nose is the best area to target. Punch it there and you are liable to lose a hand or arm – depending on the size of the shark. You'd do much better to strike at its eyes or gills since these are a shark's most vulnerable points.

6 Ask students to put the expressions on the appropriate part of the scale. When students have finished, ask them to compare with a partner. Then check the answers with the whole class, accepting any reasonable variation.

To give students practice in using the expressions, divide the class into groups and ask students to brainstorm a further life-and-death scenario, e.g. your plane is hijacked. Students present their situation to the other groups, who suggest possible courses of action, using some of the expressions from this exercise.

ANSWERS

(order of likelihood from more likely to less likely)
a, h, e, c, i, d, f, j, b, g, k

7 Tell students to read the words in the first box and say which are both verbs and nouns (*mistake, bet, point, move*). Tell them to see all the words as nouns when completing expressions a–n. When they have finished, call out the letters and a student's name at random in order to check the answers. Model the pronunciation of any expressions which students found difficult and drill as necessary.

ANSWERS

a bet   b circumstances   c idea   d point   e thing   f move
g mistake   h think   i Resist   j Put   k Make   l Take
m Forget   n do

8 Elicit examples of extreme situations from the recent news and examples of common workplace problems. Give further practice of the expressions in 6 and 7 by eliciting possible pieces of advice for each situation.

64   10 MAKING DECISIONS

BUSINESS COMMUNICATION

Check/Pre-teach: *iceberg, bungee jump, cord, to snap, to take the credit, to back up (data), to be passed over*. Divide the students into pairs and get students to take turns to present their problem and give advice. Monitor the activity and take feedback notes. Elicit examples of the best pieces of advice/solutions. Give feedback on the use of the key language and overall fluency before highlighting important or common errors.

1:1 Check/Pre-teach any tricky vocabulary, as outlined above. Ask your student to read the worst-case scenarios and the workplace dilemmas. Give them time to make decisions and take notes. Ask your student to give you a mini-presentation on the advice they would offer. Comment on the student's advice and engage in discussion.

The decision-making process

In this section, students read and comment on an anecdote about decisions made at meetings. A recording presents a number of businesspeople involved in decision-making at three different meetings. Students then focus on the key language used in the recording.

1 Ask students to read the anecdote by John Adair about the head of General Motors and elicit the point being made. Ask students if they agree and elicit any other problems with group decisions, e.g. people go along with the majority view rather than risk expressing their own opinion.

ANSWER
A quick agreement may not be the right decision.

2 2.30–2.32 Write the three topics from the listening on the board: *an industrial dispute, political instabilities* and *a product recall*. Elicit examples of these from students' experience or from recent news, e.g. some years ago, British Airways staff objected to clocking-in times; companies are often unwilling to invest in war-torn countries/regions; Nestlé and Perrier have both experienced product recalls.

Check/Pre-teach: *to phase in, backlog of orders, to be plunged into (war), to be aware of, to overlook, drastic, to affect, I dread to think ..., harm*. Tell students they are going to listen to three extracts from meetings and that you will play each extract twice. The first time, ask students to listen for the main topic on which the decision is being made (1 what to do if the unions vote to go on strike, 2 whether or not to pull out of a production plant in Somalia due to possible civil war, 3 whether or not to recall all cars sold of a particular model on safety grounds). Now ask students to read the questions in 2. Play the recording again, pausing after each extract for students to complete the task. Check answers with the whole class.

ANSWERS
1 a There's a backlog of orders.   b C (Per)
2 a Closing down the production plant in North Africa.
   b Local people losing their jobs.
3 a Neither Simon's nor Matt's.   b yes

2.30
Meeting 1
A: Right, as you know, our last offer to the union was a 3% pay rise and a two-hour reduction in the working week to be gradually phased in over the next 18 months. The ball is now firmly in their court. Ragnar, do you have any idea which way they'll vote?
B: Word is they'll turn it down. In fact, they might even be considering taking industrial action.
A: A strike?
B: I don't know, Dan. It's a possibility.
A: With the current backlog of orders a strike's the last thing we need!
C: Now, let's not jump to conclusions. They haven't announced the result of the vote yet.
B: My sources are usually accurate, Per.
A: Look, time is short. If the vote goes against us, I want us to be able to come straight back with an improved offer. So let's put our heads together and see what we can come up with.

2.31
Meeting 2
A: Okay, we've weighed up the various pros and cons. Now it's time to reach a decision and stick to it. Our latest information is that the political situation in Somalia is worsening. In fact, it may only be a matter of days before the country is plunged into civil war. The proposal is that we should pull our people out of there immediately.
B: Now, wait a minute, Richard. I don't want us rushing into anything. This whole issue requires long and careful consideration. This is our biggest production plant in North Africa and we're talking about closing it down here.
A: I'm well aware of that, Hans. But I take it we're all in agreement that our first priority is to safeguard the well-being of our personnel.
B: Of course.
A: Well, then, I don't see we have any option but to give this proposal our full backing.
C: Aren't we overlooking something here? I mean it's all very well talking about flying our management team home and closing the plant, but what about our factory workers? They'll all be out of a job.
A: I'm afraid our responsibility to local workers is different, Andrea. When it comes to the crunch, we have to look after our European staff first ...

2.32
Meeting 3
A: Okay, you've all seen the results of the road tests. It looks like the two-litre model has some kind of a steering problem and we may have to authorize a total product recall while we conduct further tests.
B: Isn't that a bit drastic, Simon? I mean, it's only a slight steering problem, isn't it? And it doesn't seem to be affecting the smaller-engined models.
A: Well, that's what we're here to discuss, Matt. With a safety issue like this I don't think we should

10 MAKING DECISIONS 65

BUSINESS COMMUNICATION

take any chances, but I'd like your input on this before committing us to any definite course of action. Laura?

C: Hmm, I'm in two minds about it. I mean, I agree with you that the safety of our customers must come first. But if we take the whole series off the market, I dread to think what the newspapers will do with the story. At this stage I think we should keep our options open. And these test results aren't conclusive, are they?

A: Well, no, but I don't think we can just sit on the fence here. In the long run, failing to act quickly could do us a lot of harm.

B: So what do you suggest?

A: Well, in the absence of more reliable data, I think I'm going to have to go with my gut instinct on this one. I'm just not prepared to put our customers' lives at risk …

3 Ask students to work in pairs to complete the idioms and then check the answers.

ANSWERS

a court   b conclusions   c crunch   d fence

4 Ask students to replace the words in bold with words from the box. Be prepared to play the recording again if necessary. Check the answers and the pronunciation of any difficult items. To get the students to practise the language of decisions, divide them into groups and ask them to devise three scenarios each involving a decision, e.g. decide on a venue for the next Olympics from the following five cities: …; decide on a venue for a new HQ; choose between high-, medium- and low-risk shares, etc. Students give their scenarios to the other groups, who discuss them and try to reach a decision, using the language from 3. Students report back on their decision, giving reasons for their choice.

ANSWERS

a Look, **we're running out of time**. So let's **pool our ideas** and see what we can **suggest**.
b Okay, we've weighed up the various **advantages and disadvantages**. Now it's time to **come to** a decision and **stand by** it.
c **We need to take our time on this**. This whole issue requires **serious thought**.
d I take it **we unanimously agree** that **the main thing** is to safeguard the well-being of our personnel.
e Well, then, I don't see we have any **alternative** but to give this proposal our **complete support**.
f I'd like your **opinions** on this before committing us to any definite **plan** of action.
g I'm **undecided** about it. At this stage **I don't think we should make a decision**.
h Well, in the absence of more reliable **information**, I think I'm going to have to go with my **intuition** on this one.

Language links

Direct students to the *Phrase bank* in the *Language links* section on page 69 for more on the language used in decision-making.

Crisis management

In the final section, students discuss the kind of crises which companies can face. They do a jigsaw reading activity using short texts on a crisis at McDonald's and Mercedes and decide where the missing articles (*a*, *an* and *the*) should go in the texts. The unit ends with a case study of a crisis at the Coca-Cola company. Students listen to two recordings to get information about the case and then roleplay a strategy meeting. A final recording tells students what actually happened in the Coca-Cola case and allows them to compare their recommendations with the decision the company took.

1 Check/Pre-teach: *fraud, boycott, insider trading, the monopolies commission* (a body who investigates monopolies), *lawsuit, sabotage*. Divide the class into groups and have them brainstorm recent examples.

2 Focus students' attention on the title of the texts. Check the literal meaning of *to spill* and highlight the play on words in the title – the original expression is *to cry over spilled milk* (to waste time worrying about a past mistake that can't be changed). Check the literal meaning of *to roll* and the meaning of the expression *to be on a roll* (to be having a lot of success with what you are doing).

Divide the class into AB groups and assign the McDonald's text to group A and the Mercedes text to group B. Tell students that *a, an* and *the* are missing from each text. Get students to predict from the title what the crisis in their text might be and then to read the text quickly to check, ignoring the lack of articles at this stage.

Ask the groups to discuss where they think the articles go and remind them there are 25 missing articles in each text. Ask students working on the same text to exchange books to check that their answers are the same. Check the answers with the class.

1:1 Select one of the two texts for your student to read and analyse for missing articles. If articles are a problematic area for your student, issue the other text for homework. Your student can read out their answers. Finally, comment on the student's performance and give feedback as necessary.

ANSWERS

A McDonald's crying over spilled coffee
In 1994 Stella Liebeck, **a** New Mexico grandmother, ordered **a** coffee at **a** McDonald's drive-through restaurant. Minutes later, sitting in her car in **a** car park, she accidentally spilled **the** coffee – heated, in response to customer preference, to **a** scalding 180°F – and suffered severe burns requiring surgery. **A** crisis was about to unfold.

When McDonald's refused to take responsibility for paying **the** woman's medical bills, she went to **an** attorney and sued **the** company. At **the** trial **the** jury found McDonald's liable and awarded $200,000 in compensatory damages (less $40,000 for negligence on Liebeck's part) and **a** massive $2.7 million in punitive damages because of what they saw as McDonald's unacceptably dismissive attitude.

One might have expected **the** bad publicity to ruin McDonald's, but instead newspapers leapt to **the** company's defence, declaring

10 MAKING DECISIONS

what nonsense **the** court's verdict was. 'America has **a** victim complex,' announced **the** *San Francisco Chronicle*. **The** punitive damages were later reduced by **the** judge to $480,000 and, while awaiting **the** appeal, **the** parties made **an** out-of-court settlement for **an** undisclosed sum. But by then **the** 'three million dollar coffee-spill' had already passed into corporate legend.
a = 8, an = 3, the = 14; total = 25

B Mercedes on a roll

In **the** automotive industry **the** trend for many years has been towards **a** smaller, more economical vehicle. So in **the** autumn of 1997, Daimler-Benz introduced **a** new economy model, **the** Mercedes 'A Class'. It was **a** car designed to compete with **the** ever-popular Volkswagen Golf. But just before **the** November launch, disaster struck.

A Swedish auto magazine had conducted what they called **an** 'elk test' on **the** new car. **The** test is standard in Sweden to make sure cars can steer to avoid large deer crossing **the** road. But at just 60 kph **the** 'A Class' overturned, injuring both **the** test drivers. **A** storm immediately blew up in **the** press and on TV, as buyers waiting to take delivery cancelled their orders. For Mercedes it was not only **a** financial but **an** image crisis too.

Daimler responded quickly, adding wider tyres, **an** electronic stability mechanism and stronger anti-roll bars – all at no extra cost to **the** customer. **A** highly successful advertising campaign and public support from Niki Lauda, ex-formula one racing champion, helped to restore consumer confidence in **the** 'A Class' but at **a** cost of hundreds of millions of dollars.
a = 8, an = 3, the = 14; total = 25

> **Language links**
>
> Direct students to the *Language links* section on pages 68–69 for further explanation of the use of articles, and an exercise to practise them.

3 Ask students to make notes on the key points in their text as preparation for giving a summary of it and also to think of what lessons can be learnt from the crisis. Ask students to cross-group so that the A students summarize their story for the Bs, and vice versa.

4 Students match the verbs to the words they collocate with. Ask students to divide the actions into good and bad advice. Check the answers with the class.

ANSWERS
b stay calm   c delegate responsibility   d buy time   e blame someone   f be decisive   g admit nothing   h take charge   i make promises   j act quickly   k collect data   l be honest

5 2.33–2.35 Ask students to work in small groups. As a lead-in to the task, write some of the key words from the recording on the board: *global dominance, a loss of consumer confidence, contaminated, officially banned, consignments seized by officials*. Get students to predict what the crisis is. Play the first recording through once so that students can check their predictions.

Step 1 2.33

Ask students to read questions a–e and answer as many as they can. Play the recording again so students can complete their answers. Check answers with the class.

ANSWERS
a one billion
b aggressive, powerful
c People have become ill after drinking contaminated Coke.
d Belgium, France, Luxembourg, The Netherlands
e $376 m [2% of $18.8 billion]

Step 2 2.34

Ask students what they think might have happened next. Write students' predictions on the board. Check/Pre-teach: *bottling plants, toxicologist, psychosomatic, to deliberate, denial*. Play the recording once and get students to check their predictions. Play the recording again and have students answer the questions a–e. Check answers with the class.

ANSWERS
a +25% – how much the Dow is up; -13% – how much Coke and Pepsi are down
b Untypically, Coke and Pepsi were both behind the market.
c nothing unusual
d The 200 cases are probably psychosomatic.
e rivals Pepsi & Virgin Cola

Step 3

If necessary, before the meeting elicit a summary of the crisis at Coca-Cola and write the key information on the board. Have students read the article and agenda on page 121. After students have skimmed the texts, check they know the words *nauseous/nausea*. Have students brainstorm the options the company has. When students are ready, they hold the meeting. Monitor and take feedback notes.

> **1:1** In preparation for the meeting, ask your student to summarize the current crisis. Tell your student to read the agenda on page 121 and make notes. Structure the meeting so that it begins with a short student presentation of his or her ideas. Record the presentation, if possible. Comment on your student's ideas, then discuss and agree on an action plan. Finish the lesson by listening to your student's presentation and giving language feedback.

Step 4

When all groups have finished their meetings, ask one member of each group to present their recommendations.

Step 5 2.35

Check/Pre-teach: *irreproachable, pesticide, mad cow disease, fungicide, to take measures, to withdraw, public relations coup*. Tell students they are going to find out what action Coca-Cola took. Play the recording and elicit reactions.

> **Language links**
>
> Direct students to the *Language links* section on page 68 for more practice of useful marketing vocabulary.

BUSINESS COMMUNICATION

2.33
Step 1

The mighty Coca-Cola has been the world's number one brand for so long, it's hard to imagine anything threatening its position of global dominance. One of the company's own publicity brochures proudly declares: 'A billion hours ago human life appeared on Earth; a billion minutes ago the three great monotheistic religions emerged; a billion seconds ago the Beatles performed on the Ed Sullivan Show – a billion servings of Coca-Cola ago was yesterday morning.' Quite a claim. And one that makes a loss of consumer confidence unthinkable.

But take yourself back to May 1999. The unthinkable has just happened. Hundreds of people in Belgium and France have become ill after drinking what they claim is contaminated Coke. And when the cause of the problem cannot quickly be established, the famous soft drink is officially banned in both countries as well as Luxembourg and the Netherlands. The price you pay for being the brand leader is that customers expect quality, as Coca-Cola's CEO is the first to admit. 'For 113 years,' he says, 'our success has been based on the trust that consumers have in that quality.' Now that trust is shaken.

In fact, the four countries banning Coke only represent 2% of the company's $18.8 billion in annual sales. But within a week consignments exported from Belgium to other countries as far apart as Germany and the Ivory Coast have also been seized by officials. Though no definite proof of contamination has yet been found, the panic is starting to spread ...

2.34
Step 2

1999 is not a good year for soft drinks companies. Though the Dow is up 25%, both Coke and Pepsi, normally well ahead of the market, are down by around 13%. Coca-Cola is not going to rush into a highly expensive product recall.

In any case, early examinations of the Belgian bottling plants find nothing unusual and an official toxicologist's report concludes that the 200 cases of sickness are probably psychosomatic.

But while Coca-Cola is deliberating over what action to take, rivals Pepsi and Virgin Cola are quick to fill the gaps left on the supermarket shelves. And Coke's refusal to react until it has conducted a thorough investigation is starting to look like a denial of responsibility ...

2.35
Step 5

This is how Coca-Cola actually handled the problem.

Initially, full-page advertisements were taken out in European newspapers to reassure the public that the quality of Coke was 'irreproachable'. This was not totally successful as the public at that time could still remember a similar contamination scare at Perrier some years before and all the talk was of pesticides on fruit and mad cow disease.

But, fortunately, the source of the Coke contamination was eventually traced to a strange fungicide on cans shipped from Dunkirk and poor carbon dioxide at Coca-Cola's bottling plant in Antwerp, which makes the Coke taste a little different but does no real harm. It wasn't the Coke itself but the cans that were contaminated.

Coke took the necessary measures and, at enormous cost to the company, all 17 million cases of Coke were withdrawn. Finally, in a spectacular public relations coup, and as an apology to the Belgians who had been ill, Coca-Cola offered a free one-and-a-half litre bottle of Coke to each and every one of Belgium's 10 million citizens! Coke was immediately back in the stores.

Language links

ANSWERS

Vocabulary
Marketing
The marketplace
1 booming – thriving, healthy – buoyant, volatile – unpredictable, weak – sluggish, flat – depressed
3 a marketing b market c distribution d advertising e brand
4 a advertising agencies b market forces c marketing mix d distribution channels e brand stretching
5 a market **challenger** b competitive **advantage** c retail **outlet** d mass **market** e price **sensitivity** f leading **brand** g subliminal **advertising** h price **war** i niche **market** j public **relations** k consumer **analysis** l permission **marketing**
6 a market challenger b price sensitivity c niche market d retail outlet e subliminal advertising f permission marketing
7 1 target 2 enter 3 compete in 4 dominate 5 be squeezed out of 6 break back into 7 come up against 8 take on 9 outclass 10 succumb to 11 fight back against 12 destroy

Grammar
Articles
1 / 2 / 3 a 4 the 5 / 6 / 7 / (or a) 8 the 9 the 10 an 11 a 12 the 13 / 14 / 15 /

Phrase bank
Decision-making
1 b, k, p 2 f, g, l 3 a, h, m 4 c, i, q 5 e, j, n
6 d, o, r

11 Stress

Learning objectives

This unit is about stress in the business world.

Students begin by discussing a cartoon and the attitudes to stress that the cartoon shows. They then consider their own experience of attitudes towards stress in the workplace. They listen to a talk on stress management and complete a chart showing the effects of stress on performance. They listen again and match photos of work environments to the three levels of stress.

Students then consider their own levels of stress. They read an article on helping colleagues manage stress and match headings to the correct paragraphs. They then consider appropriate and inappropriate behaviour when counselling colleagues about stress.

Students listen to eight short dialogues of meetings between managers and their employees. In each one, the manager is dealing with a situation in which the employee is stressed. Students decide if the manager is doing things correctly or incorrectly. They listen to the recording again and complete some useful expressions.

Finally, students take part in a roleplay to practise helping a colleague in a stressful situation.

Digital resources: Unit 11

Online Workbook; Extension worksheets; Glossary; Student's Book answer key; Student's Book listening script; Fast-track map

1:1 Before starting this unit, discuss the culture of your student's current workplace to see if they think it is stressful and, if so, why. For example, there may be unrealistic sales targets, too few employees, etc. If it isn't a stressful place to work, find out why not. Ask: *What factors make it stress-free?* This discussion will also provide you with useful background information about the student's company and working life.

Warm-up

Write the word *stress* on the board and ask students to build up a word map of useful phrases, such as: *stressful, stressed, to de-stress, to deal with stress, stress-related*, etc.

1 Put students in pairs to discuss the cartoon and answer the questions. Elicit students' ideas.

SUGGESTED ANSWERS

a The woman is stressed and aggressive. She is shocked by the man's reaction.
b The man is relieved that the woman's stress-related condition will not have a negative effect on work. He is unsympathetic and insensitive; he does not realize or care that training a replacement will only increase the woman's level of stress.
c The woman clearly feels that the company/management are responsible for her stress. The man feels that managing stress is a personal issue for the employee to resolve, one that cannot be allowed to interfere with productivity. In other words, any stress an employee suffers from should not be allowed to affect their performance at work.

2 Tell students to think about the difference in attitude shown by the man and the woman in the cartoon – they are good examples of how employees can react when there are different levels of sympathy to stress. Attitudes to stress are likely to vary in different work cultures, and between management and employees. Ask students to think about places they have worked and discuss the question about attitudes to stress with a partner. Ask some students to share their experiences.

3 Tell students that they are going to study a chart and then interpret it. Give them a moment to look at the chart. Elicit what each axis represents (the vertical axis shows employee performance from low to high; the horizontal axis shows levels of stress). Ask students to discuss with a partner their ideas on what it shows. Elicit students' ideas, e.g. no stress may mean poor performance; there is a level of optimum stress; too much stress is negative. Find out if students agree with the idea that a certain amount of stress can be a good thing.

4 2.36 Tell students they will hear part of a talk on stress. Play the recording so that students can listen and label the coloured areas on the chart. Check answers with the class. Find out if the term *eustress* is new for anyone.

ANSWERS

1 Under-stressed
2 Eustress or good stress
3 Distress

2.36

Now, this next slide shows how performance varies with the level of stress. At very low levels, as shown by the yellow area, performance, health and motivation are low. This state is referred to as Under-stressed; it may be experienced by people who are unemployed, or who have very boring jobs with too little to do.

As the level of stress increases, in the green area, performance improves and people feel more motivated. This state is known as Eustress, that's E-U-S-T-R-E-S-S, or 'good stress'. Many people need

11 STRESS 69

PEOPLE SKILLS

a moderate amount of stimulation and pressure in order to perform at their best.

However, if the level of stress increases beyond a certain point it becomes destructive and reduces levels of performance, motivation and health. This red zone is called Distress. The first step in managing both your own and other people's stress is learning to recognize the symptoms of Distress.

5 **2.36** Check that students know the words *stimulation* and *destructive*. Play the recording again. Ask students to match the photographs with the stress level on the chart. Check answers with the class. Find out what students feel about the jobs in the photographs. Ask: *Could you imagine doing any of these jobs? Do you know anyone who has an especially stressful job?*

ANSWERS

1 Under-stressed – photo b
2 Eustress – photo c
3 Distress – photo a

6 Provide an example of the symptoms of distress for each of the three categories, body, mind and behaviour: *body – itchiness; mind – being anxious; behaviour – shouting at someone*. Give students one or two minutes to continue their lists individually. Then, put students in pairs to compare their lists. Check answers with the class and collate them on the board.

POSSIBLE ANSWERS

Effects on the body	Effects on the mind	Effects on behaviour
Headache	Anxiety	Overeating or under-eating
Nausea	Restlessness	Angry outbursts
Skin rashes	Loss of concentration	Poor personal hygiene
Sweating	Indecisiveness	Social withdrawal
Muscle tension or pain	Lack of motivation or focus	Speech impediments
Chest pain	Irritability or anger	
Fatigue	Sadness or depression	
Stomach upset	Nightmares	
Sleep problems		

7 Ask students to think about how they manage their own stress and if they know any good techniques for doing this. Put students in pairs to discuss their ideas. Elicit some of their ideas, e.g. taking time to jog or cycle, going to the gym to do exercises that increase your heart rate, and so on.

8 Tell students that they are going to read an article entitled *Helping colleagues manage stress*. Check that they are familiar with the word *strain*. Ask students to read the paragraph headings, skim the article and match the correct headings to each paragraph. Check answers with the class.

ANSWERS

1 Share feelings
3 Ease the strain
2 Identify the source
4 Facilitate change

1:1 Before reading, do a collocation building exercise with your student. Write four verbs on cards of one colour: *facilitate, ease, share, identify*. Write four nouns on cards of another colour: *change, the strain, feelings, the source*. Ask your student to create four verb + noun collocations. (Note: it is possible to say *identify feelings*, but *share the source* is unlikely.) When your student has made the collocations, tell them that these are the headings they should match with the paragraphs in the article.

9 Check that students know some of the key vocabulary in the article, such as: *contagious, to keep (something) on track, judgemental, to probe, to keep (things) in perspective, counselling*. Ask students to read the article again and consider how many of the techniques they discussed in 7 are mentioned. Elicit feedback from students.

10 Ask students to use information from the article to give reasons why they shouldn't do the things listed. Go through each of the points in the list, eliciting an answer from students at random. As you go through the list, encourage students to add any more reasons they can think of not to do some of the things in the list. Ask if students agree with the information in the text.

ANSWERS

You shouldn't:

- force your advice on colleagues because this pressure may just increase stress; finding their own solution will be more effective.
- defend yourself as this will reinforce the conflict and the person's feeling of loss of control.
- probe, because you must respect the fact that a colleague's problems may be very personal; they should not feel under pressure to reveal anything they prefer not to discuss.
- ask leading questions, because you may misunderstand the problem or be serving your own interests rather than helping a colleague to deal with their stress.
- minimize the problem, because you cannot measure or predict a colleague's feelings about the relative importance of events and situations.
- provide answers, because they may not be appropriate and you prevent the person from learning to find solutions to problems, which can be as important as the solution itself.

11 **2.37** Tell students that they are going to hear a recording of eight managers counselling their employees. Ask students to decide if the managers are doing things correctly or incorrectly. Check that students know what a *leading question* is. Play the recording. Check answers with the class.

Ask students to read the list of advice (a–h) that the managers are following, or should follow. Ask them to match a manager to each one. Play the recording again so that students can check their answers and, if necessary, pause the recording at each change of speaker to give students time to complete the task. Go through the grid and check answers with the class.

70 11 STRESS

PEOPLE SKILLS

ANSWERS

Manager	✓/✗	Advice
1 Mark	✓	c
2 Jacky	✗	d
3 Corey	✓	a
4 Brett	✗	b
5 Jo	✗	h
6 Perry	✗	g
7 Chris	✓	f
8 Georgie	✓	e

🔊 2.37

1
A: I'm sorry, Mark, you must think I'm so unprofessional!
B: Not at all. You're frustrated because the customer keeps changing his mind. It's perfectly normal, and it's better to get it off your chest.
A: Thanks.

2
C: I just never seem to finish my 'to do' list. There just aren't enough hours in the day.
D: You obviously need to prioritize. HR run a really good time-management course. If I were you, I'd register straight away. In fact I'm surprised you haven't already done it!
C: Oh, yeah. Erm, thanks, Jacky.

3
E: Look, Corey, even if I write the whole thing again, I'm sure it still won't be good enough for you!
F: I understand how you feel. Would it help if Martha took over some of your regular work for a couple of weeks? That would give you more time, and then maybe you could work from home some days?
E: Oh, yes, that would be great. Erm, thanks.

4
G: Brett, I just can't go on like this!
H: What's the matter?
G: I don't ... I don't want to talk about it.
H: Was it Pete Jennings? Has he upset you again?
G: Mm.
H: Was it something he said? D'you want me to talk to him?
G: No!! ... erm, no ... thanks.

5
I: Listen, Jo, how can you ask me to transfer to London when you know my partner has just found a good job here?
J: Well it's hardly my fault! I don't decide company policy; I'm just trying to do my job.
I: Oh, right! Well thanks!

6
K: That's the third time this week I've left after 8 pm. I'm burning out here, Perry!
L: It's just the time of year. It's always like this in November. You'll get used to it. Anyway, it's not as bad as January.
K: Oh great – thanks!

7
M: What's the matter?
N: I've just had my head bitten off by Production. I ordered the wrong components again. I can't seem to go a week without putting my foot in it. I must be stupid or something!
M: Oh, come on! It could happen to anyone. You're just going through a difficult period. It was an honest mistake, there's no need to feel guilty about it.
N: Yeah, I suppose so. Thanks, Chris.

8
O: I'm never going to meet the new sales objective. It's just not fair!
P: Not fair?
O: Yeah, just because Marcus is always over target, you've raised everybody's objectives! I mean come on, Georgie, we're not all sales superstars like he is!
P: Hmm. What would happen if you didn't meet your target?
O: Well I wouldn't get my bonus for a start!
P: Uh huh. How big a problem would that be?
O: Well ... not really that disastrous actually, since the basic's gone up. It's just the principle, isn't it? But yeah, if you look at it like that, I suppose it's not the end of the world. Thanks.

12 🔊 2.37 Ask students to try to complete the missing words. Play the recording again for students to check their answers, pausing after each extract.

ANSWERS
1 perfectly 2 chest 3 feel 4 help 5 happen
6 guilty 7 happen 8 big

13 Tell students that they are going to take part in two roleplays. Each roleplay will give students practice in helping to counsel a colleague with stress. Put the students in pairs, A and B, and ask As to turn to page 118, and Bs to turn to page 136 and read the first roleplay. Give students a few minutes to prepare their role. Monitor and provide any language help, as necessary. When the students are ready, give them about five minutes to perform the roleplay. Monitor the roleplays and take notes on language use, as well as on any successes and failures in terms of following the advice suggested in the article.

Follow the same procedure for setting up the second roleplay, in which students exchange roles. Finish the lesson by providing feedback on both stress management skills and language.

1:1 Proceed with both roleplays, your student taking the role of Student A and you of Student B. Record the conversations and then play them back in order to evaluate how successful they were in terms of providing advice and the accurate use of language. If you cannot record the meetings, spend a few minutes after each roleplay debriefing it, i.e. reflecting together on how successful it was.

11 STRESS

MANAGEMENT SCENARIO C

Pitch and persuade

Learning objectives

This scenario is based on the skill of being able to persuade someone successfully.

Students begin by discussing their own experience of persuasive people and the techniques they use. They then watch a video of Peter Neubauer making a pitch to his boss, Sue, which fails. They consider the things he did incorrectly, and how he could improve his persuasive skills.

Students watch a second video in which Peter's pitch is successful in persuading Sue to do more in the area of social media.

Finally, as a post-viewing task, students have a committee meeting to discuss how to help staff adapt to a merger, and then evaluate their own performances.

Digital resources: Management Scenario C

In company in action C1–C2 and worksheet; Extension worksheets; Glossary; Student's Book answer key; Student's Book listening script; Fast-track map

Warm-up

Build a mind map on the board based on the verb *persuade*. Make sure you include important words such as: *persuasive, persuadable, persuasion*. Check students know some of the trickier words by creating meaningful sentences with them.

1 Be ready to give students an example of a persuasive person you know, and why. The reasons that they might be persuasive include their use of facts, reasoning, common sense arguments, or emotional arguments. When students have discussed the questions, elicit some answers.

1:1 Ask your student to talk about their experiences of being persuaded by someone, or persuading someone themselves. Be ready to give examples of your own, such as a sales person who persuaded you to buy a product you didn't really want. Encourage your student to identify any techniques they have used themselves.

2 As a lead-in to the reading, ask students which social media sites they use (e.g. Facebook / Twitter / LinkedIn) and why. Tell students they are going to read an article on the power of social media sites, which Cassie recommends to her boss, Peter. Check or pre-teach any tricky terms, such as: *donors, batches, leverage* (the power to make someone do what you want). Give students time to read the article and decide if the statements are true, false or not stated. Ask students to compare their answers with a partner. Go through the answers with the whole class, asking students to justify their answer with information from the text.

ANSWERS
a F – Cassie discreetly suggests the idea might be useful.
b F – no longer
c T
d D

3 **C1** Explain to students that they are going to watch Peter making a pitch to Sue in the video. First, give students time to read the list of points. Check that students know the word *precedent*. Play the video and ask students to tick the points that are mentioned. Then ask students to compare their answers.

ANSWERS
a three-day conference	✓
a budget cut	✓
recruiting new staff	✗
return on investment	✓
an important interview	✗
an urgent decision	✓
waste water treatment	✗
a precedent for non-profit organizations	✓

C1

Peter: They haven't called yet, then?

Emma: No, we're a few minutes early, actually.

Sue: I hope they'll be on time. I have a train to catch at five. By the way, you couldn't fill in these forms for me, could you? We're supposed to send them back today.

Peter: Sorry, Sue. I've got a big meeting tomorrow, and I've got stuff to prepare. Couldn't Cassie deal with it?

Sue: No, I don't think she knows enough about it. I'll just have to do them on the train.

Peter: Right. Um, Sue, I need to talk to you about fund-raising for the Eastern India project.

Sue: Well, it'll have to be next week. I'm off to a conference in Manchester for three days.

Peter: Oh. You don't have any time later?

Sue: Sorry, no. Stuff to prepare, you know.

Peter: So when can I make my presentation? It's pretty urgent; we need your decision as soon as possible.

Sue: Well, how about now?

Peter: Now?

Sue: Yes. You've heard of elevator pitches? Well now's your chance! You've got about two minutes before the conference call begins!

72 C PITCH AND PERSUADE

MANAGEMENT SCENARIO

Peter: Well, um, my, er, presentation is in three parts, er …
Sue: Two minutes, Peter!
Peter: Right. Er, basically, I think a social media campaign is the best way to raise funds to install solar-powered water pumps in the villages in Eastern India, and I want to launch …
Sue: Hold on, I thought we already had government funding for that project?
Peter: Well we did, but they cut it by 50%.
Sue: So why didn't you say so? Go on.
Peter: Anyway, er, studies show over 40% of social media users are sympathetic to helping people in the developing world get access to clean water. At the moment, women and girls are walking miles in very high temperatures to fetch water for their families. Unfortunately, that doesn't mean that the water is fit to drink …
Sue: Okay Peter, I've been there, I know what it's like. How will social media help us raise money?
Peter: Our plan is to encourage the community of current small and mid-level donors to leverage their interest by building shared-giving relationships, a kind of MLM business model that will …
Sue: Sorry Peter, you've lost me there. MLM?
Peter: Multi-level marketing. Basically, instead of Blue Rock appealing directly to potential donors, we identify supporters or fans who each recruit their own team of donors, who then recruit from their own circle of friends and family, and so on, and so on …
Sue: You mean like pyramid schemes? I'm not sure that's something we want to be associated with.
Peter: No, you don't understand! We're not selling anything, Sue! We're just giving donors the satisfaction of making a bigger contribution to improving people's lives, don't you see?
Sue: Has it been done before by the nonprofit sector?
Peter: Well, sure, there are lots of fundraising applications for good causes …
Sue: For example …?
Peter: Well, off the top of my head … there's DonationConnect, and Giveabit, and … can I get back to you on that?
Sue: Hm. What sort of investment are we talking about here?
Peter: Well, the app service and setting up the mobile website are going to be quite expensive, but the ROI should compare favourably with our conventional strategies. Anyway, what we want to do is …
Sue: Sorry Peter, time's up.
Emma: Hello, Emma Lambert?
Charles: Hi Emma, it's Charles.
Emma: Oh hi Charles. Sorry, can I just put you on hold for a few seconds?
Charles: Sure.
Sue: You said you need a quick decision?
Peter: Yes. Can we go ahead?
Sue: I'm sorry, Peter, I'm not ready to commit to such a big change. Plus, I'm not sure our supporters are ready for social media. Let's talk again when I get back from Manchester, okay?
Sue: Hello, Charles? Sue here. Sorry about that, we're ready for you now.

4 + 5 C1 On the second viewing of the video, students have a chance to develop their listening by exploring the content in more detail. Ask them to read through the questions first. Let students watch the video again, this time making notes on the answers to the while-viewing questions. Put students in pairs to discuss their answers. Check students' answers by asking individual students to read out their answers, and encourage other students to add any further relevant information.

ANSWERS

4 a Because she has 'stuff to prepare'. Perhaps also because Peter was reluctant to fill in the forms for her, she is reciprocating.
  b to install solar-powered water pumps in villages in Eastern India
  c She doesn't want Blue Rock to be associated with pyramid schemes.
  d the app service and setting up a mobile website
  e She is not ready to commit to such a big change and she thinks their supporters are not ready for social media.
5 1 b 2 a 3 f 4 e 5 c 6 d

6 Put students in pairs to brainstorm the ways in which Peter could improve his pitch. Ask students to make a list of dos and don'ts for trying to persuade someone. For example, Peter could be brief – an 'elevator pitch' is much shorter than a presentation. He could also offer to help Sue before starting out, as this puts her 'in his debt'. Ask individual students to read out their ideas one by one and list them on the board.

7 The students will read two emails, one from Peter to Emma asking for advice, and the second providing Emma's ideas on effective persuasion. First, tell students to check that they know the trickier words in the boxes, such as: *jargon, scarcity, reciprocity*. Also deal with any tricky words and phrases in the memo, such as: *to put someone on the spot, to lean* and *credentials*. Then ask students to read and complete Emma's email. Monitor and answer any queries. When students have finished, ask them to compare Emma's tips with theirs in 5, by going through the collated list on the board.

ANSWERS

1 details 2 overview 3 discussion 4 structure
5 specific 6 jargon
a Reciprocity b Liking c Scarcity d Authority
e Consistency f Social proof

8 C2 Establish that in the second video clip, students will see Peter make a second pitch. Check any difficult or new vocabulary, such as: *humanitarian, water pumps, pyramid selling, webcasts*. Play the video and pause it after each of the phrases. Let students study the list and match the phrases to the pieces of advice in Emma's email. Elicit the correct answers.

C PITCH AND PERSUADE

MANAGEMENT SCENARIO

ANSWERS
a Reciprocity b a reason to listen c he is sincere d being likeable by respecting Sue's point of view e Authority or Social proof f short but specific g Scarcity h a call for action

🎥 C2

Emma: How was the conference by the way?

Sue: Good. But absolutely exhausting, you know what these things are like. And I have to fly to New York tomorrow!

Peter: That's a pretty heavy schedule!

Sue: Yeah. Oh, and I still haven't managed to fill in these stupid forms!

Peter: Leave them with me, I'll deal with them.

Sue: Well, that's very kind of you, Peter. Much appreciated.

Peter: No problem.

Sue: Anyway. You wanted to talk to me again about the Eastern India project. It'll have to be quick I'm afraid, I've got another meeting in five minutes.

Peter: That's fine; two minutes will be plenty! Okay. Did you know 68% of social media users will take time to learn about a humanitarian project if they see a friend post about it?

Sue: Really?

Peter: Yes. As you know, the objective of this project has been to install solar-powered water pumps in Eastern India. Now, the problem we've been facing is the government funding we were promised has been cut by 50%. We think – and by the way, this was Cassie's idea, so she should take the credit – we think the solution is to ask our existing supporters to use their social media contacts to build giving circles.

Sue: I'm still worried it sounds a bit like pyramid selling.

Peter: I know exactly what you mean. We certainly don't want to compromise our reputation and our relationship with our loyal donors. But let me reassure you on that point, this strategy is already being used very successfully by high-profile non-profits like the WWF, UNICEF and the Museum of Modern Art.

Sue: Oh, I see.

Peter: So, how does it work? First, we invite our supporters to post on social media about our work and how they've helped us with their donations. We encourage them to find four or five people who show interest in what we're doing and form what's called a giving circle. We also provide them with an app. that they can pass on to their friends and contacts. I know you'll have questions about cost, return on investment and so on, so I've put all the details in this handout.

Sue, Emma: Thanks.

Peter: Now, the great benefit of using social media to build these circles is they just keep growing and growing. Each new supporter to a giving circle passes the word on to their own circle of friends, who then become a new giving circle – and so on, and so on. So, what are we waiting for? As I mentioned, this strategy is already being used by top NGOs – if we wait till everyone's doing it, it won't be so effective. And the sooner we start, the sooner we can be pumping clean water into those villages. That's why I'm asking you to give the go-ahead before you leave for New York! Do you have any questions?

Sue: Only one. That was great, Peter. But why didn't you pitch it like that first time round?

9 Divide the class into small groups of around four students. Give each group a few minutes to read the different options for spending the money, and to choose one. Monitor the discussions and help students where necessary, encouraging them to provide their own ideas. Check that each student has selected a different idea.

Give students 5–10 minutes to prepare their pitch. When they are ready, ask them to take turns pitching. Monitor the activity and take notes. When students have finished, and the group has voted, ask someone from each group to report back to the whole class on which was the successful project pitch.

Ask students to turn to page 127 in order to access the two checklists – one for 'pitchers' and one for 'influencers'. Students complete the checklists. For example, they can evaluate their own performance as pitchers as well as completing the checklist for 'influencers' for one of their colleagues. Sum up by asking what went especially well in the winning pitches, i.e. which techniques were effective in terms of persuasion.

Finish the lesson by providing useful language feedback, as necessary.

1:1 Ask your student to take the role of the pitcher. Record the session and then go back over it in order to provide feedback on language. If it is not possible to record the pitch, use the pitching and influencing checklists on page 127 to reflect together on how successful the meeting was.

C PITCH AND PERSUADE

12 Emailing

Learning objectives

The growth of email has radically changed the nature of business communication. This unit looks at appropriate email style and gives students practice in composing and replying to emails.

Students discuss their reactions to various short extracts about emailing. They then make a list of their top three emailing tips.

Students listen to a podcast about the dynamics of emailing and then analyse two emails in the light of the text, correcting the mistakes in one of them, and rewriting the other to make it more appropriate.

Students then focus on email style, selecting the best expressions to use in a model message and writing a reply. A recording about email blunders provides listening practice and a springboard for discussion. Finally, students take part in a written fluency task and exchange emails.

The grammatical focus is on future forms and the lexical focus is on prepositional phrases.

Digital resources: Unit 12
Online Workbook; Extension worksheets; Glossary; Phrase bank; Student's Book answer key; Student's Book listening script; Fast-track map

---

In this first section, students read some short texts from the business press about emails and using computers, and discuss their reactions. The students then make and compare lists of their top three emailing tips.

1:1 Before starting this unit, check that it's appropriate for you and your student to exchange email addresses and emails. If it is, you can insert language feedback into your student's emails in a different text colour. Or you can copy and paste an email thread into a Word document, which can also be used to give feedback. Sometimes, email communication is virtually instantaneous, allowing you both to communicate quickly in a class activity, such as a roleplay. If your emails tend to sit on a server for a while before being delivered, you may wish to send and receive emails between lessons instead.

Warm-up
Ask students how many emails they receive a day and if they think they could now live without email at work.

Read the quotation from the author, Robert Cormier. Check that students can explain the humour in the quotation and elicit examples of other tasks which need to be done right first time, e.g. air traffic control. Point out that, in business writing, we should allocate time for checking and redrafting. The same is true for writing emails, but in reality, of course, many are written and sent in haste.

1 Students read the extracts and note down their reactions to each of the questions. Then divide the group into pairs to discuss their answers. Hold a short whole-class feedback session and encourage students to mention any particularly interesting points which arose. With weaker groups, you may wish to check/pre-teach: *trash, to wane, outburst*.

2 Students do this individually and then compare in small groups. They could select their favourite tips and write them on a board to display to the class.

Writing emails

In this section, students listen to a podcast which suggests that the sloppier the email, the more likely the writer is to be successful. They then focus on two emails, correcting the grammar, spelling and punctuation mistakes in one and deleting unnecessary words in the other.

1 As a warm-up exercise, ask students to read the article. Put students in pairs to discuss their responses. Feedback as a class.

2 2.38 As an introduction to this section, ask students to list the pros and cons of rewriting an email.

Pros: accuracy reduces the possibility of misinterpretation, rewriting can improve the tone and avoid causing offence

Cons: loss of speed, accuracy may be unnecessary because people see email as 'speech-writing'

Check/Pre-teach: *sloppy, dash off, emoticon* (emotion + icon). Ask comprehension questions such as: *What's the surest way of reaching the top of the corporate ladder?* Ask students to listen to the podcast and match the people and email types. Get students to compare their answers in pairs, then check the answers with the class.

ANSWERS
a 3 b 6 c 5 d 1 e 4 f 2

According to the podcast, badly written emails are a sign of leadership potential because they tend to be written by high status employees with little time to spend on writing perfect emails. Well-written emails are a sign of a corporate loser – someone who has too much time to spend writing emails. Using emoticons means people won't take you seriously.

BUSINESS COMMUNICATION

🎵 **2.38**

Welcome to the *In Company* Business Podcast Career Spot.

Forget about spelling, switch off your grammar-check, and you just might email your way to the top of the corporate ladder. According to research by Professor David Owens of Vanderbilt University into what your email says about your career prospects, sloppy, hastily written emails are a clear sign of leadership potential. 'High-status people in a company' he says, 'send short messages and they have the worst grammar and spelling in the firm. This isn't because they are the least educated. They just don't have time to waste on the small stuff.'

Owens's study shows that high-fliers invest more time in 'face-mail', face-to-face meetings with those they need to liaise with or persuade. This leaves them just a few brief moments during the day to dash off emails confirming what was decided, making last-minute changes and tying up any loose ends. Frequently the emails of natural-born leaders are no more than a phrase: 'Fine by me', 'Let's do it!', 'Okay, see you at the meeting'.

The neatly paragraphed 300-word email with a 5Mb attachment, on the other hand, is strictly for corporate losers. The message it sends is: my job is so undemanding and lacking in challenge or responsibility, I have hours to craft this email into a work of art. 'Reply to all' usually indicates a time-waster, whilst anyone who uses the 'blank carbon copy' to secretly involve the boss in emails to colleagues, is a poor player of office politics and definitely not to be trusted.

Owens's research also reveals that anyone who has a habit of forwarding jokes or sending animated electronic greetings cards is destined never to reach the level of senior management. An overuse of smileys and other more elaborate emoticons further undermines professionalism and guarantees you won't be taken seriously. According to Owens, office jokers play an important social role – they boost morale and are unlikely to be fired, but they don't very often get promoted.

But is it really true that bad email is good? A study attributed to Cambridge University and widely circulated on the Internet, claims that bad spelling, at least, is not much of a barrier to communication. And surveys suggest that when native English speakers receive emails from non-natives, the last thing they care about is the grammar. So, if you want to stay on the executive fast-track, don't waste your time on email – you're supposed to be much too busy!

3 Elicit from students a description of how they approach emails, e.g. length, formality, use of abbreviations, etc.

4 Ask students to quickly read the two emails and say which was probably written by a junior manager. Ask the students to justify their choice based on the information in the podcast in 1 (the message in the second email is accurate but overly long and complicated; it uses an emoticon; the writer could have said everything in the message in a quick call or face-to-face).

> **ANSWER**
> the second one

5 Focus attention on the abbreviations in the *Glossary*. Elicit other examples of common abbreviations used in emails, e.g. *atb* (all the best) and ask students if they use abbreviations in the same way when emailing in their own language.

Elicit the first two mistakes in the email (see below). Students correct the remaining mistakes. Remind them to mark the paragraph breaks and add in a subject line. Ask students to compare their answers with a partner and then check the answers with the whole class.

Refer to the answer key to check where the paragraph breaks should go and elicit possible subject lines, e.g. Rome Expo/Copenhagen conference.

> **SUGGESTED ANSWER**
> **Subject: Rome Expo**
> Steve
> Can you **update** me on where you are with **the** Rome Expo arrangements? I was unable to open the **attachment** you sent me, so **I don't** have a copy of the programme.
> As **far** as the Copenhagen **conference** is concerned I **just don't** have time **to deal** with it myself. So please can you sort this out with the Danes asap? You'll **probably need** to contact Margrethe Rasmussen at **their** headquarters in **Helsingborg**.
> Copy me in on any **correspondence**.
> Thanks **a lot. You're** a star!
> Maxine
> (BTW any news on **Gary's feasibility** study???)

6 Ask students to read the statements and note if they agree or disagree. Put them in pairs in order to discuss their thoughts. Elicit students' ideas and encourage discussion. While there are a range of possible views on these issues, it is worth pointing out that the presence of a lot of typos in the first mail didn't make the overall message impossible to understand; who you are writing to is critical, e.g. clients, colleagues, your boss, a friend; and the fact that native speakers make mistakes in emails.

7 Students delete as many words as they can from the second email, while retaining the basic meaning, and then compare with a partner. Alternatively, students work in pairs/small groups to produce the shortened version. Check the answers with the class, accepting any reasonable variation.

> **SUGGESTED ANSWER**
> (suggestions for words that could be deleted are underlined below)
> Dear Stephen,
> I do realize that you must be very busy at the moment with all the arrangements for our exhibition stand at the Rome Expo in two weeks' time, but, if you have a spare moment sometime over the next few days, could you possibly just have a quick look at the first draft of my report on the ComTech feasibility study, which I've been working

76   12 EMAILING

BUSINESS COMMUNICATION

very hard on since we last spoke? As I'm sure Maxine has already told you, it was actually due last week and I know that she needs it quite urgently, but there are just a couple of points I need to check with you, if that's okay, before I submit the final report – see attachment.

FYI, I don't know if anyone has spoken to you about it yet, but it looks like I'm probably going to be coming to Copenhagen with you, Fiona and Michael in September after all. You'll remember from my CV when you interviewed me for this position that I studied German and Danish at university and, as a matter of fact, I still speak pretty good Danish, which might just come in handy ;-) although I'm quite sure most of the Danes we'll be meeting at the conference will have no problem whatsoever with English!

KR,
Gary

> **Language links**
>
> Direct students to the *Language links* section on pages 80–81 for further explanation of the use of future forms, and exercises to practise them.

8 Ask students to add a sentence or two to personalize the email then elicit possible answers.

> **SUGGESTED ANSWERS**
>
> (BTW) Congratulations on becoming a father!
> (BTW) I heard you applied for that promotion – good luck!
> (BTW) I know you are under a bit of pressure at the moment so let me know if I can do anything to help.
> (BTW) I know Denmark quite well if you need any help organizing the visit.
> (BTW) If you fancy a game of squash one evening, just let me know.

Email style

In this section, students read another email and select the best expressions to use in terms of style. They then write a reply to the same email, working from prompts. Finally, students focus on useful expressions to use in emails.

1 Ask students who they write emails to and if they consciously change the style of writing depending on the recipient.

Remind students that a friendly, neutral style works best in email. Ask them to read the message and underline the most appropriate expressions. Check answers with the class.

> **SUGGESTED ANSWERS**
>
> 1 Dear Mr Green
> 2 I trust you are well
> 3 I would like to congratulate you on an excellent presentation.
> 4 The product demonstration was extremely well received.
> 5 However, there is one aspect which concerns me.
> 6 As it stands the packaging design may be problematic.
> 7 Would you consider changing the design?
> 8 Could we meet next week to discuss some alternative ideas?
> 9 Also, I would be grateful if you could read over the Singapore report.
> 10 Would it be possible for you to provide me the information by Wednesday 10 am?
> 11 Should you have any questions, please do not hesitate to contact Sandra Taylor in accounts.
> 12 Yours sincerely

2 Tell students to read through the prompts and point out that the mark // indicates students should start a new sentence. With weaker classes, elicit the first two sentences with the whole class. Set a time limit to encourage students to focus on fluency. If students have access to computers, encourage them to type and print out their answers. Students can exchange their emails and check them for corrections. Then check possible wording with the whole class.

> **SAMPLE ANSWER**
>
> Hi Simon
> I'm glad you enjoyed the presentation and I'm also pleased about the response to the product demo. I was disappointed to hear you are not keen on the design. I thought it was quite stylish. Let me know when you are free to discuss alternatives. I'm around most of next week.
> I'm happy to go through the report. The costing will be ready within a few days. I may need to check a few things with Sandra. Do you happen to have her extension number?
> Thanks a lot
> [your name]

> **Language links**
>
> Direct students to the *Language links* section on page 80 for more practice of prepositional phrases.

The biggest email blunders ever made

In this section, students discuss aspects of computer use and emailing, such as the spread of viruses and the sending of inappropriate or angry emails (*flaming*). This leads into a listening task on the biggest email blunders ever made.

1 Check/review the verb *to flame* (another way of saying *to fire off an angry email*) and the noun *a flame* (the angry email itself). Ask students to discuss the questions in pairs. Use the following points as prompt or follow-up questions:

a *Does your computer have anti-virus software installed? How often is it updated? Does your company have a firewall to protect the network against viruses?*

b *How tolerant is your company of the personal use of computers? Is it considered a perk? Some companies allow workers some personal use each day – is this a good solution to the problem?*

c *What other inappropriate material could be circulated via email? (company gossip, intimate messages between people who are in a relationship and who are also colleagues, etc)*

2 2.39 Check/Pre-teach: *blunder, to spread a rumour, to sue, to suspend, to reprimand, antitrust trials, to sabotage.*

Play the recording once and get students to number the items in the correct order. Check the answers.

12 EMAILING 77

BUSINESS COMMUNICATION

ANSWERS

Netscape	9	Merrill Lynch	7
Dow Chemical	5	Cerner	6
the Love Bug	1	Western Provident	3
AOL	10	Norwich Union	2
Microsoft®	8	The Pentagon	4

2.39

A: This week on CyberReport Terry Lancaster takes a look at some of the biggest email blunders ever made.

B: In April 2000 millions of computer users received an unexpected email. The subject line was intriguing. It said 'I love you.' Those whose curiosity got the better of them opened the message and unleashed what later became known as the Love Bug – a virus so lethal it has so far infected 45 million PCs and caused $8.7 billion worth of damage to computer networks worldwide.

Computer viruses like the Love Bug sound like every company's worst nightmare. But the real danger these days is not so much what can get into your email system as what can get out. You just never know where that email you now regret sending may end up.

The first high-profile blunder occurred in 1997 when employees at the Norwich Union insurance company started spreading a rumour about a competitor on their internal email system. Western Provident, they said, was about to go bankrupt. Western Provident was not about to go bankrupt, and when the emails suggesting it was came into their possession, it sued. The case was eventually settled out of court for a cool £450,000.

In yet another email blunder instance, Devon schoolgirl Claire McDonald found herself receiving emails containing top secret information from the Pentagon after being accidentally added to a cc list by a naval commander. One of the emails was offering advice to the UK on how to prevent secrets from being leaked. She received so many secret files, it caused her computer to crash!

And the corporate email blunder stories just go on. When Dow Chemical discovered hundreds of controversial emails being exchanged between members of staff, the company took no chances. It fired 74 employees and suspended a further 435.

But disciplining your staff electronically isn't always a good idea, as the CEO of Cerner, Neal Patterson, found out to his cost. When Patterson reprimanded 400 managers by email, his criticisms somehow found their way onto the Yahoo! website – for all the world to see. Cerner stock fell by 28% within the week.

And at Merrill Lynch in 2002, the company ended up paying out $100 million when Henry Blodget, an Internet stock analyst, strongly recommended buying stock in a company he had previously described, in what he thought was a private email, as totally useless.

But perhaps the most famous business emails in history came to light during the Microsoft antitrust trials. When Netscape was still operational, CEO Jim Barksdale claimed his company never wanted to collaborate with Microsoft® in the Internet browser market – until, that is, Microsoft lawyers unearthed an email from Netscape president Jim Clark to a senior executive at Microsoft® stating clearly: 'We do not want to compete with you.' And Microsoft, for its part, denied any attempt to push Netscape out of the market – until an email from Bill Gates to AOL executives was submitted as evidence. The email clearly expressed Gates' desire to sabotage Netscape. Oh, dear!

So the message is clear. With email, honesty is not always the best policy. And if you must tell the truth, think twice before clicking that send button.

A: That was Terry Lancaster talking about the biggest email blunders ever made. And now a sneak preview of the latest in wireless technology

3 Divide the class into pairs. Ask students to work together to see if they can remember any of the key information. Play the recording again to let students complete/check their answers.

With weaker groups, write up all the figures from the recording and ask students if they can remember what they represent: *45 million, $8.7 billion, £450,000, 74, 435, 400, 28%, $100 million.* Get students to choose the correct figures to answer a, b, d and f. Check answers with the class.

ANSWERS

a $8.7 billion b £450,000 c accidentally added to cc list
d 74 e Cerner's f $100 million g Jim Clark & Bill Gates

4 **2.39** Play the recording again and let students check their answers. Elicit students' reactions to the blunders. Ask follow-up questions, e.g. *Has your company suffered from the Love Bug virus? What would happen if someone in your company made any of the blunders described in the recording?*

You've got mail!

In the final section, the students take part in an email exchange exercise and so practise fluency in writing. They also get the opportunity to give peer feedback.

1 For this task, students with access to computers can key the text of their emails, and if they are on an internal network, they can write and send them to the appropriate address.

Stage 1

Check/Pre-teach: *short notice, to be a pain, up to your neck in work, to be kept in the loop, do you fancy* (would you like to). Ask students to skim all four subjects and choose the one they wish to use. Remind them they need to write to a real colleague and that they can adapt/add to the prompts.

Remind students of the need for a friendly but neutral tone and for clarity but they do not need to achieve total accuracy. Set a strict time limit so that students exchange emails at a set time. Get students to write their email.

Stage 2

Check/Pre-teach: *to stand in for.* Divide the class into pairs and ask students to read Stage 2. Tell students that they should reply as the employee standing in for the colleague.

Again, get students to keep to the same time limit as in Stage 1. Students exchange emails and write their reply. If appropriate, place the emails in a central box for collection by the recipient, rather than just swapping them between pairs of students. Be ready to deal with questions on staging/procedure but encourage students to address queries regarding the situation to the email recipient and to use language from the unit as appropriate.

Stage 3

Check students understand that the correspondence will continue until the business in hand is brought to a conclusion but suggest a maximum of five emails in total and keep to the same time limit. Again, be ready to answer procedural questions, but don't offer too much help as this will interfere with the authenticity of the task.

2 Ask students to review their partner's emails using a checklist of points to look for: tone and style, clarity, brevity, accuracy. If appropriate, set up a grading system of 1–5 for each point, where 5 is excellent. Students give feedback on each other's writing, highlighting language mistakes that caused a problem for comprehension.

If accuracy in writing is important to your students, take in the emails and give feedback on important errors.

Language links

Direct students to the *Phrase bank* in the *Language links* section on page 81 for more on useful expressions for emailing.

1:1 Discuss the four email subjects and decide with your student which email situation they wish to practise. Decide if you would like to run this activity in real time, answering the emails immediately, and continuing until the sequence is complete and the issue resolved. It is also possible to answer each email later and run the exchange over a number of days. At the end of the activity, print out the results in order to provide feedback and do any follow-up language work.

Language links

ANSWERS

Vocabulary
Prepositional phrases
1 a at   b on   c in   d as   e up   f off
2 a first glance; the whole; some respects
  b a matter of fact; general; any rate
  c no account; the top of my head; the very most; second thoughts
  d theory; practice; the contrary; any case; best
3 study them in detail,   they're pretty much in line with,   In fact,   been in touch with,   are they in favour of,   By the way,   were all for it,

Grammar
Future forms
1 1 a schedule or timetable   2 an arrangement
   3 a refusal   4 an indisputable fact
2 a He offered to help me.   b He warned me about it.
  c He promised to be there.   d He suddenly had an idea.
  e He refused to do it.
3 b, d, e, h
4 a 4   b 1   c 2   d 3
5 1 c   2 a   3 b   4 h   5 d, e, f, g
6 a We were going to fly Lufthansa.   3
  b We were meeting at three.   2
  c I was just about to leave.   1
  d I thought we'd have problems.   4
7 a, b, d

Phrase bank
Emailing
1 a Have a quick look **at** these figures and get **back to** me asap.
  b Let me know if you need any help **with** the Koreans. And copy me **in on** any correspondence **with** them.
  c Could you get **on to** our suppliers and sort something **out with** them? I'll leave the details **to** you, but keep me **in** the loop.
  d BTW, you did a great job **on** the presentation. It went **down** really well **with** the Belgians. We'll just have to wait and see what they come **back** to us **with**.
  e Could you update me **on** where we are **with** the Expo arrangements? I'm a bit **out** of touch. Can I leave it **up to** you to contact the speakers?
  f I'd like to sound you **out on** this new packaging idea. Let's meet **up** to discuss it sometime next week. BTW, I still can't seem to get **through to** Monica.
  g I haven't had time to read **through** the whole report and I'll probably need to check some of these figures **against** the computer, but leave it **with** me.
  h Thanks for your offer **of** a drink. If I can finish this report **off** by 7, I may just take you **up on** it! I could certainly do **with** one!
2 a Delegating tasks
    I'll leave the details to you.
    Would you mind taking this off my hands?
  b Asking for advice
    Can I sound you out on something?
    Can you just cross-check the figures for me?
  c Buying time
    Give me a week and I'll see what I can come up with.
    Leave it with me. I'll sort it out.
  d Requesting information
    Can you update me on where we are with this?
    Keep me in the loop.

13 Making an impact

Learning objectives

This unit focuses on effective beginnings and endings of presentations, and gives students the opportunity to use rhetorical devices in English.

Students discuss the way presenters start their talks and listen to six openings of presentations in order to evaluate their effectiveness.

Students listen to four famous political speeches, which all use rhetoric, and study the techniques used. They then listen to extracts from four ineffective presentations, rephrase them to make them more effective, and practise delivering them. Students then focus on techniques for closing presentations and present a close to the class.

Finally, a fluency task in which students create a new country gives practice in preparing and delivering a speech and in using rhetorical techniques.

The grammatical focus is on rhetorical techniques and the lexical focus is on metaphor.

Digital resources: Unit 13

Online Workbook; Extension worksheets; Glossary; Phrase bank; Student's Book answer key; Student's Book listening script; Fast-track map

---

In this first section, students focus on the openings of presentations. They listen to and discuss the beginning of six presentations and focus on the language used.

1:1 In this unit, the work on rhetorical devices used in presentations can be especially helpful for students who need to give presentations. For homework, encourage your student to think about other inspiring speeches they may have heard, look for the transcripts online and bring them to class to discuss. Your student could also bring in a presentation they need to deliver at work, and discuss with you how to change it in order to make more effective use of rhetorical techniques.

Warm-up

As a lead-in, ask if students can think of a recent speaker who had the power to persuade them, e.g. a political leader, a salesperson, or a business person who gave a presentation. Ask students if they can identify what was so good about the speaker's ability, and how exactly the speaker was able to influence them.

1 Check/Pre-teach: *to convert, to compel, orator*. Then focus attention on the quotation by Ralph Waldo Emerson. Ask students if they agree with the sentiment expressed.

2 Ask students to think of the most memorable opening to a presentation they have ever heard and elicit examples from the group. Ask the students why the opening to a presentation is important and then get them to read the book extract. Students compare their ideas with the author's (it establishes tone; it means the speaker can take charge; it should be memorable). Ask students how far they agree with the author, especially with his last sentence.

3 Point out that presentations often start with a 'hook' – something which involves the audience in some way, e.g. asking a question, asking for a show of hands. Divide the class into pairs and get students to brainstorm techniques for getting people's attention.

4 🔘 **3.01** With weaker groups check/pre-teach: *G8 countries* (the major industrialized democracies), *scary, to outperform, to resent, corrupt, on the right track, mean* (informal for *cruel*), *Total Quality* (management philosophy which gives responsibility for quality to everyone in an organization), *magnate*. Play the recording and get students to check the techniques used against their list in 3. Elicit which other techniques were used, e.g. asking rhetorical questions, getting participants to raise their hands.

ANSWERS
quoting a statistic, telling a joke, thanking people, quoting a famous person, telling an anecdote, making reference to a famous person

---

🔘 **3.01**

1 Did you know that of the world's one hundred biggest economies only 56 are actually countries? That's right, 56. The other 44 are companies! In fact, if companies were allowed to join the G8 group of the world's richest countries, Microsoft® would take the place of the poorest country! I think it's getting a little scary, don't you, when a corporation can outperform a nation? And maybe it's time to stop and ask ourselves: should business really be that powerful?

2 You know, the joke books of the world are probably full of more lawyer jokes than just about anything else. One of my favourite lawyer jokes is: this guy's having a quiet café latte at a coffee bar when an angry man starts shouting 'All lawyers are criminals!' The man jumps to his feet and cries 'I resent that remark!' 'Why?' says the angry man. 'Are you a lawyer?' 'No' says the man, 'I'm a criminal!' But I'm here to tell you that not all lawyers are corrupt. It's just 99% of them who give the others a bad name.

3 Good morning. Erm, I'd like to start off by thanking Dr Jensen, Dr Tan and Dr Martinez for inviting me to speak today. Our company has a long history of collaboration with this university and it's always a great pleasure to address the robotics experts of the future. Erm, yes, before I

begin, perhaps I could just take a moment or two to introduce you to the rest of my team, who are here with me this morning …

4   I think it was Thomas Edison who said: 'I have not failed. I've just found 10,000 ways that don't work.' Of course, Edison was an inventor, but he could just as easily have been talking about sales. In sales, our success rate is nowhere near as bad as one in 10,000. At least, it better not be! But we have to go through an awful lot of 'no sales' to make one sale. And the ability to deal with failure is the single most important characteristic of the successful sales professional. Could you just raise your hand if you failed to make a sale yesterday? … Just about everybody, right? Well, congratulations! You're obviously on the right track!

5   I was looking through the appointments pages the other day and came across this unusual job advertisement. Here it is: 'Good hours, excellent pay, fun place to work, paid training, mean boss! Oh, well, four out of five isn't bad.' Wouldn't you like to be interviewed by that boss who admits he's mean? How powerful that little touch of honesty is. And that's exactly what I want to talk to you about this morning: honesty in advertising. And how you get people's attention when you simply tell the truth …

6   Whenever I'm asked about Total Quality, I think of the story of the American steel magnate, Andrew Carnegie. It seems Carnegie was doing a factory tour one day, when he stopped to speak to one of the machine operators – a grey-haired old guy obviously coming up to retirement. 'Wilson,' he said, reading the man's name badge, 'how many years exactly have you been working for me now?' 'Thirty-nine, sir,' Wilson replied with a proud smile. 'And may I add that in all those years I made only one very small mistake.' 'Good work,' mumbled Carnegie, 'but from now on, please try to be more careful.'

5 Ask students to rank the openers in 4 in order of effectiveness. Students compare their order in pairs and then report back to the class.

6–7   3.01 When students have finished, play the recording again so that they can check their answers.

> **ANSWERS**
> a Did you know …
> b One of my …
> c I'd like to …
> d I think it …
> e I was looking …
> f Whenever I'm asked …

Presence and performance

Students start by discussing the meaning of *charisma* and then rank four extracts from famous political speeches according to how charismatic they sound. They focus on the seven 'rules' of rhetoric and analyse the rhetorical techniques used in the speeches. They then re-word extracts from ineffective business presentations and practise delivering the improved versions with maximum impact. There is a further recording highlighting techniques for ending presentations, which students analyse before practising the delivery of the final part of their own presentation.

1   Have students read the definition of *charisma* and elicit the adjective *charismatic*. Check pronunciation and make sure students produce the stress shift between the two words: *char-IS-ma*, *char-is-MA-tic*.

Ask students to think about the equivalent word in their language and then elicit examples of charismatic speakers internationally and from the students' own country. They may well mention Obama's speech in the US presidential elections.

2   3.02–3.05 Tell students they are going to hear extracts from four speeches from the second half of the 20th century given by four former leaders. (Point out that the recordings are of actors speaking in the style of the original speakers, not the original orators themselves.)

Play the recording and get students to rank them in terms of charisma. Then get students to compare their answers in pairs. Hold a short feedback session and establish which speech students thought most charismatic and why. Ask them to guess who the original speakers might be and which famous speech they deliver:

Extract 1 – John F Kennedy, 1961, from his inauguration speech as 35th president of the USA.

Extract 2 – Martin Luther King, 1963, from his address to the civil rights demonstrators who had marched on Washington.

Extract 3 – Margaret Thatcher, 1975, from her speech to the Conservative Party Conference in Blackpool.

Extract 4 – Nelson Mandela, 1994, from his inauguration statement as president of the Democratic Republic of South Africa.

With weaker groups, you may wish to deal with the following vocabulary: *to shrink, faith, devotion, endeavour, glow, rooted, creed, brotherhood, sweltering, oppression, oasis, to beg, humbled, elevated, reconciliation, to fulfil*.

> **3.02**
>
> **Extract 1**
>
> In the long history of the world, only a few generations have been granted the role of defending freedom in its hour of maximum danger. I do not shrink from this responsibility – I welcome it. I do not believe that any of us would exchange places with any other people or any other generation. The energy, the faith, the devotion, which we bring to this endeavour will light our country and all who serve it – and the glow from that fire can truly light the world. And so, my fellow Americans, ask not what your country can do for you – ask what you can do for your country. My fellow citizens of the

BUSINESS COMMUNICATION

world, ask not what America will do for you – but what together we can do for the freedom of man.

3.03
Extract 2

I say to you today, my friends … so even though we face the difficulties of today and tomorrow, I still have a dream. It is a dream deeply rooted in the American dream. I have a dream that one day this nation will rise up and live out the true meaning of its creed: 'We hold these truths to be self-evident; that all men are created equal.' I have a dream that one day on the red hills of Georgia the sons of former slaves and the sons of former slave owners will be able to sit down together at the table of brotherhood. I have a dream that one day even the state of Mississippi, a state sweltering with the heat of injustice, sweltering with the heat of oppression, will be transformed into an oasis of freedom and justice. I have a dream that my four little children will one day live in a nation where they will not be judged by the colour of their skin but by the content of their character. I have a dream today.

3.04
Extract 3

These are the two great challenges of our time – the moral and political challenge, and the economic challenge. They have to be faced together and we have to master them both. What are our chances of success? It depends on what kind of people we are. What kind of people are we? We are the people that in the past made Great Britain the workshop of the world, the people who persuaded others to buy British, not by begging them to do so, but because it was best. We are a people who have received more Nobel prizes than any other nation except America, and head for head we have done better than America, twice as well in fact. We are the people who, among other things, invented the computer, the refrigerator, the electric motor, the stethoscope, rayon, the steam turbine, stainless steel, the tank, television, penicillin, radar, the jet engine, hovercraft, float glass, carbon fibres, et cetera – and the best half of Concorde.

3.05
Extract 4

We are both humbled and elevated by the honour and privilege that you, the people of South Africa, have bestowed on us, as the first president of a united, democratic, non-racial and non-sexist South Africa, to lead our country out of the valley of darkness. We understand it still that there is no easy road to freedom. We know it well that none of us acting alone can achieve success. We must therefore act together as a united people, for national reconciliation, for nation building, for the birth of a new world. Let there be justice for all. Let there be peace for all. Let there be work, bread, water and salt for all. Let each know that for each the body, the mind and the soul have been freed to fulfil

themselves. Never, never and never again shall it be that this beautiful land will again experience the oppression of one by another …

3 Check comprehension of the noun *rhetoric* (language / techniques used to create a powerful or dramatic effect). Elicit examples of rhetorical techniques students are familiar with, e.g. repetition of sounds/words/phrases. Check/Pre-teach: *to accumulate, metaphorical*. Get students to complete the rules of rhetoric and then check the answers.

ANSWERS
1 words   2 sounds   3 opposites   4 threes   5 questions
6 points   7 language

4 Refer students to the extracts on page 84 and get students to find more examples of rhetoric, working in pairs. Check the answers with the class. As an optional follow-up task, refer students to the listening scripts on pages 152–153. Get students to choose a speech and practise delivering it for dramatic effect.

ANSWERS
Extract 1
a I do not shrink from this responsibility – I welcome it. *contrast*
b I do not believe that any of us would exchange places with any other people or any other generation. *repetition (words), group of three*
c The energy, the faith, the devotion, which we bring to this endeavour will light our country and all who serve it. *group of three, metaphor*
d And so, my fellow Americans, ask not what your country can do for you – ask what you can do for your country. *contrast, repetition (words), repetition (sounds)*

Extract 2
a I still have a dream. It is a dream deeply rooted in the American dream. *repetition (words), metaphor, repetition (sounds)*
b I have a dream that one day on the red hills of Georgia the sons of former slaves and the sons of former slave owners will be able to sit down together at the table of brotherhood. *repetition (words), repetition (sounds), metaphor*
c I have a dream that my four little children will one day live in a nation where they will not be judged by the colour of their skin but by the content of their character. I have a dream today. *contrast, repetition (sounds)*

Extract 3
a What are our chances of success? It depends on what kind of people we are. *rhetorical question*
b What kind of people are we? We are the people that in the past made Great Britain the workshop of the world … *rhetorical question, repetition (words), repetition (sounds)*
c … the people who persuaded others to buy British, not by begging them to do so, but because it was best. *contrast, repetition (sounds)*

Extract 4
a We understand it still that there is no easy road to freedom. We know it well that none of us acting alone can achieve success. *metaphor, repetition (sounds)*
b Let each know that for each the body, the mind and the soul have been freed to fulfil themselves. *repetition (words), repetition (sounds), group of three*

c Never, never and never again shall it be that this beautiful land will again experience the oppression of one by another. *repetition (words), group of three*

Language links

Direct students to the *Language links* section on page 87 for more on the use of metaphor in business English.

5 3.06 Ask students to rephrase the extracts and play the recording so they can check their answers.

ANSWERS

a main problem we're / main problem is
b so / so / and / so
c faster / cheaper / easier to use / all / reliable
d if / never / biggest / can / be the best
e is / more / are fighting / and fewer jobs
f only are / now number one
g market / company / outperformed / one / ever
h once / years of business / we ever / single one

3.06

a What's the main problem we're facing? The main problem is cash flow.
b It's so risky, so problematic, and yet so critical to our success.
c It's faster, cheaper and easier to use. But, above all, it's more reliable.
d Even if we can never again be the biggest, we can still be the best.
e The point is, more and more graduates are fighting over fewer and fewer jobs.
f Not only are we number one in Brazil. We're now number one in Latin America.
g In this market, no company has outperformed us, not one – ever!
h Not once, in over 30 years of business, have we ever had a complaint – not a single one!

6 Check students can define a *clause* (a group of words with a subject and verb). Ask students to analyse the word order and then check the answer with the class. Ask students if this technique of switching word order can be used in their language.

ANSWER

The most important words usually come at the end of clauses and the most important clause at the end of the sentence.

7 With weaker classes, model one or two examples first, highlighting the stressed words and intonation. Divide the class into pairs/small groups and get students to deliver the extracts. If possible, record the students and play back the recording, getting students to assess the delivery and how to improve on it.

Language links

Direct students to the *Language links* section on pages 87–88 for further explanation of the use of rhetorical techniques, and exercises to practise them.

8 3.07 As a lead-in, ask students which they remember most: the opening or closing of a presentation. Elicit examples of memorable closing remarks/techniques that they have seen or used themselves, e.g. using a quotation.

With weaker groups, check/pre-teach: *on the brink of, nonsense, gene therapy, handout, reputation, to diminish, ironic, to sum up, to do something justice, masterpiece*. Play the recording and let students number the techniques in the order they hear them. Check the answers and elicit the key words/phrases that helped students decide on the order.

ANSWERS

the sum up = 4   the call to action = 3   the famous quotation = 1
the emergency stop = 2

3.07

1 Ladies and gentlemen, we are truly on the brink of a revolution in bio-technology. I'm reminded of the words of futurist and science fiction writer Arthur C. Clarke: 'People go through four stages' he said, 'before any revolutionary development. Stage one: it's nonsense, don't waste my time. Stage two: it's interesting, but not important. Stage three: I always said it was a good idea. And stage four: I thought of it first.' In gene therapy we're about to enter stage four. And I'd like this company to honestly be able to say 'We thought of it first.' Thank you.

2 Uh-oh. Sorry. Looks like we've run out of time. Erm, so I'm going to have to cut it short. Er, yeah, I was hoping to show you some of the figures in our comparative study. But, erm, never mind. I think you'll find all the main points are covered in the handout. So I'll, er, I'll just leave the copies here and you can pick one up on your way out. Okay. So, sorry about that. That's it. Thanks.

3 Well, that just about brings me to the end of my presentation, except to say that the future of this company is now in your hands. For if there's one central message I'd like to get across to you this morning it's this: that this consultancy is no more and no less than the consultants who represent it. And whilst our reputation as a firm may have been damaged by the recent unfortunate events, our expertise as a team is in no way diminished. I want to see each and every one of you raising this company to new heights. I know you can. We built our reputation on crisis management, and it would be ironic indeed if we were unable to successfully manage this crisis of our own – and come out on top. So thank you very much.

4 So, how do you sum up the new Spearing Silhouette ocean cruiser? I could tell you that it has won just about every boat show in the USA and Europe this year, that the orders for it are coming in so fast we already have a five-year waiting list; that the first three names on that waiting list, though strictly confidential, include a famous Hollywood actor, a member of the Saudi Royal Family and one of the world's greatest sporting legends. I could also mention that, so impressed are they with our award-winning design, the directors of

BUSINESS COMMUNICATION

> the Museum of Modern Art are actually proposing to place a full-size model on permanent exhibition. But all that would fail to do it justice. For the fact is that the Silhouette is in a class of its own. It is a masterpiece of marine engineering. It is, quite simply, the most stunningly beautiful boat ever built. Ladies and gentlemen, I give you … the Spearing Silhouette!

9 Tell students that they will now have a chance to practise closing a presentation. They should choose one of the ways of ending in 8 and apply it to a presentation they have given in the past, or may need to deliver in the future. If students are short of ideas, elicit examples, e.g. a sales presentation on a product, a welcome speech to new employees, a merger announcement, etc.

Give students time to prepare and to rehearse the delivery. Refer them to the listening script on page 153 to help them. Monitor and help as necessary. Students deliver their closing to the rest of the class. Hold a short feedback session, encouraging students to comment constructively on each other's delivery and impact.

> **Language links**
>
> Direct students to the *Phrase bank* in the *Language links* section on page 88 for more on techniques for opening and closing a presentation.

A new country, a new start

In the last section of this unit, students take part in a fluency task in which they prepare and deliver parts of a presentation to persuade the other group members that the country they have invented is the best to live, work and holiday in.

1 As a lead-in to the task, ask students to write down where else in the world they would like to go to live and work. Find out why they chose that place. Explain to students that they are going to invent a new country and try to persuade the class that it's the best place to live, work and holiday in. Ask students to read the questions and discuss their answers in pairs. Remind students that there are lists of countries based on how ideal they would be to live in with factors such as the standard of education, and safety. Students may be able to access this information on the Internet, if available. Give students plenty of time to develop their new country's profile. Tell students to make brief notes under each heading. Remind students they can use all the tools at their disposal, such as PowerPoint or visuals. Monitor and help students with ideas or language, if required.

2 In the same pairs, ask students to prepare their presentations. Explain that the audience will be rating their performance on clarity, persuasion and impact, so students should take these factors into account in their preparation. When the students are ready, pairs take turns to give their presentations. Ask the audience to use the rating card to rate each presentation. At the end, ask the class to decide which pair gave the most persuasive performance. Hold a class vote on the most desirable place to live in, work in and visit. Give feedback on students'

use of rhetoric and on overall fluency before highlighting important or common errors.

1:1 Ask your student to prepare and deliver the presentation while you take the role of a potential investor in tourism or a business development officer. Ask questions. Record the presentation, if possible, and afterwards watch part of it with a view to giving feedback.

> **Language links**
>
> **ANSWERS**
>
> **Vocabulary**
> **Metaphor**
> 1 a takeover   battle   **war**
>   b ballpark   figure   **sport**
>   c heated   debate   **fire**
>   d economic   recovery   **health**
>   e cash   flow   **water**
> 2 a pouring b trickling c pooling d coming e growing
>   f sowing   g idea   h attack   i fight   j guns   k victory
>   l stakes   m odds   n goalposts
>
> **Grammar**
> **Rhetorical techniques**
> 1 b much   c now   d always   e here   f today
>   This is important, very important.
> 2 1 b history – past   c group – team   d advertising – promotion
>   e energy – dynamism   f prepared – willing
>   g easier – simpler
>   2 a b   b p   c t   d p   e d   f w   g s
>   They are all lists of three.
> 3 b If we don't seize this opportunity, **someone else will**.
>   c Tackling a few minor problems now will save us a whole **lot** of **major problems later**.
>   d Some people are saying we can't afford to advertise, but **I say** we **can't afford not** to.
>   e I'm not saying we're certain to succeed: what **I am saying** is we'll **never know until** we **try**.
>   f Three years ago this company was going nowhere; **today** it's **number one** in the **industry**.
> 4 a Isn't this what we need to be doing?
>   b Shouldn't we be learning from our mistakes?
>   c Deep down, don't we all know this to be true?
> 5 a advantages   b answer
>   c chances   d point
>   e problem   f result
> 6 a … is this company leaner, it's also greener.
>   b … must we panic.
>   c … have we done better than in Mexico.
>   d … exhaustive tests will we be ready to launch.
>
> **Phrase bank**
> **Opening and closing a presentation**
> 1 Would you believe it?
> 2 Now, here's a funny thing
> 3 Let me take you on a journey
> 4 Wise words
> 5 This is a true story, by the way
> 6 Is anybody out there?
> 7 To cut a long story short
> 8 Oh, and one last thing

13 MAKING AN IMPACT

14 Out and about

Learning objectives

This unit is about business travel. Students work on fluency and communication skills, and practise telling anecdotes.

Two extracts from the film *The Accidental Tourist* set the scene for a discussion on travel. Students focus on ellipsis, which frequently occurs in conversational English. They also focus on a range of expressions useful for striking up a conversation, and roleplay conversations to practise using these techniques and expressions.

Students listen to a series of travellers' tales. They review narrative tenses and the stages of a story, and go on to tell their own story / anecdote.

In the last section, two short texts provide the stimulus for a discussion on business lunches. A recording of businesspeople moving from one topic of conversation to another over dinner provides listening practice. Finally, students do a roleplay set in a restaurant and discuss a variety of topics as they aim to keep a conversation going.

The grammatical focus is on narrative tenses and the lexical focus is on the language of storytelling.

Digital resources: Unit 14

Online Workbook; In company interviews Units 12–14 and worksheet; Extension worksheets; Glossary; Phrase bank; Student's Book answer key; Student's Book listening script; Fast-track map; Quick progress test 3

In the first section, students decide which items are essential to take when travelling. An extract from the film, *The Accidental Tourist*, provides an introduction to the topic of business travel. Students discuss a recording from the same film. An exercise raises awareness of ellipsis, a key feature of native-speaker speech, which can be quite challenging. Students study ways of starting up a conversation with a stranger, before roleplaying short conversations with fellow travellers.

1:1 Ask your student how much they travel for business. This unit offers plenty of scope to discuss aspects of travel. In this unit, there are some opportunities for students to tell a story about something that has happened to them in real life.

Warm-up

Ask students to read the quotation from Mark McCormack. Elicit possible interpretations, e.g. you can beat homesickness by keeping home in mind.

1 Divide the class into pairs and give students two minutes to brainstorm a list of essential travel items.

2 Lead in to the text by writing the following prompts on the board and asking students what they would pack for a five-day business trip: *number of travel bags, number of suits, number of books/magazines*.

Ask students to read the text quickly and compare what they would pack with the advice given in the text. Check/Pre-teach: *detergent, laundry, spot remover, handy, devastate, everything but the kitchen sink*. Ask students to read the text again and answer questions a–f in pairs or small groups. Hold a short feedback session, eliciting interesting/funny anecdotes for questions b and f, and the best advice for question d.

Ask students to describe the tone and register of the text (humorous and ironic) and to give examples of how the writer achieves this, e.g. *you won't fall into the hands of unfamiliar laundries, grey … is handy for sudden funerals, always bring a book as protection against strangers*.

3 Check/Pre-teach: *sarcastic, fussy, witty, bitter, paranoid*. Ask students to choose the relevant adjectives, giving reasons for their answers.

SUGGESTED ANSWERS

a bit paranoid, antisocial, fussy, gloomy, private, well organized, witty

4 3.08 Draw students' attention to the *Glossary* entries. Tell students they are going to read the text and listen to the extract at the same time. Ask them to tell you what coincidence links Loomis and Leary. Ask students to comment on what passenger type Loomis is: a chatterbox, enthusiastic and complimentary.

ANSWER

Loomis has read and is a fan of Leary's book.

3.08

Traveller: I'm sorry I'm so fat. Name's Lucas Loomis.
Leary: Macon Leary.
Traveller: You a Baltimore man?
Leary: Yes.
Traveller: Me too. Greatest city on the earth. One of these seats is not really enough for me. And the stupid thing is, I travel for a living. I demonstrate software to computer stores. What do you do, Mr Leary?
Leary: I write travel guidebooks.
Traveller: Is that so? What kind?
Leary: Well, guides for businessmen – people just like you, I guess.
Traveller: 'Accidental Tourist'!
Leary: Why, yes.

BUSINESS COMMUNICATION

Traveller: Really? Am I right? Well, what do you know? Look at this. Gray suit – just what you recommend, appropriate for all occasions. See my luggage? Carry-on. Change of underwear. Clean shirt. Packet of detergent powder.
Leary: Oh, good.
Traveller: You're my hero. You've improved my trips a 100%. I tell my wife, going with The Accidental Tourist is like going in a cocoon.
Leary: Well, this is very nice to hear.
Traveller: Times I've flown clear to Oregon and hardly knew I'd left Baltimore.
Leary: Excellent.
Traveller: I see you have your book for protection there. Didn't work with me, though, did it?

5 Refer students back to the text and ask them to scan the conversation to find the correct expressions. Check the answers. As an optional follow-up activity with groups that are keen on drama and roleplays, get pairs of students to act out the dialogue. If available, you could also play the relevant extracts from a DVD of *The Accidental Tourist*.

ANSWERS

a Is that so? b I guess.
c Why, yes. d Well, what do you know?

6 Focus on the first sentence as an example with the whole class. Elicit both the word that is missing (*The*) and the type of word (article). If appropriate, introduce ellipsis as the term for the omission of words.

ANSWER

pronouns, articles, auxiliary verbs

7 Students work individually to delete the unnecessary words in the dialogues before checking with a partner.

ANSWERS

a A: ~~Is~~ everything okay with your meal, sir?
  B: ~~It's~~ delicious. ~~It~~ couldn't be better.
b A: ~~Do you~~ need anything else, sir?
  B: ~~I~~ don't think so, thanks.
c A: ~~Are you~~ ready to start?
  B: Yeah, ~~I'm~~ just coming.
d A: ~~Do you~~ mind if I switch the reading light on?
  B: ~~It~~ doesn't bother me. I think I'll get another coffee. ~~Do you~~ want one?
e A: ~~I~~ saw you earlier in the fitness centre. ~~Have you~~ been here long?
  B: ~~No,~~ I just got here yesterday. ~~Are~~ you here on business too?
f A: ~~Have you~~ got a light?
  B: Sorry, ~~I~~ don't smoke.

8 Elicit any advantages of striking up a conversation with strangers. Ask students how they feel about starting up conversations with strangers.

9 Students work individually to match the sentence halves. You can have students practise the pronunciation of the sentences, getting students to underline the stressed words and mark in the intonation pattern with arrows.

ANSWERS

1 e 2 d 3 b 4 l 5 k 6 f (i) 7 c 8 j 9 g
10 i (f) 11 h 12 a

10 Ask students to match the six ways of starting a conversation with a stranger with the expressions in 9.

ANSWERS

a make an observation	3, 9	b pay a compliment	10, 6
c make a request	1, 2	d ask for information	5, 12
e offer assistance	7, 8	f make an apology	4, 11

11 Check/Pre-teach: *hyperactive, the red-eye* (a plane that flies during the night), *bumpy, casting meeting, to skip dinner, there goes* (your relaxing flight), *turbulence*. Divide the class into AB pairs and refer Speaker A to page 125 and Speaker B to page 132. Give time to read and take notes on their roles and prepare for each of the conversations in turn. Remind them to choose a suitable opener for each conversation from 9.

Tell students that they should try to keep each conversation going for a minute or two. With weaker classes, model one of the roleplays with a strong student first. Monitor and take feedback notes.

When students have finished, elicit feedback from each pair on the outcome of their conversations. Elicit from students how easy or difficult it was to get started and to keep the conversation going.

1:1 Decide if you will do all three roleplays with your student. In advance of each roleplay, change the seating so that you are next to each other. Remind your student of the different ways of opening a conversation with a stranger, outlined in 9. Give your student time to prepare each of the roleplays by turning to page 125 and reading the information for Speaker A. You will need to refer to Speaker B's information on page 132.

Travellers' tales

In this section, students listen to four travellers telling stories about strange events which happened on flights and then focus on the use of narrative tenses in telling stories/anecdotes. Students put storytelling expressions into a logical order. They do an exercise on matching active listening expressions before telling their own story.

1 3.09 Elicit examples of strange/frightening experiences students have had when flying. Check/Pre-teach: *runway, hammering* (noise), *fuselage, lifejacket drill, to divert, to not have a clue about something, nuisance*.

Before students listen, get them to read questions a–f and predict any possible answers. Write up students' ideas on the board. Play the recording through once and get students to check their predictions.

Play the recording a second time, pausing between each speaker, in order for students to complete their answers. Check answers with the class.

BUSINESS COMMUNICATION

> **ANSWERS**
> a The pilot was hammering on the fuselage to get in the plane.
> b The air force jet might have shot them down.
> c They did the lifejacket drill even though they weren't flying over water.
> d The pilot.
> e She was asked to sit on the toilet during take-off.

🔊 **3.09**

1 Emma

A: So Emma, what's your worst flying experience?
B: Well, I think the worst one's probably flying back from Bangladesh to Heathrow. It's quite a few years ago now, but I can still remember it. We were at the gate, ready to taxi to the runway, and suddenly there was this terrible hammering noise from outside the plane.
A: A hammering noise?
B: Yes, and the strange thing was that the cabin crew just seemed to be ignoring it. But all you could hear was this bang, bang, bang on the fuselage. After a while, some of the passengers were starting to get nervous, me included.
A: I'm not surprised.
B: Anyway, eventually, after we'd been sitting there for about 10 minutes with no announcement and the plane still not moving, I said something to one of the stewards and they went and opened the door to see what was going on.
A: And what happened?
B: The pilot got in!
A: You're joking!
B: No, they'd locked him out. Seems quite funny now, but it didn't at the time.

2 Enrique

A: Enrique, what's the worst flight you've ever been on?
C: Definitely the time I was flying from Malaga to Stansted in the UK. This was around the time of security alerts on international flights and people were very nervous about flying.
A: Oh, yes, of course.
C: I was travelling on business, but most of the passengers were British tourists.
A: Uh huh.
C: Anyway, we were cruising at 30,000 feet and I looked out of the window and saw this French air force fighter plane flying alongside us.
A: What? Oh, yes, I read about this. Didn't they think the plane had been hijacked or something?
C: Well, apparently, air traffic control had lost radio contact with our plane, so they weren't sure what was going on and they weren't taking any chances. I mean this French jet was armed with missiles and everything.
A: Sounds terrifying!
C: It was.
A: So, what happened?

C: Well, the jet was there for about 10 minutes checking us out. Fortunately, the captain of our plane managed to keep everybody calm. And anyway, to cut a long story short, everything turned out okay. We even landed on schedule!
A: But I bet you were glad to be back on the ground, weren't you?
C: You can say that again!

3 Joe

A: Joe, have you had any bad experiences on planes?
D: Oh, yes, several. One flight I was on, I couldn't understand why they were making us go through the lifejacket drill for landing on water.
A: But don't they always do that?
D: What, on a domestic flight from Manchester to London?
A: Oh, right. I see what you mean.
D: I'm not sure which flight path they were planning to take but it goes nowhere near the sea. But that's nothing compared to one of my recent trips to Frankfurt.
A: What happened there, then?
D: Well, we didn't land in Frankfurt.
A: You were diverted?
D: No, no, the pilot just landed in completely the wrong country!
A: What, you mean he didn't know?
D: Hadn't got a clue. Just about everybody on the plane was looking out the windows and saying 'Er, look, I'm sorry to be a nuisance, but this isn't Frankfurt.'
A: So where did you land?
D: Luxembourg.
A: Oh, my goodness! I don't believe it!

4 Selina

A: Selina, you've flown all over the world. You must have some stories to tell.
E: Hmm, quite a few. I'll never forget the time I was flying in Asia and the cabin crew asked me to sit on the toilet during take-off.
A: What?
E: Yeah, they wanted my seat next to the emergency exit.
A: Doesn't inspire much confidence in the airline, does it?
E: Not a lot, no. And then, to top it all, I ended up sitting next to a guy with a rattlesnake in a basket!
A: Incredible!
E: Yes, that's what I said. Apparently, he just brought it on as hand luggage.

2 Students work individually to complete the exercise and then check their answers in pairs. Encourage students to say why they chose each tense. Check the answers with the whole class.

> **ANSWERS**
> a were starting b we'd been sitting c I said d went e opened
> f was going g happened h got i they'd locked j didn't

14 OUT AND ABOUT 87

BUSINESS COMMUNICATION

3 Tell students only to count the correct answers in 2. Check the number of uses of each tense and elicit examples from the recording (see below). Ask students to explain the use of tenses.

ANSWERS	
Past Simple	6 (*said, went, opened, happened, got, didn't*)
Past Perfect Simple	1 (*they'd locked*)
Past Continuous	2 (*were starting, was going*)
Past Perfect Continuous	1 (*we'd been sitting*)

Language links

Direct students to the *Language links* section on page 95 for further explanation of the use of narrative tenses, and an exercise to practise them.

4 Give students a few moments to consider the questions.

Language links

Direct students to the *Phrase bank* in the *Language links* section on page 95 for more on the language used in sharing anecdotes.

5 Write the four stages of a narrative on the board: *opener, context, emphasis, close*. Prepare students for the fluency activity by telling them a story of your own, using this narrative structure and some of the expressions in the box. After you have finished, ask the students if they remember which phrases you used at each stage.

Ask students to categorize the expressions and then check the answers by asking individuals to read out the phrases. Highlight intonation and voice range.

ANSWERS			
Opener:	e	**Context:**	h and i
Emphasis:	a, b, d and j	**Close:**	c, f and g

6 Students choose the correct expression. Check answers with the class.

ANSWER
Seems quite funny now, but it didn't at the time.

Language links

Direct students to the *Language links* section on page 94 for more practice of storytelling techniques, such as using more interesting adjectives and adverbs, and exaggerating.

7 Ask students what *active listeners* do. This includes nodding, making encouraging noises and reacting to what the speaker is saying. Ask students if these features are important in their language. Find out if silence is important when someone else is speaking and how people react to short interjections.

Tell students to look at the two halves of the phrases and match them. Model correct stress and intonation to help students sound natural.

ANSWERS
a You're joking!   b I don't believe it!   c Oh, my goodness!   d So, what happened?   e Sounds terrifying!   f I see what you mean.

8 Give students a few minutes to think of an appropriate travel experience. Refer students back to the stages in 5 and get them to note down key words and phrases as preparation for telling their story. Set a time limit of four or five minutes for the preparation stage. Ask a confident student to start the storytelling and try to make sure all students have an opportunity to speak. With bigger classes, students can work in groups to tell their stories.

The business lunch

The students discuss the most expensive business meal they have had before reading about two surprising stories connected with dining out. They listen to a recording of a business meal in which the topic keeps changing and this gives practice in listening for gist. A final fluency activity gives the students a chance to roleplay keeping a conversation going at a restaurant.

1 Tell students about the most expensive meal you have ever had and then get students to discuss the questions in pairs. Elicit any interesting examples from the class.

2 Ask students how long a typical business dinner lasts with clients and how much businesspeople usually pay for a meal at a local restaurant. Students then scan the texts to find how long one lunch lasted (five hours) and how much the most expensive business lunch cost (£44,000).

Students read the texts again and then discuss the questions. Elicit a range of opinions and then ask what would happen in the students' own company, e.g. *Would an employee be sacked for taking such a long lunch?*

3 3.10 To set the scene, ask students to tell the group about their favourite restaurant and why they like it.

Tell the students that you will play each extract twice and that during the first listening they only have to identify the general topic. Encourage them not to worry about understanding every word. Play the recording once and tell students to note down the topics.

ANSWERS
a the weather   b their meal   c a film   d their workload

3.10
a
A: Ugh, isn't it dreadful? And we'd got plans for the weekend as well. Thought we might have some friends round for a barbecue.
B: Well, it's always the same, isn't it? You plan anything, it always lets you down. And it was so fabulous yesterday.
C: Yes, wasn't it? Never would have thought it could turn so nasty in just 24 hours. But that's Britain for you, I suppose. Heatwave in the morning, a

88   14 OUT AND ABOUT

downpour in the afternoon and a howling gale by dinner time. Unbelievable weather!

b

A: What on earth is that?

B: Don't think you'd like it? Look, it's seasoned with a bit of cinnamon and dried mint.

A: Smells off to me.

B: Nonsense! It's really delicious. How about trying it?

A: Cinnamon sounds a bit odd. And dried mint? As seasoning?

B: Well, that's normal for Middle Eastern dishes! Ian is giving it a go, so why don't you? It's really good!

A: Hmm. All right, if you insist! But if you ask me, cinnamon belongs in sweets!

B: Oh, give it a chance, Roger! We'll order you something else if you really can't handle it.

c

B: No, it's not my thing at all, I'm afraid.

A: Oh, but I thought it was marvellous! And it was so well done. Because it must have been a very difficult adaptation, don't you think?

B: Hmm, yeah. It went on a bit, though, didn't it? I mean, what was it, two and a half hours?

A: Well, I found the whole thing absolutely fantastic. Brilliantly directed. And the special effects were incredible!

B: Yes, well, they were good, I'll admit, but they've all got those nowadays, haven't they? I mean it's all just CGI digital animation. Like all those sci-fi, superhero things ...

d

B: I'd really appreciate it, because I'm just snowed under at the moment, what with all this backlog to deal with.

A: Yes, I'm sorry to have dumped all that on you. Couldn't think of anyone else I could trust. And with the deadline coming up so fast ...

B: It's no problem, but if you could let me borrow Kim for a couple of hours, I'm sure that together we could polish the whole thing off that much faster.

C: You overworking this poor boy, Susan? That's how she lost her last assistant manager, you know, Ian.

A: Oh, ignore Roger. I'll speak to Kim about giving you a hand as soon as we get back to the office.

B: Thanks.

4 3.10 Play the recording again and ask students to write down the key words. With weaker students, do the first extract with the whole class as an example. Students compare their words in pairs and then check against the listening script on page 154. Clarify the meaning of any new vocabulary and encourage students to note down any useful words and expressions.

5 Tell students they are going to roleplay a conversation over a business lunch. Focus attention on the expressions in the box and elicit possible ways of continuing, e.g. a gerund, a preposition, a noun/noun phrase, and elicit complete examples.

Before starting, ask the students to think of ideas for each of the topics in the boxes. Encourage them to write down key words as prompts. Then divide the class into groups and get them to sit at different tables. Allow about ten minutes for the roleplay. Monitor and take feedback notes.

Give students feedback on how they handled changing the subject and keeping the conversation moving.

1:1 For the roleplay, transfer the discussion topics onto cards and place them on the table, face down. Set a timer on your mobile phone (e.g. for one minute). Explain to your student that you will have a conversation and that you have to try and keep it going for as long as possible. Each time the timer rings, you and/or your student should gently move the conversation to another topic. Do a practice run first. If possible, record the conversation so that you can do some language analysis later.

Language links

ANSWERS

Vocabulary
Storytelling
Descriptive power
1 b really fascinating c absolutely delighted d quite inedible
 e utterly miserable f drop-dead gorgeous g absolutely fabulous h utterly astonished i absolutely hilarious
 j absolutely ancient k utterly furious l absolutely filthy
2 a funny b beautiful c expensive d enjoyable
 e disappointing f quiet g dangerous h difficult

The art of exaggeration
3 2 you should have seen 3 I'm telling you 4 like something out of 5 is literally 6 me tell you 7 I'm not exaggerating 8 Talk about 9 out of this world 10 you'll never believe

Grammar
Narrative tenses
1 thought 2 had identified 3 hadn't conducted 4 seemed
5 were switching 6 went away 7 came up with 8 hadn't realized 9 were 10 sounded 11 wasn't selling 12 were
13 had it been thinking of? 14 had been developing
15 needed! 16 was

Phrase bank
Sharing anecdotes
1 Opener: a, c, f   Context: h, i, m
 Emphasis: e, g, j, k   Close: b, d, l

Reactions
2 a I'm not **surprised**! b I can **imagine**! c How **odd**!
 d What a **nightmare**! e You're **joking, right**? f Sounds **awful**! g You can't be **serious**! h I don't **blame** you!
 i Wow, that's **amazing**! j Oh, I see what **you mean**! k Were you **really**? l So, what **happened**? m Oh, my **goodness**!
 n Lucky **you**!

14 OUT AND ABOUT 89

15 Delegation

Learning objectives

This unit is about delegation in the business world.

Students begin by discussing the attitudes to delegation shown in a cartoon. They then consider what kind of information is needed when you delegate a task to someone, and read a blog entry on good practice in delegation.

Students listen to three managers delegating tasks. They take notes on what each manager specifies, and any points they omit. They then consider the differences in management style.

Next, students listen to part of a presentation about management styles and complete a diagram. They listen to the three managers again, and decide which delegation styles they use.

Students discuss their own preferences in terms of management style when working with a superior, and when someone is working for them.

Finally, students take part in a roleplay to practise delegating tasks.

Digital resources: Unit 15

Online Workbook; Extension worksheets; Glossary; Student's Book answer key; Student's Book listening script; Fast-track map

1:1 There are essentially two approaches to this unit. You may wish to concentrate on discussing good practice in the area of delegation if the student delegates to people in their team or those working for them. Alternatively, students lower down the company hierarchy may be more interested in the different styles of delegation shown by those above them in the hierarchy, i.e. focusing on good delegation techniques as well as delegation techniques that could be improved.

Warm-up

Write the word *delegate* on the board and ask students to discuss with a partner the following points: 1 *Who delegates? Why? What types of task?* 2 *What went well when you delegated?* 3 *What went badly?* After students have discussed these points, elicit some of the students' answers.

1 The unit begins with students giving their reactions to a cartoon which takes a humorous look at delegation. Put students in pairs to discuss the cartoon and answer the questions. Elicit students' ideas.

SAMPLE ANSWERS

The woman has absolutely no motivation because there is no chance of success.

The manager knows she has no chance of succeeding but either doesn't care or deliberately wants her to fail.
The woman is disappointed because her manager is putting her in a no-win situation. She feels she cannot trust him because what he says is completely contradictory: how can the project be 'of the utmost importance' if she is not given the method, the means or the time to complete it?

2 Ask students to think back to the *Warm-up*, when they spoke about what went well and what went badly when delegating tasks. Ask students to discuss the question with a partner and then ask some students to share their ideas. You could draw on the SMART objectives acronym, that tasks are best when they are: Specific, Measurable, Achievable, Realistic and Time-related. So, when delegating, you can give a time limit, etc. Collate students' ideas on the board.

3 Tell students they are going to read a blog post called *Delegation: provide a clear action plan*. Explain to students that they have to match the headings to the paragraphs in the blog post, so they should skim the blog quickly (e.g. in two minutes) to do this task. Check answers with the class.

ANSWERS

1 Objective   2 Method   3 Means   4 Deadline   5 Check

4 Ask students to read the blog post again and then look at the list of students' own ideas collated on the board in 2. Ask students to tick off any of the ideas they came up with.

5 Ask students if they can remember any synonyms for employee from the article. Write their suggestions on the board. Then, ask them to underline all the words in the text which mean employee. Put students in pairs to discuss the three questions. Elicit students' ideas and write them on the board under the headings: *in company / suppliers / customers / colleagues / boss*. Make students aware of any connotations or differences in meaning or use of these words, e.g. subordinates have less power or authority than others; staffers is an American term and is not so common in British English.

ANSWERS

staff, team, people, staffers, folks, co-workers, subordinates, peers, associates, team member, colleague

6 3.11 Tell students that they are going to hear three managers delegating tasks. Give them a minute to transfer the headings from the action plan in 3 into the left-hand column. Check that students know the words *timeframe* and *feasible*. Play the recording and ask students to tick which points the managers specify. Play the recording a second time, pausing from time to time to allow students time to process each point. Put students in pairs to compare their answers then check answers with the class. Ask students if they can think of any reasons why two managers omitted some points.

90   15 DELEGATION

ANSWERS

	Manager 1 / Daniel	Manager 2 / Gina	Manager 3 / Pete
1 Objective	✓	✓	✓
2 Method		✓	
3 Means		✓	
4 Deadline	✓	✓	
5 Check	✓	✓	✓

1 Daniel is an experienced team member and already knows what Method and Means to use.
2 Gina is new in the job, so needs a complete action plan.
3 Pete knows the task very well and is clearly very autonomous, so only needs to be told the essentials of the action plan.

3.11

1
A: Daniel, can I have a quick word?
B: Yeah, sure.
A: We've just had confirmation for the Ericsen order. You worked on it last year with Maggie, didn't you?
B: Yes, that's right.
A: So this year, I'd like you to handle it on your own. Are you comfortable with that?
B: Yes, no problem.
A: Great. So basically, the deliverables are exactly the same as last year. You'll find all the specifications in the file. The only difference is we got a bit squeezed on price this time, so if we can manage to keep costs down as much as possible, that would be great.
B: Okay, I'll do my best. What's the timeframe?
A: We've scheduled delivery for July 31st. Do you think that's feasible?
B: Yes, should be fine. I'll get started straight away.
A: Excellent. Let's schedule a meeting every couple of weeks, then, so we can look at any problems together and think about ways of keeping costs down, okay?
B: Sure.

2
C: Hi Gina, how's it going?
D: Not too bad, thanks. But there's a lot to remember!
C: Yes, well, everybody says the first week is the hardest; it gets better, believe me!
D: Okay, that's good to know!
C: Listen, could you call these people as soon as you can? They're old customers, so you don't need to tell them a lot about the product, just try to get appointments for me. Tell them we've got a special offer on upgrades, so I'd like to meet them. You've got my schedule, haven't you?
D: Yes. Shall I email them first?
C: No, just keep calling until you can speak to them personally. You'll probably have to call some of them back outside office hours; if you need to work overtime, that's fine, just keep a note of the extra time you put in, okay?
D: All right.

C: I'd like us to contact everyone on the list by this time next week. Book the appointments into my schedule as you go, and we'll see how you're getting on when I get back from Spain on Friday, okay?
D: Okay.
C: If you have any questions while I'm away, feel free to ask Mandy. Is that all right?
D: Erm, yes. That seems fine.
C: Brilliant. Thanks, Gina, I know you'll do a great job!

3
E: Technical support?
F: Pete? Frank here.
E: Uh-oh!
F: Yeah. Look, I know it's late, but the server's down again at Captain Discount.
E: Oh for goodness sake! All right, I'll get over there asap.
F: Thanks, mate. Give me a ring when you've finished, would you? Just to let me know how things stand?
E: All right. Will do.
F: Cheers.

7 Draw a 'staff development' timeline on the board with the following points on it: *one month, six months, one year* and *two years*. Ask students to read and think about the four management styles in the box. Then, ask individual students to come out to the front and write each at the correct place on the timeline. See if the other students agree. Do not check students' answers at this stage.

ANSWERS
one month – Directing   six months – Coaching
one year – Supporting   two years – Delegating

8 3.12 Write the terms *directive style* and *supportive style* on the board and ask the students if they can explain the difference, i.e. one is telling someone what they need to do, the other is more 'hands-off', where you ensure the employee has the tools to do their job. Explain to students that they are going to listen to a presentation about management styles. Check they know the words *axis* and *quadrant*. Students listen and complete the diagram. Play the recording again and ask students to check their answers in 7.

ANSWERS
1 Directive style   2 Supportive style
3 Directing   4 Coaching
5 Supporting   6 Delegating

3.12

This next slide shows how you can adapt your management style to different members of staff. The horizontal axis indicates an increasingly directive style from left to right, and the vertical axis measures a supportive style, less at the bottom and more at the top. So, as you can see, there are four quadrants representing four main management styles. At the bottom right we have Directing. Here the focus is on giving very explicit instructions: you tell people exactly what you want them to do, why, how and when they should do it, and you follow them very closely to make sure they do it right. It's the kind of approach you need for young, inexperienced or new members of your team.

As people get to know the job, you can gradually move up into the top right quadrant, which is Coaching. Here you can spend less time telling them what to do, and more time working with them to develop their skills. Gradually you can then move to the top left quadrant, which is Supporting: here your main role is to make sure that they have the resources they need to do the job, and of course to continue setting objectives and checking achievement. If there are problems, you may sometimes need to move back towards a more directive style.

Finally, the most experienced and expert members of your team will be happiest with a Delegating style, here in the bottom left-hand quadrant. They are almost completely autonomous, setting their own objectives and evaluating their own results. Of course, they will always welcome a few words of support and thanks from time to time.

1:1 Before starting the roleplays, decide which ones you will do with your student. Note that in roleplays 1 and 3, Speaker A (page 119) makes a decision beforehand; in roleplays 2 and 4, Speaker B (page 132) makes a decision beforehand. Making these decisions is a good way for your student to choose something useful and relevant to their own job. Point this out to your student when they are preparing.

Proceed with the roleplays you have selected, taking the role of Speaker B. Record the conversation and then play it back in order to help with the completion of the delegation checklist on page 137. If it is not possible to record the conversation, then complete the checklist by reflecting on the task together.

9 3.11 Play the recording of the three managers from 6 again and ask students to identify the management style of each of the managers. Put the students in pairs and ask them to compare their answers. Check answers with the class and ask students to give a reason for choosing a specific answer.

ANSWERS
1 Coaching
2 Directing
3 Supporting or Delegating

10 Ask students to discuss the questions with a partner. Elicit students' ideas and examples.

11 Tell students that, in the last part of the lesson, they are going to work with a partner to practise delegating tasks. They can decide on the most appropriate style of delegation for each situation.

Put students in AB pairs. Ask As to turn to page 119 and Bs to turn to page 132 and read the first role card. Give students a minute to prepare their role. Monitor and help clarify anything, as necessary. When students are ready, give them about three minutes to perform the roleplay. Monitor and take language notes, as well as noting any successes in terms of appropriate delegation style. Continue as above through some more or all four roleplays.

When students have finished the roleplays, tell them to turn to page 137 and complete the delegation checklist for each roleplay. Then, ask students to compare their evaluations. Ask students to tell you to what extent they agreed with each other in their feedback.

Finish the lesson by providing feedback on both delegation skills and language.

MANAGEMENT SCENARIO D

Change champion

Learning objectives

This scenario is based on the issue of managing change in organizations. In the pre-viewing tasks, students begin by discussing their own experiences of change management. They then discuss the steps in implementing change and read an email from the CEO of Blue Rock. They watch a video in which two employees talk about the email from their own viewpoint and complete a PowerPoint slide about managing change. Students then look back at the original email in order to identify the mistakes the writer made in managing change. Students watch a second video and answer comprehension questions. As part of the post-viewing tasks, they focus on the language of change management. Finally, after they have re-written the email in a more collaborative style, students take part in a meeting about changes in their company.

Digital resources: Management Scenario D

🎥 In company in action D1–D2 and worksheet; Extension worksheets; Glossary; Student's Book answer key; Student's Book listening script; Fast-track map

Warm-up

Ask students to think about some big changes that have happened recently in society. In pairs, ask them to think of some reasons why so many people have problems coping with these changes.

1:1 Ask your student to talk about their experience of being in a situation in which some kind of change happened. Provide some ideas, such as a change of direction at a company that was not popular with all staff or the introduction of a new product or new working practices. Give your student time to think of a situation, and ask them to describe to you what changed and why.

1 Write the term *change management* on the board and tell students they will be thinking about this issue in life and at work. Ask students to discuss the question in pairs.

2 Check any new vocabulary such as: *feasible, incentive, tools*. Give students time to study the cartoon, decide on their answers and compare ideas with a partner.

ANSWERS
a I can't do it   b I won't do it   c I'll try to do it   d How do I do it?
e I want to do it   f Yes, I did it!   g I will do it   h I can do it

3 In this task, students read an email from Sue Jensen to all staff at Blue Rock about a change in company policy, and insert the missing punctuation. First, check that students know the term *reimbursement*. Check answers with the class.

ANSWER
To: All staff
Re: Travel and entertainment
As from the first of next month, several changes will be introduced to our travel policy and expense claims procedures.
As in the past, all travel must be approved by senior management. However, our travel bureau's contract has been terminated and staff should make their own bookings and arrangements. Please note that, from now on, only economy class travel will be reimbursed. Hotel accommodation should no longer exceed a three-star rating or local equivalent. Staff are also reminded to use public transport in preference to taxis whenever possible and to obtain separate receipts for all meals and other necessary expenses.
Finally, when entertaining visitors or local contacts you will now need to provide a justification statement and a guest list containing names, titles and occupations of every guest.
I know I can count on you all to ensure these changes are implemented as smoothly as possible.
Sue Jensen (CEO)
Blue Rock

4 Give students time to re-read the email carefully. Ask students to answer the four questions.

ANSWERS
a staff should make their own travel bookings; only economy class travel will be reimbursed; hotel accommodation should not exceed a three-star rating; staff should provide a justification statement and a guest list when entertaining
b all travel must be approved by senior management; staff should use public transport in preference to taxis whenever possible; staff should obtain separate receipts for all meals and other necessary expenses
d they won't be able to get the best deals on travel bookings
they don't have time to book their own travel
they don't want to pay in advance for business expenses
economy class is too uncomfortable / tiring
it may be impossible to find a three-star hotel
it may be inconvenient, embarrassing or culturally inappropriate to ask for their guests' details (for the guest lists)
the extra paperwork will be time-consuming

5 🎥 **D1** Students now watch a video in which Sue talks to Jack Wright from Operations. First, ask students to read the list of problems. While watching, ask students to number the problems in the order they are mentioned.

ANSWERS
1 a computer problem   2 imposing changes   3 booking flights
4 company credit cards   5 public transport   6 admin time

D CHANGE CHAMPION   93

MANAGEMENT SCENARIO

🎥 D1

Jack: Here's the Somalia file you wanted.

Sue: Oh, thanks. Er, Jack, you're good with computers, can you have a look at this?

Jack: Sure. What's the problem?

Sue: There's something weird happening here. I've lost all the punctuation in this email.

Jack: Um, Sue ... you're not going to send it out like that, are you?

Sue: Well, no, obviously – I'll have to put all the punctuation back first.

Jack: I don't mean the punctuation – I'm talking about why you're imposing all these changes.

Sue: I'm not imposing anything, Jack, I'm simply asking people to follow slightly different procedures. Besides, people always resist change at first, but they soon get used to it.

Jack: Well, I don't think they're going to like it, that's all I'm saying.

Sue: Oh, come on, it's just admin procedures! What's not to like about it?

Jack: Well for a start, I don't mind laying out the cost of a meal or a couple of nights in a hotel, but I don't see why I should have to pay for my own flights!

Sue: We're not asking you to pay for flights, Jack; just to make your own booking instead of going through the travel bureau. You know, online – it's pretty straightforward!

Jack: True, but have you tried booking a flight online without a credit card? Or are you planning to give us all a company card?

Sue: Hm, I hadn't thought about that.

Jack: And taking public transport instead of a taxi when you're travelling alone in a place like Africa or India – it can be pretty risky!

Sue: Obviously we understand there are exceptions ...

Jack: Well, I'm sorry, but that's not exactly the message that comes across! And do you realize how much time this is going to take, all this bureaucracy? I came to work here so I can help people have access to clean water, not spend all my time filling out expense claims!

Sue: Oh, come on, Jack. I don't understand why you're reacting so strongly!

Jack: Well, don't take my word for it, ask other people. It seems to me if you send this email out as it stands, you're going to have a rebellion on your hands!

Sue: What was all that about?

6 Students work with a partner to decide what attitudes and feelings are revealed by the phrases.

SUGGESTED ANSWERS

- *pretty risky* – Jack feels that public transport can be dangerous when travelling alone in some countries, especially for women
- *What's not to like about it?* – Sue obviously hasn't thought about what the changes will mean for people
- *that's not exactly the message that comes across* – Jack feels that Sue's communication style is rigid and unfeeling

- *don't take my word for it* – Jack feels sure that other people will share his reactions
- *they soon get used to it* – Sue seems to think that people's feelings and resistance to change are unimportant

7 Tell students that they will now study part of a presentation which introduces a series of steps for managing change. Ask students to check through the words in the box, and then study the PowerPoint slide and decide which words are missing. They can compare their answers with a partner.

ANSWERS

1 benefits   2 need   3 champions   4 resources   5 communicate

8 Put students in pairs to reflect on what Sue did. Ask students to list any mistakes Sue made, according to the PowerPoint slide in 7. Tell students to add any advice they would give her.

SAMPLE ANSWERS

Sue has not explained why the changes are necessary.
She has not mentioned benefits to staff or the organization.
She has not consulted people or recruited change champions.
She has not thought about what tools and resources people will need.
She has not planned how she will monitor and consolidate the change.

She should:
- involve other people in decisions before communicating changes.
- adopt a more personal and collaborative style.
- try to predict and understand people's objections and fears.
- plan a strategy to help people implement the changes.

9 🎥 **D2** Tell students they will now watch a video of Sue talking to Ed Ryan in which Ed gives her useful advice about successfully managing change. In the first viewing, ask students to listen out for the additional piece of advice that Ed gives Sue (on top of the five steps to managing change). Ask a student to call out their answer.

ANSWER

to improve the style by making it less impersonal and more collaborative

🎥 D2

Ed: Hi Sue – you said you wanted a word?

Sue: Hello, Ed. Yes, have a seat. I showed this email to Jack and he went crazy! I don't get it. You know this organization as well as anyone – what's the big deal?

Ed: All staff ... changes will be introduced ... travel must be approved ... staff are also reminded ... ensure these changes are implemented ... uh-huh. Well, I think I can see why Jack took exception.

Sue: You can?

Ed: Yeah. And to be honest, I think you'll upset most people if you send it out like this.

Sue: What do you mean, like this?

Ed: Well, let's just say the style is kind of ... impersonal? Lots of passives, staff should do this or that ...

Sue: All right. I was in a hurry. I'll make it more ... collaborative.

Ed: Right. More we's, fewer you's!

Sue: Sorry?

94   D CHANGE CHAMPION

MANAGEMENT SCENARIO

Ed: We are going to do this together, rather than you will do this alone!

Sue: Okay, I take the point. But I still don't understand why he got so upset about a few small administrative changes.

Ed: You know, even very small changes can become big issues when people don't see the benefits.

Sue: Yes, I suppose so.

Ed: People need to know why.

Sue: Why we're changing the procedures? Well it's obvious, isn't it? Raising funds is getting more and more difficult, so we need to make every penny count! Every pound we save on travel is an extra pound we can spend on wells and pumps in Africa and Central America. Jack knows that!

Ed: Of course he does. But you didn't mention it, and people aren't going to think about that when you're telling them to book their own flights or use public transport – they'll just see the inconvenience for them. You've got to get people on your side first: explain why we need to make the changes, and show them the benefits for everyone.

Sue: Like having more control over when and how they travel?

Ed: Exactly.

Sue: Yes, I suppose I should've mentioned that.

Ed: It would definitely help. Of course, what might be even better would be to actually identify the people most directly concerned before you start making the changes.

Sue: You mean the people with the most air miles? People like you?

Ed: Well, yeah, people like me. We can probably make helpful suggestions, become your 'change champions'.

Sue: And help convince the others the changes are a good idea? I understand. Talking of helpful suggestions, Jack was worried about using his own credit card to book flights. But we can't give everybody a company credit card – any suggestions?

Ed: Well, yes. You know you can get those virtual credit card numbers? You give people a one-time use number to book their flights, the company's billed and nobody can ever use that number again.

Sue: Now that's really clever. Thanks Ed. I appreciate it.

Ed: Well, you've got to provide the tools and resources people need. One other suggestion …

Sue: Yes?

Ed: How about circulating the figures on how much we've saved each month? Maybe even get people together to discuss which projects need that extra money?

Sue: To keep communicating and consolidating the new procedures? Yes, you're right. Thanks Ed. You're a real change champion! I owe you one, okay?

10 📹 D2 Ask students to read the four while-viewing questions and note down their answers. Pause the video at key moments to allow students to make notes.

ANSWERS

a using 'we' to be collaborative rather than 'you' to isolate individual staff members

b to save money on travel and entertainment expenses in order to be able to spend more money on projects

c virtual credit card numbers which allow staff to have their plane tickets paid directly by Blue Rock

d to continue communicating and consolidating the new procedures

11 Ask students to read the phrases and tell them that each one corresponds to one of the Change Management steps in the PowerPoint slide in 7. Ask students to match these. Check the answers with the class.

ANSWERS

circulating the figures 5   the people with the most air miles 3
virtual credit card numbers 4   more control over when and how they travel 2   get people on your side 1

12 Ask students to work in pairs to rewrite Sue's original email in a more collaborative style. Monitor the activity and offer guidance and correction.

SAMPLE ANSWER

To: All staff
Re: Travel and entertainment

As you may know, the company is losing a large amount of money each month on unnecessary travel. I am sure you agree that this money can greatly benefit our essential work in improving lives.

Therefore, from the first of next month, several changes will be introduced to our travel policy and expense claims procedures.

I have been working closely with some of you who travel most, and we have agreed that it is best to stop using our regular travel bureaus. Staff should in future make their own bookings and arrangements. In order to help everyone, we are introducing a system of virtual credit card numbers. If you have any questions, we will happily help you with the new procedures.

Many things will remain the same. All travel must still be approved by senior management. The system of using public transport in preference to taxis whenever possible and obtaining separate receipts for all meals and other necessary expenses is the same.

Please note that from now on only economy class travel will be reimbursed; hotel accommodation should no longer exceed a three-star rating or local equivalent. We hope this will save money. Also, when entertaining visitors or local contacts you will now need to provide a justification statement and a guest list containing names titles and occupations of every guest.

We will post information on how much is saved each month. Any ideas on how to use this will be gratefully received. There'll be a prize for the best idea!

Thanks in advance for helping us implement these changes.

13 Assign students a letter, A or B. Tell As to look at the information on page 134 and Bs to look at the information on page 136. Give students a few minutes to prepare their ideas, with As working together and Bs working together.

Divide the class into small groups for the two meetings. Make sure each group has some A and B students in it. Monitor the meetings and take language notes.

When students have finished, tell them to turn to page 124 and complete the checklists. Finish the lesson with feedback on students' performance and language.

D CHANGE CHAMPION   95

16 Teleconferencing

Learning objectives

This unit is about doing business at a distance using teleconferencing. Teleconferencing uses telecommunications to link up people at two or more venues. There are two opposing views on teleconferencing: one is that it will change the way people do business across distances, the other is that people will always want to meet face-to-face.

Students discuss whether people really need to travel in order to do business. A text presents a videoconferencing system and students answer questions and discuss some of the key language. They then listen to a short commercial for a teleconferencing system and discuss its suitability for different kinds of meetings.

Further listening practice is provided by a recording about a business crisis and students study phrasal verbs and idioms from the recording, as well as looking at the implications. A continuation of the first recording presents an emergency teleconference. Students complete the missing information in the minutes of this meeting.

In the final section, students read another case study of a crisis at an advertising company and roleplay a teleconference to devise an action plan.

The grammatical focus is on reporting and the lexical focus is on teleconferencing and personnel and production.

Digital resources: Unit 16
Online Workbook; Extension worksheets; Glossary; Phrase bank; Student's Book answer key; Student's Book listening script; Fast-track map

In this first section, students discuss the need for business travel, given the possibilities afforded by telecommunications. The view of a teleconferencing entrepreneur is presented in a short text, and then students read a web page presenting a videoconferencing system. Students discuss the texts and then listen to a short commercial for a teleconferencing system and decide on its suitability for different types of meetings.

1:1 Ask your student about their experience of teleconferencing. Is it something they have to do? If so, do they use a particular system at their company? (Common teleconferencing systems used in the business world include WebEx, Adobe Connect and Blackboard Collaborate.) Many students may also use Skype in their non-professional lives. In the final roleplay of this unit, there is scope to replicate the experience of holding a web conference.

Warm-up

Elicit examples of technology used in business travel, e.g. a GPS, street or underground maps on a smartphone, an email facility on a mobile phone. Find out what technology students use when travelling and which equipment they think is most useful.

Focus attention on the quotation by John Naisbitt and ask students if they agree with it. Ask students if they, or their colleagues, use teleconferencing in place of business travel.

1 Ask students to discuss the questions with a partner and then elicit opinions about business travel. Will people always want to visit a place / meet others face-to-face? Do the students think teleconferencing will replace face-to-face communication? Ask students to report on what is happening in their own company about travel budgets – are they being cut?

2 Before asking students to read the text, check/pre-teach: *to eliminate, to dispute*. After students have read the text, find out if they agree with George Mackintosh that people need at least one face-to-face meeting but after that, videoconferencing will be enough, and even improves on telephone and email. Ask follow-up questions, e.g. *How often do you do business with people you have not met face-to-face? Will teleconferencing increase with the current threat of terrorism? Has business travel decreased in your company since the latest recession kicked in?*

As an optional follow-up task, divide the class into AB groups: group A writes to their CEO to recommend a reduction in business travel by 50% and investment in Geoconference, and group B writes to protest against the intention to buy facilities from Geoconference. With weaker classes, get students to brainstorm arguments for and against before they draft their letter.

3 Ask students to read the two questions and then scan the web page in order to find the answers. Ask students to read the web page again intensively. You may wish to check key vocabulary such as: *collaborate, competitive edge, hemispheres*. Find out students' initial reactions to this technological solution.

ANSWERS
a The paradox is that technology has shrunk the world in terms of communication, but to stay abreast and maintain relationships, we need to travel more.
b TelePresence allows for real time, face-to-face communication at a distance.

4 Students scan the web page for the three expressions.

ANSWERS
a business operations
b competitive edge
c technological solution

BUSINESS COMMUNICATION

5 🔊 **3.13** After playing the recording, ask students to work in small groups to think about each of the meeting types. Encourage them to discuss any advantages and disadvantages. Ask them to draw on their own experience of videoconferencing. Each group reports on its findings. Encourage discussion.

3.13

A: Since you're new here, I want you to meet your teams in London, Bangalore and Tokyo. You need to do it right away.
B: Oh, I'm really looking forward to meeting them, but it's going to take a week or more to get to all those places.
A: Actually, they're right down the hall.
B: Oh! ... A video conference.
A: I wouldn't call it that.
B: No?
A: I think you'll be pleasantly surprised.
B: Wow.
A: Hello, everyone. This is Patricia.
C: Hello from London. Tania and Owen here.
D: I'm Mohan. This is Seema. Greetings from Bangalore.
E: And I am Hiro with my colleague Kumi from Tokyo. Hajimemashite!
B: I really feel like I'm in the same room with all of you.

Voiceover
This isn't the future. It's right now. With Cisco TelePresence you feel like you're sitting across the table from other meeting participants. Seeing them in full life-size images. Making direct eye contact. Hearing them talk left and right ... and centre. Making everyone sound like they're in the same room. TelePresence creates an in-person meeting experience over the network, where the quality's so good, it's as if you took a conference table and just split it in half.

Language links

Direct students to the *Phrase bank* in the *Language links* section on page 106 for more on useful expressions for teleconferencing.

6 Put students in pairs to discuss the two questions about their own experiences of the types of meetings mentioned in 5, and of using teleconferencing equipment. Elicit some of the students' experiences.

Trouble at the plant

In this section, students listen to a conversation about a crisis at a fictitious company, Oriflamme. They answer comprehension questions, then focus on some of the phrasal verbs and idioms used by the speakers. They then listen to an emergency teleconference in which the management team consider solutions to the problem. The students do a comprehension check exercise and complete the minutes taken after the conference.

1 🔊 **3.14** Elicit what type of materials would be stored at the plant, e.g. chemicals, perfumed oils, wax, and get students to brainstorm what kind of crises could occur, e.g. machinery problems, an accident, etc. Check/Pre-teach: *heat exchanger, leakage, oil heater* and get students to predict what has happened. Play the recording through once and elicit the answer to question a. Ask students to read questions b–d and see if students can answer these questions. If not, play the recording a second time. Check the answers with the class.

ANSWERS
a There's been a leakage so they need to shut down the plant.
b There was a risk of explosion.
c It cost the company millions.
d He and Monica should fly back to Germany.

3.14

A: Ugh! Who on earth can that be? Where's the ... the light switch! Ow! Er ... hello?
B: Pete, is that you?
A: Er, yes. Who is this?
B: It's Max.
A: Max! ... Max, it's ... it's two o'clock in the morning!
B: I'm sorry, Pete, but this is an emergency.
A: Well, it had better be, I've got to be up in a few hours.
B: I think you'd better get up right now, Pete. All hell's broken loose here. We're going to have to shut down the Hamburg plant immediately.
A: What!
B: It's the heat exchanger. We've got a leakage between the hydrogenation section and the oil heater. There's nothing we can do but stop all production straightaway. Otherwise, the whole thing could go up!
A: But Max, do you have any idea what you're saying? If you authorize a plant shutdown, everything grinds to a halt. We'll have container lorries backed up from Hamburg to Lübeck!
B: Pete, do you think I don't know that?
A: Tell me this isn't happening. It cost us millions last time ... Okay, look, I have no idea how long it will take me and Monica to get a flight, but we're on our way.
B: I think that's best, Pete.
A: I'll phone you to fix up a teleconference once we're airborne. Contact Françoise and Otto right away, will you? There's not a moment to lose ...
A: Monica? It's Pete. Look, I'm sorry to get you up at this unearthly hour, but there's been a disaster at the Hamburg plant. Yeah. Better get dressed. I'll tell you about it on the way to the airport.

2 Ask students to work in pairs to guess the words from the synonyms. Check the answers. Point out that further collocations can be generated with the verbs, e.g. *to shut down machinery / a business / a hospital / a school; to go up in smoke/flames; traffic/cars can be backed up.*

16 TELECONFERENCING 97

BUSINESS COMMUNICATION

> **ANSWERS**
> a down b up c up

3 Ask the students to work individually, then check their answers with a partner. Point out that some of these expressions are informal.

> **ANSWERS**
> a earth b hell c halt d moment e hour

4 Elicit ideas from the students, listing the implications of the crisis at the plant. Get students to think about the immediate implications and the wider business context, e.g. safety issues at the plant, a loss in consumer confidence.

5 Check/Pre-teach: *adverse, backlog, bottleneck, hazard*. Get students to match the columns. Check the answers with the class, making sure students have the stress in the correct place. Check how many of the expressions students included in their list in 4.

> **ANSWERS**
> a a backlog of orders b a production bottleneck c a safety hazard d a fall in productivity e a damaged reputation f adverse publicity g lost man-hours h delayed deliveries

Language links

Direct students to the *Language links* section on page 105 for more practice of vocabulary relating to personnel and production.

6 Ask students to discuss an action plan for Oriflamme, listing at least five points, e.g. transferring stock from other parts of the company, offering clients some kind of incentive, etc. Divide the class into pairs/small groups and get them to exchange ideas. Remind them that their aim is to reduce the negative implications listed in 5. Get students to agree on the three most important action points and the order of priority. Students then present their action plan to the class and see if they can decide on the approach they think the company should take.

7 3.15–3.17 Get students to recap on the situation at the Oriflamme plant and review the names of the people involved (Peter, Monica, Francoise, Max and Otto).

Extract 1

Check/Pre-teach: *to get through, rescue plan, up and running, replacement, to fit*. Tell the students to read questions a–c, then play extract 1. Check the answers with the whole class.

> **ANSWERS**
> a Otto
> b on the plane from Vancouver
> c at least three days

Extract 2

Check/Pre-teach: *to clear, in reserve, overstretched, shortfall, to build a reputation*. Tell students that in the next extract various actions/solutions are discussed. Write up the following in a random order on the board: *safety checks,* *rewriting production plans, discussing reserve stock, buying from a competitor*. Play the extract through once and get students to put the topics in the correct order as they hear them.

Before playing the extract again, ask students to read questions a–c. Elicit any answers they can give from memory and then play the recording again.

> **ANSWERS**
> a Pretty bad. The whole area has had to be cleared.
> b There's not enough stock in reserve.
> c negative, hostile

Extract 3

Ask students to read questions a–c and to guess who or what Handelsmann is and to predict possible answers to questions a and c. Play the recording through once and get students to check their predictions. Play the recording again and check the answers with the whole class.

As a follow-up task, write the following words on the board and ask students to brainstorm some verbs which collocate with them: *favour, conference call, secure, backlog, posted* (e.g. *to do a favour, to make/book/organize a conference call*). Write the options on the board. Play extract 3, pausing if necessary and ask students to check which expressions were used (*make up a backlog, owe a favour, make secure, schedule a conference call, keep someone posted*).

> **ANSWERS**
> a Oriflamme helped them in a similar situation.
> b No, the area has been made secure.
> c to keep him informed if the situation changes

3.15

Extract 1

A: Okay, so we're just waiting for Otto. Françoise, you told him when to call in, right?

C: Yes, I did. Perhaps he's still at the plant or he may just be having problems getting through.

B: Pete, where are you and Monica?

A: Just left Vancouver about half an hour ago, Max. Should be back in thirteen hours or so.

C: Pete, I think we should just start.

B: Yes, I think so too.

A: Okay, we really need to talk to Otto, but let's go ahead and get the meeting started and hopefully he'll join us later on … Right, well, as you all know, we've had a serious mechanical failure at the Hamburg plant and, basically, we've had to shut it down. There'll be time for a proper analysis of what went wrong later but right now we need a rescue plan. Max, could you first of all just fill us in on what's going on? When can we expect to get the plant up and running again?

B: Well, Pete, it's difficult to say at the moment. My technicians tell me they can't get a replacement heat exchanger for at least 48 hours. And then it'll have to be fitted, of course. We're probably looking at three days.

D: Three days!

A: It's worse than I thought. And is that your best estimate? Three days?
B: I'm afraid so, Pete.
A: Well, that's that, then. But I want us back in production no later than Thursday, Max. Okay?
B: Okay, Pete, I'll see what I can do.

🔊 **3.16**

Extract 2

E: Excuse me, Mr Manser has joined.
A: Otto! Thank goodness you got through. Have you been to the plant yet? What's the situation there?
F: It's pretty bad Pete. We've had to clear the whole site for the fire service to run safety checks.
A: I see. Otto, is there any chance we can rewrite our production plan? I mean, can we make sure our key customers get priority on orders?
F: I'm already working on that. The problem is it doesn't look as though we'll be able to meet any of the orders completely.
A: What's the stock situation?
F: Not good.
A: Oh, great. Just what I needed to hear. Don't we keep any stock in reserve for this kind of thing?
F: What, for a complete plant shutdown? No, Pete, we don't.
A: Okay, okay. Well, what about transferring stock from one of our other European plants?
F: It'd take too long. And, besides, they're already overstretched as it is.
A: Right ... Monica, is there any point in us buying in traded goods from another supplier to cover the shortfall? Just for the time being.
D: You mean buy product from our competitors to keep the customers happy?
A: Just for the time being.
D: Pete, you know how I feel about buying from the competition. How are we supposed to build a reputation with our customers if we end up selling them other people's products instead of our own?
A: It's not as if we haven't done it before, Monica. And what alternative do we have?

🔊 **3.17**

Extract 3

A: Okay, now, we've got to make up this backlog of orders somehow. How about Handelsmann?
C: Er, can I come in on that?
A: Go ahead, Françoise.
C: Well, I've already been on to Handelsmann. They owe us a favour, actually. We helped them out a few years ago when they were in a similar situation, if you remember. Anyway, it looks like they may be able to do something, but probably not until tomorrow morning.
A: Well, at least that's something, I suppose. Okay, get back to them and see if we can hurry things up a bit. And get somebody in after-sales to ring around all our biggest customers and smooth things over with them.

C: Okay, I'll see to it now.
A: Now, Max. Are you sure this thing can't just be fixed? I mean, if I gave your technical people, say, 24 hours ... Max, you still there?
B: Still here. I've just been told the leakage area has now been made secure.
A: Well, thank goodness for that. Anyway, okay, that's it for now. We're going to try and get some sleep. I suggest we schedule another conference call for midnight European Time. But, Otto, keep me posted if there's any change in the situation, won't you?
F: Will do, Pete.
A: Okay, thanks everyone ...

> **Language links**
>
> Direct students to the *Language links* section on pages 105–106 for more practice of reporting.

8 Before doing the exercise, check with students if they keep minutes of meetings and if they think it's a worthwhile task. Ask why it's particularly important to minute the Oriflamme teleconference (to deal with the crisis quickly and to make sure everyone knows what to do).

Tell the students to read the minutes of the teleconference. Draw attention to the convention of using initials. When the students have completed the gaps, tell them to check their answers with a partner before doing a whole-class check.

With a larger group, divide the class into four and give one part of the report to each group. Then ask the students to regroup in order to exchange answers. When the students have finished, check answers with the class.

ANSWERS

Details 1: confirmed, authorized, informed, assure
Action 1: keep
Details 2: estimated
Action 2: ensure
Details 3: proposed, pointed, agreed
Action 3: reach, report
Details 4: opposed, mentioned, okay'd
Action 4: follow, smooth

Desert island blues

In this final fluency activity, students roleplay directors of an advertising agency who have to deal with a crisis. They work in groups and read two of six emails in order to learn about the background to the problem, which has arisen while filming an advert in an exotic location. The students prepare for and hold a teleconference to decide on an action plan.

As a lead-in to the topic, elicit examples of product endorsement by famous people, e.g. sports personalities and trainers, actresses and beauty products, etc. Ask if students believe that such endorsements help to sell products. Before Step 1, set the scene by asking students

BUSINESS COMMUNICATION

to read the background information in the rubric. Ask check questions such as the name of the company, the client, the location and the product.

Step 1
Check/Pre-teach: *to run up costs, post-production, to overrun, hold-up, drastic, in the can* (filmed and ready to be shown), *footage, secluded, to scout for, handler, lethal, through the grapevine, set building*. Divide the class into groups of three. Assign each student a letter: A, B or C. Ask students to add their names to the organigram. With larger groups, have students work together in pairs on the same role.

Step 2
Ask students to read their roles and their respective emails: A reads emails 1 and 2 on page 125, B reads emails 3 and 4 on page 133, and C reads emails 5 and 6 on page 135. Deal with vocabulary queries as necessary and check pronunciation of the proper nouns given in the scenario and emails. Write the following prompts on the board and give students time to make notes in preparation for the teleconference:

- key points to update colleagues
- important figures to quote
- suggested action points and order of priority

Step 3
Ask students to read the agenda. Ideally, use phones with a conferencing facility, or set up the seating for a teleconference, so participants sit in a group but don't look at each other. Remind the A students to act as CEO and chair the meeting. They also need to specify who speaks at any one time. Ask all students to read the agenda and set a time limit of thirty minutes for the teleconference. Monitor and take feedback notes.

When the activity has finished, give the students a few seconds to think about the task, the outcome and their own performance. Then ask each group in turn to report back on what went well and what could have been improved. Give feedback on overall fluency before highlighting important or common errors.

1:1 One of you takes the role of the Creative Director and the other takes the role of the Account Director. Hold the teleconference and try and agree on a strategy to put forward to the CEO. Make sure you both read the emails from the CEO first.

Language links
Direct students to the *Language links* section on page 105 to do a puzzle to revise some of the teleconferencing language in this unit.

Language links
ANSWERS
Vocabulary
Teleconferencing
1 a waiting b ahead c fill d moment e can
  f working g point h feel i being j alternative
  k come l been m can n ring o now p change

Personnel and production
Organizational issues
2 a human resources   b job satisfaction
  c appraisal interview   d fringe benefits
  e promotion prospects   f incentive scheme

Operations management
3 raw **materials**
  safety **regulations**
  zero **defects**
  stock **control**
  quality **circle**
  finished **goods**
  assembly **line**
  supply **chain**
4 a raw materials b assembly line c quality circle
  d supply chain

Grammar
Reporting
1 a they had managed to distribute poverty equally.
  b he had opinions of his own, strong opinions, but (that) he didn't always agree with them.
  c he would not tolerate intolerance.
  d it wasn't pollution that was harming the environment – it was the impurities in our air and water that were doing it.
  e he had committed a crime – what he had done was fail to comply with the law.
2 Anna questioned the need for the training programme. Niels was of the same opinion.
  Anna raised the issue of the training budget. Jon replied that he hadn't come to a decision yet.
  Jon confirmed that the project had been given the go-ahead.
  Jon wondered if it was a good idea to bring in consultants.
  Anna was against it.
  Both Anna and Niels recommended reviewing the situation.
  There was some initial opposition to the spending cuts.
  The issue was finally resolved.
  There was unanimous agreement on the proposal.

Phrase bank
Teleconferencing
Across
2 introduce 4 ahead 6 trouble 8 recap
13 interruptions 14 hear 16 agreed 17 postpone
18 vote
Down
1 waiting 2 input 3 covers 5 agenda 7 finished
8 running 9 come 10 lost 11 favour 12 straight
15 welcome

17 Negotiating deals

Learning objectives

Everyone negotiates informally to some extent: with a partner about where to eat out, in discussions with their boss and/or colleagues, and so on. Many business English students need to negotiate formally, and this unit looks at the language and skills necessary to do this successfully.

Students test their skills as negotiators in a two-stage fluency task, and then listen to feedback being given on the same negotiation. They then focus on and practise compound adjectives.

Students study different tactics in negotiating and discuss their effectiveness. They listen to extracts from negotiations to identify the strategies being used. Language work focuses on bargaining, showing disapproval and idioms, and further listening practice is given on negotiation strategies.

In the final section, students discuss music, read an article on the music industry, and identify useful language. This leads on to a fluency activity in which students roleplay a negotiation between a rock band and a record company.

The grammatical focus is on the language of diplomacy and persuasion, and the lexical focus is on the language of negotiations.

Digital resources: Unit 17

Online Workbook; In company interviews Units 16–17 and worksheet; Extension worksheets; Glossary; Phrase bank; Student's Book answer key; Student's Book listening script; Fast-track map

---

In the first section, pairs of students practise negotiating by doing a short roleplay, while an observer takes notes on the language they use. The students repeat the roleplay, but with a change in their relationship; students discuss the differences between the two negotiations. A recording provides an analysis of this negotiation by a management trainer, and students then focus on some of the language used in the recording, including compound adjectives.

1:1 In many negotiations, two parties are involved. This is an ideal situation for one-to-one teaching, with the teacher playing one of the roles. If you have a video camera, mobile phone or tablet with the possibility to film or to record audio, you can access the exchanges between you and your student afterwards, in order to identify mistakes and to select pieces of language to be reformulated. With video, you can also encourage the student to observe and comment on body language during the negotiation.

Warm-up

Find out which students need to negotiate formally in their work, and if they find it easy or difficult, and why. For those students who don't negotiate formally, ask them to think of a situation in which they needed to use their negotiating skills and find out how it went. Focus attention on the quotation from Don Herold and elicit what the implication is for negotiators (keep up good relations with people, as you may want to deal with them again in the future; consider the long-term implications of a discussion).

1 Divide the class into groups of three: Student A, Student B and an observer. If the group does not divide into threes, assign the role of observer to two students.

a Check/Pre-teach: *to go mad for, a surge of panic, to slip your mind, to mumble, to grab*. Refer the A students to page 126 and the B students to page 127. Tell the observers that they will need to make notes on the stages/tone of the negotiation and on the language used. Students roleplay the negotiation and the observers take notes. Monitor but don't offer help or interfere.

b Ask the negotiators to comment on whether an agreement was reached and to highlight the main problems. Elicit comments from the observers on the key stages and whether the tone changed during the negotiation. Write up examples of key language on the board.

c Refer Students A and B from each group to the extra information on page 123. Get them to try the negotiation again and remind the observers to note down the stages and key language, and any changes in body language, tone of voice, etc.

d Elicit feedback on the second negotiation. Ask students if it was easier to reach a compromise and, if so, why. Ask the observers for their comments, eliciting any additional/different stages and how the key language changed.

2 3.18 Ask students to predict what the management trainer will say. Play the recording through once and get students to check if their predictions were correct.

Check any difficult words: *opponent, encounter, issue* (problem/point for discussion), *vice versa, to pre-empt, deadlock, deserving*. Tell students that this time they should take notes under the following headings:

1st negotiation:	objective	tactics
2nd negotiation:	objective	tactics

Play the recording again and get students to complete their notes. Check the answers and then ask students if they agree with the trainer's analysis.

17 NEGOTIATING DEALS 101

BUSINESS COMMUNICATION

3.18

The activity you just did is designed to demonstrate the critical importance in the negotiating process of relationship building.

In your first negotiation you probably didn't think much about your opponent's interests. And why should you? After all, it was just a stranger who you'd never meet again. But by concentrating on only one objective, you reduced the whole encounter to a single issue negotiation with little room for manoeuvre. This made it a simple zero-sum game – if I get what I want, you don't, and vice versa.

In order to win at all costs, perhaps you became hostile and tried to pre-empt negotiation altogether by just grabbing the box off the other person. Or maybe you gave in completely, deciding it simply wasn't worth the hassle. Many professional negotiators act the same way if they think they are negotiating a one-off deal. As the negotiation ended in deadlock, perhaps you became desperate and resorted to emotional blackmail, inventing all sorts of reasons why your kid was more deserving than the other kid.

In the second negotiation, on the other hand, there was a long-term relationship you wanted to maintain. The circumstances were exactly the same, but the prospect of one of you 'losing' was no longer an option. By accepting the need to reach some kind of compromise, you were able to turn a head-on conflict into a problem-solving meeting. Now your main objective was to generate options in the hope that you could create a win-win situation, where you both got something you wanted.

3 Students form the collocations and then match them to the definitions. Get students to practise the compounds by asking follow-up questions.

ANSWERS

a	a single-issue negotiation	one where only one topic is being discussed
b	a long-term relationship	one that lasts
c	a win-win situation	one from which both sides feel they've gained
d	a one-off deal	one that happens only once
e	a zero-sum game	one where one side wins what the other side loses
f	a head-on conflict	one which is very direct

4 Students complete the phrases, working individually or in pairs. Check the answers by playing the recording again or referring students to the listening script on page 156. Check pronunciation of difficult words, e.g. *manoeuvre*, *hassle* and get students to practise the expressions by writing questions. Students work in pairs to ask and answer their questions.

ANSWERS

a manoeuvre b costs c hassle d deadlock
e blackmail f compromise

Language links

Direct students to the *Language links* section on page 112 for more on the vocabulary of negotiations.

Negotiating style

In this section, students match the names of high-pressure tactics in negotiations to their relevant descriptions and then discuss the tactics. They listen to extracts from negotiations and identify which tactics are being used. Students then complete exercises on the language of bargaining and on ways of showing disapproval. Further listening practice is provided by a recording of experienced negotiators talking about negotiating strategy and the section ends with a focus on idioms used in the recording.

1 Ask students if they have ever been on a negotiation skills training course. Encourage those who have to give examples of the techniques covered. For students with little or no experience of negotiating, name some of the techniques in 1 (e.g. *the good cop, bad cop approach, the take-it-or-leave-it challenge*) and get students to guess how the tactics work. Check/Pre-teach: *ploy, concession, to keep a straight face, to jeopardise, nasty*. Students work in pairs to match the tactics and descriptions.

ANSWERS

1 d 2 b 3 a 4 c 5 h 6 f 7 e 8 g

2 Check if anyone in the group has been faced with high-pressure tactics and, if so, what strategies they used. Put students into groups. Get students to brainstorm possible responses to each of the tactics in 1. Hold a class feedback session and elicit possible answers.

Ask students which tactics they think are high-risk and why. Also find out if students think any of the tactics are unethical. Students then select one tactic which they would like to try out and one which they think is beyond their negotiating skills.

3 3.19–3.20 Check/Pre-teach: *volume, case, trial order, pack, margin, premium* (high quality), *unique, unit, installation*. Tell students that they will hear each extract twice. Before students listen, give them the names of the characters in random order (see bracketed text below) and ask the following gist questions: *Who is negotiating? What product is under discussion?* Play the recording through once and check the answers (1 Ms Barrett/Mr Koivisto; a new brand of carbonated water; 2 Rob Hayes/Gavin and his negotiating partner; precision tools).

Tell students to now focus on the tactics used in each extract and on how successful they are. Play the recording again and check the answers.

ANSWERS

Extract 1 7 3   Extract 2 6 5

---

102   17 NEGOTIATING DEALS

BUSINESS COMMUNICATION

🔊 3.19
Extract 1
A: Okay, so, do I take it we're in agreement on volume?
B: Er, well, just a minute, wouldn't it be a good idea to talk prices before we go any further?
A: Yes, of course. But in principle you're happy about taking forty cases, right?
B: Er, well, in principle, yes, if the product's as good as you say it is …
A: Splendid, that's settled then.
B: … But, look, getting back to price for a moment. This would be just a trial order, you understand? Sale or return. Until we see how it sells. So, can you give us some idea of what kind of figure you were thinking of?
A: €50.
B: €50 per case.
A: Er, no. Per pack.
B: Per pack? There seems to have been a slight misunderstanding. A pack is just twelve bottles, right?
A: Yes, that's right.
B: Is this meant to be some kind of joke or something? €50 per pack? That's over €4 a bottle. By the time we've added a decent margin, you realize we're looking at a retail price of €7 minimum. How am I supposed to sell a one-litre bottle of water for €7, Mr Koivisto?
A: Ms Barrett, O-Zone is an innovative, premium product. A pure oxygen-enriched drink. We're not talking about a bottle of Perrier here.
B: Well, that's as may be, but €7!
A: O-Zone is an exciting opportunity to get in at the start of a new trend in luxury health drinks.
B: Well, there's no way on earth I'm paying you €4 for a bottle of oxygenated water, Mr Koivisto. With respect, your prices are simply not competitive.
A: Ms Barrett, there are no competitors in this market. O-Zone is a unique product and at €4 – well, I'm afraid that really is our absolute bottom line.
B: So you're saying it's take it or leave it?
A: I'm afraid so.
B: Well, then, I think I'll have to leave it …
A: What …? Now, just a minute. You said on the phone you might want 100 cases.
B: That was before I knew your water was more expensive than Chanel No 5, Mr Koivisto. Okay, look, let's set the price issue to one side for the moment, shall we? Tell me a bit more about the product …

🔊 3.20
Extract 2
A: Okay, I'll tell you what I'll do. If you order 250 units today, I can offer you not our usual five but a 6% discount, free delivery and I'll throw in twelve months' free parts and service as well. Now, I can't say fairer than that, can I? Of course, that's only if you can give me the order today. Can't hold the offer, I'm afraid.

B: Well, erm, Robert, isn't it?
A: Rob. Call me Rob.
B: Well, now, Rob, we appreciate the free service and delivery, but to be honest with you, what we'd really like to see is a bit more movement on price. I'm afraid a 6% discount is not quite what we had in mind. We were hoping for something a bit closer to ten.
A: 10%? I don't think I could stretch as far as that. Not unless this was a substantially bigger order.
C: Oh, come on! You'll have to do a lot better than that, Mr Hayes. You're not the only precision tool manufacturer, you know.
B: Hold on, Gavin. Let's hear Rob out.
C: Well, frankly, I think we're wasting each other's time here. We've already been offered a much better deal by Magnusson's.
B: Now, wait a minute, wait a minute. Surely we can sort something out here. Rob, would you be willing to meet us halfway?
A: How do you mean?
B: Well, if you were to offer us an 8% discount, we might be in a position to increase our order, say, by fifty units. But we'd need to see a bit more flexibility on terms of payment. Maybe on installation costs too.
A: Erm, well, I suppose there may be some room for manoeuvre there. I'd need to check. Can you give me a moment to have another look at the figures?
B: Sure. In fact, let's take a short time-out, shall we? And meet back here in, say, half an hour?
A: Okay, fine.
C: I still say we'd be better off going with Magnusson's.

4 Ask students to work in pairs, with student A completing a–j and student B completing k–t. Then, ask students to check their answers with their partner.

ANSWERS
a Okay, so, do **I take it we're in agreement on** volume?
b Wouldn't it be a **good idea to talk prices before we go** any further?
c But in **principle you're happy about taking** 40 cases, right?
d Look, **getting back to price for a** moment.
e Can you give us some **idea of what kind of figure you were** thinking of?
f There **seems to have been a slight** misunderstanding.
g With **respect, your prices are simply not** competitive.
h I'm afraid that **really is our absolute bottom** line.
i Let's set the price **issue to one side for the moment**, shall we?
j I'll throw **in 12 months' free parts and service as** well.
k Now, I **can't say fairer than that,** now can I?
l What we'd really like to **see is a bit more movement on** price.
m A 6% discount **is not quite what we had in** mind.
n We were **hoping for something a bit closer** to 10%.
o I don't think **I could stretch as far as** that.
p Surely **we can sort something out** here.
q Would **you be willing to meet** us halfway?
r We might **be in a position to increase** our order.
s We'd need to **see a bit more flexibility on** terms of payment.
t I suppose **there may be some room for manoeuvre** there.

BUSINESS COMMUNICATION

5 This exercise highlights some of the nuances of expression in the language in 4. Students work individually to answer the questions and then discuss their answers in pairs.

Point out that the use of *seems/appears*, modifiers like *quite/a bit*, modal verbs like *may/might/would*, etc are characteristic of a tendency to 'soften' language when negotiating in English. Ask students follow-up questions to compare negotiating styles in their own language. Ask students to categorize some of the language in 4 under functional headings, e.g. recapping on details, asking for/ checking figures, indicating that you are not satisfied, asking for a better deal, making an improved offer, etc.

ANSWERS
a With respect …; I'm afraid …   b It makes the statement less direct.   c less negotiable   d easier   e both   f They want to soften the impact of negative information.   g They now leave almost no room for manoeuvre.

Language links
Direct students to the *Language links* section on page 113 for more on the language and grammar of diplomacy and persuasion.

6 Ask students to complete the expressions in a–d. Check the answers with the class, reminding students that they may wish to avoid using these expressions completely unless they are dealing with people they know very well.

ANSWERS
a joke + something   b way + earth
c lot + that   d other + time

7 3.21–3.23 As a lead-in to the listening task, ask students to brainstorm tips for successful negotiating, e.g. stay calm, be clear about what you want, be prepared to compromise, etc. Collate the best ideas into a 'top ten' and write them on the board. Play the recording through once and get students to tick off any of the tips that are mentioned by the negotiators.

Check/Pre-teach: *one-off deal, tough, to pause, to give away (your strategy), defensive, trap*. Ask students to read the questions in 7. Then play the recording, pausing between speakers. Students check their answers by comparing with a partner. Ask students which of the three speakers they agree with most and why.

ANSWERS
Speaker 1
Win-win isn't a realistic outcome because many business negotiations are one-off deals, so win-lose is the commonest outcome.
A friendly attitude can be counter productive because the opponent reads into what is possible by your attitude: so, the friendlier you seem, the higher their expectations.

Speaker 2
Silence is more powerful than talking because it can make your opponent uncomfortable and force them into giving a concession. Listening is 'gold' because you learn more.

Speaker 3
You can avoid pointless debates by not trying to justify your position, but rather, explore mutual interests and options.
The two most useful phrases in a negotiation are: 'If …, then …?' and 'What if …?'

3.21
Speaker 1
Well, frankly, I get a bit tired of hearing people go on about win-win negotiating. I mean, let's face it, a lot of negotiations are basically win-lose, and your opponent's interests are the last thing you should be worrying about. Buying a house, a car, double-glazing – all win-lose situations. And you'd be surprised how many business negotiations are basically one-off deals as well. In my opinion, in a win-lose situation the tougher you are – without actually being aggressive – the further you'll get. That's because your opponent takes your attitude as an indication of what's possible and what's not. And the friendlier you seem, the higher their expectations will be. It's like the old saying: give them an inch and they'll take a mile.

3.22
Speaker 2
'You always know who is going to win a negotiation – it's he who pauses the longest.' I forget who it was who said that but it's pretty good advice – basically, shut up! And remember that silence is very often your best weapon. It's a very difficult argument to counter. Faced with prolonged and uncomfortable silences, your opponent is liable to make another concession or give away their strategy or weaken their own position by becoming defensive. So play your cards close to your chest. Talk less, learn more. There's an old Swedish proverb: 'Talking is silver. But listening is gold.'

3.23
Speaker 3
I think the biggest trap less experienced negotiators fall into is to turn the whole negotiation into a debate, which it isn't. This is sometimes called 'positional negotiating'. Both sides end up arguing the whys and the wherefores, rationalising their position, trying to justify themselves. They can talk till the cows come home but it's a complete waste of time. Besides, you're not there to convince your opponent that you're right. He doesn't care if you're right or not. And neither should you. You're there to explore both sides' interests, generate options and trade concessions – preferably giving away things that mean little to you but a lot to him and receiving the opposite in return. This is 'interest-based negotiation' – discovering the needs, desires and fears behind your opponent's position and working on those. The two phrases you need most of all are: 'If …, then …?': If I give you that, then what do I get? And 'What if …?': What if we looked at this another way? What if we did this instead?

BUSINESS COMMUNICATION

8 Ask students to discuss the meanings of the idioms in pairs. If necessary, refer students to the listening scripts on page 157 where the idioms appear in context, before checking the answers.

> **ANSWERS**
> a If you give people a little of what they want, they will then try to take a lot more.
> b Don't tell people what you are thinking or planning.
> c Keep pushing until you get an agreement.

> **Language links**
> Direct students to the *Phrase bank* in the *Language links* section on page 113 for more on negotiating language.

Negotiating a recording contract

In this final section, students discuss music and test their knowledge of pop trivia. They read a text about the music business and work on useful vocabulary. A listening task about a meeting at a record label provides the background to the final fluency activity.

1 As a lead-in to this section, divide students into pairs and ask them to compare musical tastes.

2 Students work in pairs to answer the questions. Check/Pre-teach: *acumen, music rights, airplay, a rip-off* (informal for *an unfair deal*), *at stake, reputedly*. Ask students to re-read the text and then summarize the main points of each paragraph, working in pairs.

> **ANSWERS**
> a The Rolling Stones
> b Madonna, Elton John, Celine Dion, Garth Brooks
> c Michael Jackson's *Thriller*
> d Bing Crosby's 'White Christmas'; the version of 'Candle in the Wind' Elton John sang at the funeral of Princess Diana
> e The Beatles' 'Yesterday'

3 Ask students to look back at the text to find the words and phrases a–k. Remind students to look for a word in the same part of speech as the definition and to use the context to help them identify the meaning.

> **ANSWERS**
> a gross revenues   b steadiest income stream   c blockbuster
> d royalties   e a string of top ten hits   f a sell-out gig
> g out-earning   h up-and-coming   i dazzled by the prospect of stardom   j the small print   k clashes

4 🔊 **3.24** Write the names of the people in the recording on the board: *Tess, Mr Ronnie Logan, Kate, Miles*. Check/Pre-teach: *A&R people* (artist and repertoire – people who look for new talent in the music industry), *to snap up* (to quickly take the opportunity to make a deal with an artist), *to sniff around* (in this context, to try to make contacts), *demo* (demonstration material), *inconsistent, tricky, a class act, glamorous, to tune into*. Let students read the four questions first and get them to predict the type of language they will hear and possible answers to the questions. Play the recording through once and let students check their answers in pairs. Play the recording again before checking answers with the class.

As a link to the fluency task in 5, ask students to review the strengths and weaknesses of the band. Refer students to the listening script on page 157 and have them underline any useful vocabulary for negotiating the recording contract in 5, e.g. *a demo, musical identity, a class act,* etc.

> **ANSWERS**
> a A lot of other record companies were at the concert and may sign them first.
> b An excellent lead singer; musically strong; good-looking.
> c The band doesn't have an identity; the drummer's bad.
> d The band is about to get massive publicity on cable TV.

🔊 **3.24**
A: Tess?
B: Mr Logan. It's Kate and Miles to see you.
A: Ah, good. Send them right in.
C: Hi, Ronnie.
A: Kate, good to see you. You're looking great as usual. Miles, come on in. Erm, sit anywhere you like. Can I get you something to drink?
C: Do you have an Evian?
A: No problem. There you go. Miles?
D: I'll just have a black coffee.
A: Good idea, Miles! You really look tired; coffee ought to perk you up! So, I hear you two had quite a late evening at the Marquee.
D: You could say that.
C: Ronnie, you have to sign this band. You could hardly move for A&R people last night. If we don't snap them up, someone else will. I saw Jimmy Armstrong from Sony sniffing around.
A: Uh huh. Well, he usually is.
C: Yeah, and EMI were there as well. This band's hot. You listened to the demo I sent you, right?
A: I did.
C: And?
A: Well, ...
C: Oh, come on, Ronnie. These guys are the best thing to come out of Ireland since U2 and you know it.
A: I wouldn't go as far as that, Kate. They sound a little inconsistent on the demo. They need to work on a clear musical identity, if you ask me.
C: Well, maybe they need a little help in that direction. We can work on that. But you have to admit the lead singer's voice is just amazing. In fact, they're musically really strong all round.
A: Okay, I'll give you that. Apart from the drummer, that is, who's pretty second-rate. So he'd have to go.
C: She.
A: She? They have a female drummer? Interesting. Well, anyway, she's no good.
C: Could be tricky to fire. She's the lead singer's girlfriend.

17 NEGOTIATING DEALS 105

BUSINESS COMMUNICATION

A: Hm. I'm going off them already.
C: Ronnie, believe me, The Penitents are a class act. And I'm not easily impressed, you know that.
A: True, you're not. Miles, meet the woman who turned down Oasis.
D: Fine by me. I never liked them.
C: I thought we weren't going to talk about that any more.
A: Okay, okay. Well, what do The Penitents look like? No, let me guess. Like they haven't eaten a hot meal for a week and they cut their own hair, right?
D: Not at all. The lead guitarist looks like Keanu Reeves. The drummer's fabulous even if her drumming's a little off. In fact, they're all pretty glamorous. Ronnie, I have a good feeling about this one.
A: Okay, call their manager and set something up. But not next week. I'm at the MTV awards.
C: Okay, I'll do that. Oh, and by the way, you might want to tune in to VH1 at eight this evening. They're being interviewed live.
A: They are? Well, why didn't you say so before? Look, give me their manager's number, I might just call him myself this afternoon …

5 As a lead-in to the roleplay, write the following words on the board: *song rights, royalties, advance, airplay fees, backlist*. Elicit relevant examples from the music industry. Check/Pre-teach: *to stand to make a lot of money, vulnerable, exploitation, rumour, commitment, to commission, net receipts, the bubble bursts* (a positive situation turns negative), *paparazzi, to retain, to offset, split*.

Divide the class into AB Teams. Refer Team A to their negotiating brief on page 126 and Team B to page 137. Have students read their brief carefully, underlining the key information. Give students plenty of time to prepare and take notes. Ask students to discuss the importance of each of the objectives 1–8 and to categorize each point as T-I-E (*tradeables, ideals, essentials*). Give students a few minutes to review the negotiating tactics on page 108 and to decide if they want to use any of them.

Arrange the seating to reflect a meeting room. Explain that the meeting will take place at Starburst's offices, so Team B should be ready to welcome Team A. Set a length of 45–60 minutes for the negotiation and appoint a chairperson. Write the following agenda on the board:

1 Welcome and purpose of meeting.
2 Discussion of potential contract for / management of *The Penitents* to cover: line-up, term, royalties, deductions, advances, territory, touring, song writing.
3 Final decisions and action points.

Monitor and take feedback notes. When the negotiation has finished, ask the students to think about what went well and what they would do differently next time.

1:1 Decide in advance whether your student will be representing Team A, The Penitents, or Team B, Starburst Records. Both sides will need time to prepare. See page 126 for Team A and page 137 for Team B. Take the role of chairperson and issue the agenda. Set a time limit on each agenda point of approximately five minutes.

Language links

ANSWERS

Vocabulary
Negotiations
Sounding out your opponent
1 a of   b with   c for   d about   e at   f towards

Discussing terms
2 price, discount, credit, volume, transportation, packaging, documentation, guarantee, consignments, maintenance, delivery time, payment terms, spare parts, exchange rate, after-sales service, penalty clauses
3 *penalty clauses is not needed*   1 volume   2 discount
3 payment terms   4 credit   5 exchange rate   6 price
7 transportation   8 documentation   9 delivery time
10 guarantee   11 maintenance   12 spare parts   13 after-sales service   14 consignments   15 packaging

Negotiating procedure
4 1 atmosphere   2 procedure   3 position   4 interests
5 phase   6 proposals   7 concessions   8 deadlock
9 time-out   10 strategy   11 table   12 options
13 breakthrough   14 details   15 champagne

Grammar
Diplomacy and persuasion
Negotiation 1
B What sort of figure did you have in mind?
A We were thinking of somewhere in the region of $12 per unit.
B To be honest, I'm not in a position to go quite that low at this stage.
Negotiation 2
A We were promised 90 days' free credit.
B With respect, it was understood you'd be placing a rather larger order.
A This doesn't seem to be getting us very far. I'm afraid we must insist on free credit.
B Unfortunately, I'm unable to offer you that unless you're prepared to increase your order slightly.
Negotiation 3
A We had been hoping for some kind of commitment from you today.
B At this point that might be a bit difficult. We're not entirely happy about these service charges.
A But it was assumed you were okay about those.
B I'm afraid not. Look, shouldn't we go over these figures again?

Phrase bank
Negotiating
a idea b kind c closer d principle e agreement f willing
g sort h manoeuvre i stretch j position k movement
l flexibility m throw n fairer o mind p line q respect
r getting s side t misunderstanding u cross-purposes

106   17 NEGOTIATING DEALS

18 Mediation

Learning objectives

This unit is about mediation in the business world.

Students begin by discussing a cartoon and the attitude to mediation that it shows. They then consider the qualities of a good mediator. They brainstorm a list of causes of conflict at work and read an article on this subject. They then focus on some of the new vocabulary in the article. Students read the article again, and identify any types of conflict that are relevant to their own situation.

Next, students listen to a manager trying to resolve a conflict and answer a set of questions. They complete the missing words in a description of the stages of a mediation session and match expressions to these stages.

Students then listen to a second meeting involving a mediator. Students predict the outcome, and check by listening to the end of the meeting.

Finally, students take part in a roleplay to practise their mediation skills.

Digital resources: Unit 18

Online Workbook; Extension worksheets; Glossary; Student's Book answer key; Student's Book listening script; Fast-track map; Quick progress test 4

1:1 This topic area is tricky to approach from a one-to-one perspective, since mediation requires three people. However, mediation often involves 'time out' between the mediator and one of the parties. In a one-to-one situation, it is possible to roleplay this latter type of discussion.

Warm-up

Write the word *mediate* on the board and ask students to tell you what it means. Ask students if they can list situations which involve mediation, e.g. a political war over territory, a work context involving conflict.

1 Put students in pairs to discuss the cartoon and answer the questions. Elicit students' ideas.

SAMPLE ANSWERS

Obviously, there's some hostility between them! The woman is mediating – trying to help them reach an agreement by finding common ground between them.

2 Ask students to brainstorm the qualities of a good mediator. Elicit students' ideas and collate them on the board. Ask students to select and agree on the three most important qualities, and underline these.

SUGGESTED ANSWERS

Ideal qualities include: patience, tact, credibility, empathy, alertness, flexibility, calmness, self-control, initiative, perseverance.

3 Put students in pairs to brainstorm causes of conflict at work. Do not check answers at this stage.

4 Explain that students are going to read an article called *8 Causes of Conflict at Work*. Ask students to skim read the article and look for the ideas they thought of in 3. Ask students to call these out and write them on the board. When students have finished reading, ask them about any other conflict areas mentioned in the article. Add these to the list.

5 Ask students to look at the underlined words in the article. Put them in pairs to try and work out any unknown words from the context. Elicit students' conclusions and answer any queries they have.

ANSWERS

a relatively hassle-free day = a day with comparatively few problems
at each other's throats = to be attacking each other constantly
to top it all = 'the final straw'
slashed = cut drastically
there's friction = there's a problem between two people
thrive on chaos = do well when there's no ordered way to do things
a personality clash = a situation where two people cannot get on due to who they are
a recipe for disaster = a situation which can only end badly
a crippling workload = a situation with a huge amount of work

---

1:1 Before dealing with the highlighted words, do a phrase-building exercise with your student. Write the following on cards: *thrive (on) / chaos / personality / clash / recipe (for) / disaster / crippling / workload*. Check your student knows the words by asking them to generate sentences, e.g. *I have a heavy workload*. Then ask them to match the cards to create collocations. Your student may be familiar with these phrases but, if not, they can work out the meaning from the context in the article.

6 Give students a few minutes to read the article again, slowly and carefully. Put students in pairs to discuss if they have ever been in any of the conflict situations in the article and, if they have, to say if and how it was resolved.

7 3.25 Tell students they are going to listen to a manager trying to resolve a conflict in the workplace between Henri and Elena. Check that students know the word *obsessed (with doing something)*. Ask students to read the questions and listen to the manager attempting to resolve the dispute. Check answers with the class.

ANSWERS

a Henri and Elena have completely conflicting styles of working. Henri likes to go at his own speed, working on different parts of the project at the same time. Elena prefers to work

18 MEDIATION 107

PEOPLE SKILLS

systematically, finishing one part of the project before moving on to the next.

They also have conflicting roles. Henri doesn't want Elena's help. Elena sees it as her job to help him.

b Possible solutions include: letting Henri continue with the project alone (but with instructions to work faster); replacing Elena with someone Henri finds it easier to work with; taking the project off Henri and giving it to Elena or finding some way of mediating the situation so that they can work better together.

c The manager James's first mistake is that he is not holding a proper structured meeting to sort this conflict out. He makes it clear that he's busy and wants a quick solution. He lacks patience and empathy. Also, he doesn't control the meeting well, allowing people to interrupt each other and lose their temper. The atmosphere is negative. People simply blame each other, rather than try to make progress.

3.25

A: Okay, take a seat. Now, look, you both know why we're here. Henri, you've been struggling to get the Panama project completed for weeks.

B: What? ...

A: No, hear me out, Henri. I've got another meeting in an hour and we really must sort this situation out today. In fact, I probably should have intervened earlier. Now, for one reason or another, you've been having difficulty bringing this project to completion. I brought Elena in to help you out, thinking it would make your life easier. And since then you two have done nothing but fight, and the project seems to be further behind schedule than ever! Now can somebody please tell me what on earth's going on? Elena?

C: Well, it's Henri. He's totally disorganized. I mean, I'm not surprised he's so far behind schedule. He can't work to a deadline. We've got no proper milestones in place for this project. I've tried working with him, but it's just hopeless ...

B: I am not totally disorganized, Elena. Just because you're obsessed with ticking boxes at every stage of the project, and I'm not, does not make me disorganized. In fact, I never asked for your help in the first place. I was getting along just fine without you, thanks very much.

C: How could you be 'getting along just fine'? Why do you think I was brought in?

B: I've no idea. I certainly didn't request your assistance.

A: People, people ...

C: And I didn't ask for the job either, Henri. I've got better things to do than sort out your problems!

A: Right, everybody just hold it right there!

B: Okay, that's it! I've had enough of this! I'm sorry, James. If you want to discuss this matter with me in private, we'll need to arrange another meeting.

A: Henri ...

B: I'll be in my office if you want me.

A: Well, that went well!

8 First, check that students know the word *to impose (on someone)*. Then give them a few minutes to complete the stages of a mediation using the verbs in the box.

ANSWERS
1 opens, describes, sets 2 speaks, listens, prevents
3 identifies, generates 4 holds
5 encourages, imposes 6 writes, gets

9 Put students in pairs and ask one of them to read out the first six sentences in 9. The listener assigns each phrase to one of the six stages in 8. Students then change roles for the last six sentences.

ANSWERS
a 3 b 5 c 1 d 5 e 4 f 3 g 6 h 3 i 2 j 3 k 1 l 5

10 3.26 Students listen to a second meeting, this time with a mediator, Kaye. Check that students know the words *impartial, reassured* and *to storm in*. Divide the class into As and Bs. Ask As to take notes on the issues for Henri and Bs to do the same for Elena. Then students, in AB pairs, summarize the issues for their partner. Play the recording again and ask students to rate Kaye's performance on a scale of 1–10. Elicit students' evaluations and ask them to justify why they chose this number.

ANSWERS
Henri. The main issues for him are:
He thinks Elena doesn't know enough about the project.
He thinks it is his project, and he doesn't like sharing responsibility.
He thinks Elena is trying to take over the project.
He needs more time and some extra IT support.
Elena. The main issues for her are:
Henri does not show her respect.
She needs to make sure the project is completed on time and on budget (it's currently five weeks behind schedule).
She has three other projects to deal with.
Henri never provides her with progress reports.
The mediator is good and should score at least 8 out of 10. She follows a clear procedure. She is empathic and a good listener. She is in control of the session and stops any emotional outbursts.

3.26

A: Okay, let's get started, shall we? Well, I'm Kaye and, as you know, James has asked me to mediate this session. He thought that maybe someone from a different department might be in a better position to help you resolve your issues. Is that okay with both of you? Okay, good. Now, it's Elena and Henri, isn't it? All right, well, first of all, let me say, that everything you say in this meeting is totally confidential. Nothing goes outside this room. And, of course, I'm completely impartial in all this. I have no personal interest in how you resolve your differences. I'm just here to try and make sure we explore every option, okay? Now, one or two rules to make this meeting more productive. We'll speak one at a time if possible. So please try not to interrupt each other. If you've anything to say, make a note of it, so you can make your point when it's your turn to speak. And if you need to talk to me privately at any stage, just let me know. All right? Now, Henri, let's start with you, shall we? How do you see the situation? ...

B: ... So, frankly, I don't see what kind of help Elena can possibly offer when she hasn't been involved in this project, knows nothing about it, in fact ...

108 18 MEDIATION

C: Now, hang on, Henri! I know as much about this project as you do. I ought to by now, for heaven's sake – I've been working on it 24/7 for the last three weeks! You see what he's like? Just no respect for anybody else's point of view.
A: Okay, I understand your position, Elena. But just let Henri finish what he has to say and I'll come back to you in a moment, okay? Now, Henri, as I understand it, you're not happy about sharing responsibility for this project with Elena, is that right?
B: Well, of course, I'm not. It's my project. James had no right bringing Elena in at all. I had everything under control. I just needed a little more time. Maybe some more IT support would have been a nice idea too. What I didn't need is someone else coming in and taking over!
C: I have not taken over!
B: Only because I haven't let you!
A: Okay, clearly, we have a misunderstanding about roles here. Elena, what was your brief from James when he brought you in?
C: To make sure this project is completed on time and on budget. At the moment, it's five weeks behind schedule.
A: But James did not ask you to take charge of the project?
C: Well, of course he didn't. I can't take responsibility for all this. I've got three other projects I'm involved in at the moment.
A: So you agree with Henri that this is his project and that you're just trying to do what you can to prevent any further delays?
C: That's right.
A: Henri, are you reassured by what Elena just said?
B: Well, ... yes, all right. I mean, if she'd just made that clear at the start instead of storming in.
A: All right. And, Elena, can you see how Henri might have thought you were taking control?
C: Well, I suppose so.
A: Good, we seem to be making some progress.
C: Look, Henri, I'm just trying to bring a bit of organization to this project. I mean, you're great on the creative side, but you have to admit you're not strong on the details. We're still sorting out things from phase one and we're supposed to be on phase three!
B: I've got all that covered, Elena.
C: So you say, but how do I know that? You never send me progress reports or anything ...
A: All right. It looks to me as though what we have here is a conflict of working styles. Shall we talk about that a bit more?

11 Find out what the students would do. There are no clear lines of authority in this situation – it isn't clear who answers to who. This needs clarifying, and having one person with overall charge of the project must form part of the solution. Give students a few minutes to discuss the options with a partner and then elicit some of their solutions. Collate them on the board.

12 3.27 Tell students they will now hear what actually happened. Play the final part of the audio to find out the outcome. Elicit students' reactions. Compare this solution with students' solutions on the board in 11.

ANSWER
Henri will remain in charge of the project and be solely responsible for meeting deadlines. He will send weekly reports to Elena, who will help out on the details where necessary. They may also have daily informal meetings to keep themselves up to date on how things are going. **Elena** will get Henri the extra IT support he needs, so he has more time to do the creative work and Elena can get on with her other projects.

3.27
A: ... Okay, so, can I just summarize what you've agreed? Henri, you're going to remain in charge of this project, but you're going to send weekly reports to Elena, so she can keep track of progress – especially on the details – and help out just where she's needed. Otherwise, though, meeting deadlines is going to be your responsibility – and yours alone. Is that acceptable to both of you? Okay, now it's just a suggestion, but you might like to consider having scheduled daily chats over a coffee just to keep everyone up to speed.
C: Good idea.
B: Yes, sure.
A: Now, Elena, you've agreed to get that extra IT support Henri requested, which will free him up to concentrate on the creative side of things, and free you up to get on with some of your other projects. Now, does this new arrangement sound like something you can both live with?
C: Yes, I think so.
B: Okay, let's give it a try.
A: Great, now I'll ...

13 Students take part in one or more roleplays of disputes at different levels of complexity: a simple dispute about work styles, a more complicated dispute on training and a very complex dispute about rationalization. In each roleplay, students work in threes. Give students a minute to prepare their role referring to pages 126–127. Remind the mediator to review the techniques covered in 8. When they are ready, give students about five minutes to perform the roleplay. Monitor and take notes. Before the third roleplay, check that students know the word *rationalization* (the reorganization of a company to improve efficiency). Finish by providing feedback on both mediation skills and language.

1:1 Ask your student to read both roles A and B in each situation and decide which advice they would offer each party. Hold a meeting in which your student is the mediator and you are Speaker A, and a second meeting in which your student is the mediator and you are Speaker B. Afterwards, discuss possible outcomes of any follow-up meeting.

MANAGEMENT SCENARIO E

Moral quarrel

Learning objectives
This scenario is based on the issues of assertiveness and to what extent political pressure becomes a bribe. Students begin by discussing a Chinese proverb and then read a memo about a meeting on international aid. Students watch a video in which Blue Rock employees discuss sponsoring three African students to do university courses in Europe. Students then consider how the participants behaved in terms of three types of behaviour: non-assertive, assertive and aggressive. They watch a second video and study one employee's ability to mediate. Finally, students have a meeting or conference call involving a mediator, and then evaluate their own performances.

Digital resources: Management Scenario E
In company in action E1–E2 and worksheet; Extension worksheets; Glossary; Student's Book answer key; Student's Book listening script; Fast-track map; End of course test

Warm-up
Draw three circles on the board and write the following terms inside them: *non-assertive*, *assertive* and *aggressive*. Ask students to tell their partner about a meeting they went to in which one of the participants behaved in one of these three ways: what was the issue and what happened?

1:1 Ask your student to talk about their experience of being at a meeting in which someone has behaved in one of the following three ways: non-assertive, assertive and aggressive.

1 Give students time to read the proverb and discuss the question about international aid with a partner. Go through the answers with the whole class.

2 Tell students that they will read a set of incomplete minutes taken at a meeting in Kampala in which Ed Ryan of Blue Rock promises support for an educational project. Ask students to read the minutes of the meeting, complete the missing words and then answer the questions.

ANSWERS
1 congratulated 2 announced 3 urged
4 emphasized 5 agreed
a Ed Ryan
b Cooperation on local water projects may not be continued if Blue Rock does not sponsor African students in the UK.
c to have an agreement validated by Blue Rock in time for the next meeting on April 16

3 **E1** Tell students they will watch a video of a meeting at Blue Rock's headquarters in which participants discuss whether or not to sponsor three students from Africa. Remind students who is at the meeting and ask them, on the first viewing, to say who is 'for' sponsoring the African students, who is 'against', and if anyone is neutral.

ANSWERS
For: Ed and Jack   Against: Cassie, Peter and Emma

E1
Cassie: You can't be serious, Ed!
Ed: Why not? It's my budget, after all.
Peter: Ed, this is just totally impossible!
Jack: Why, just because you say so?
Peter: Look Jack, you're new here, but we've been through all this before …
Emma: Listen you guys, can you keep the noise down a bit? We're trying to work next door …
Cassie: I'm sorry Emma, but this is important! We're trying to stop Ed making a big mistake.
Ed: Trying to undermine my village wells project, you mean!
Jack: Yeah! What do Marketing know about this anyway?
Cassie: Oh don't be ridiculous!
Peter: Oh now, wait a minute …
Emma: Whoa! Hold on a minute! What's going on here, Peter?
Jack: Marketing are trying to muscle in on Operations …
Cassie: They're being totally unreasonable, they just won't listen …
Peter: Look, this is really unnecessary, you …
Ed: Cassie and Peter are just being very narrow-minded …
Emma: Stop it, all of you! This is ridiculous! Shouting at each other like a bunch of schoolkids won't settle anything. I can see I'm going to have to mediate here. So let's talk this through. And one at a time, please. Now Peter, what's this all about?
Jack: Ed was just trying to …
Emma: Jack, I asked Peter, not you.
Peter: Thank you. Well, in a nutshell, Ed's agreed to pay for three African students to go to university in the UK.
Ed: Because if we don't, it could put the village wells project in danger!
Jack: Exactly!
Emma: Look, do you want me to try to help, or not? You can't keep interrupting or we're never going to get anywhere!
Ed: You don't know what you're talking about!
Jack: Nobody asked your opinion anyway!
Cassie: Exactly. They're just talking nonsense!

110 E MORAL QUARREL

Emma: Stop! That's enough! If you can't have a civilized conversation, I'll have you all out on the streets collecting donations! Not you, Peter, of course. Now, Peter; please explain why Blue Rock can't pay for university courses.

Peter: Well, as Ed discovered while he was enjoying the sunshine in Kampala last week, the Africans are very keen to train young engineers in the UK. Now, that's all well and good, but Blue Rock's supporters donate their money to help the poorest people in Africa. We can't afford to be seen spending their money on expensive university courses for the intellectual elite.

Cassie: Who just happen to be the sons and daughters of the politicians!

Ed: That's nonsense Cassie and you know it! You've got to think long-term; Africa can't continue to depend on foreign aid. If you want good engineers you've got to train the brightest and the best.

Emma: But don't you realize that could be considered as corruption?

Ed: Don't you start!

Jack: Yes, if you're going to mediate, you really shouldn't be taking sides!

Cassie: She's not taking sides; she's just stating the facts.

Jack: Facts! Huh! Well we could do with some facts, instead of half-baked opinions!

Emma: Look, I'm not going to sit here and be insulted! I was only trying to help …

Jack: Well clearly it isn't working, is it?

Emma: But that's not my fault! You and Ed are being totally unprofessional!

Jack: This is a complete waste of time!

Emma: No, it isn't!

Jack: Yes it is!

Emma: No, it isn't!

Cassie: Surely they have their own education budgets! Why should we have to pay?

Ed: Because if we don't, they might stop cooperating with the village wells project!

Cassie: But that's blackmail!

Ed: No, it's politics.

Cassie: It's blackmail!

Ed: It's politics!

Emma: Where are you going Peter?

Peter: I'm getting Sue in to sort this out. This is out of control!

4 🎥 **E1** Before playing the video again, deal with some of the more idiomatic language. Have students read the statements and choose the best answers.

ANSWERS
1 b   2 c   3 b   4 a   5 a   6 c

5 Give students time to put the words in the correct order. Check answers. Then, put students in pairs to decide how to reformulate each of the sentences to make them 'assertive', rather than 'aggressive'.

ANSWERS
a Can you keep the noise down a bit?   *We're finding it difficult to concentrate in the next office.*
b Jack, I asked Peter, not you.   *Jack, can we let Peter finish, then we'll come to you?*
c Look, do you want me to try to help, or not?   *Let's agree on some ground rules, shall we?*
d I'll have you all out on the street collecting donations!   *Let's try to find a solution so that we can focus on helping people in Africa, okay?*
e Don't you realize that could be considered as corruption?   *How do you think our donors will react to that idea?*
f You and Ed are being totally unprofessional!   *Let's try to stay calm and objective, shall we?*

6 Tell students to read the assertiveness tips on the PowerPoint slide and check: *dominance, submission, veto*. Ask students to match the beginnings and endings of the sentences. Check the answers.

ANSWERS
1 b   2 e   3 d   4 f   5 a   6 c

7 Issue students with a list of assertiveness mistakes, as follows: aggressive language / blame / judging without evidence / general arguments, not specific / threats

Ask students to match them to appropriate examples from the video, for example: *don't be ridiculous!; marketing are trying to muscle in on Operations; that could be considered as corruption; because if we don't, it could put the village wells project in danger*

If necessary, play the video again. When students have finished, ask individuals to explain why they matched the mistakes with the examples.

SUGGESTED ANSWERS
- Language, attitudes and body language were aggressive: *this is just totally impossible, don't be ridiculous!*
- Participants accused, blamed and criticized each other: *Marketing are trying to muscle in on Operations; Cassie and Peter are just being very narrow-minded.*
- They made judgements without providing any evidence: *as Ed discovered while he was enjoying the sunshine in Kampala last week; We can't afford to be seen spending their money on expensive university courses for the intellectual elite – Who just happen to be the sons and daughters of the politicians! But that's blackmail!*
- Their arguments were general, not specific: *you have to train the brightest and best; that could be considered as corruption*
- They made threats rather than offering incentives: *Because if we don't, it could put the village wells project in danger!*

8 🎥 **E2** Tell students that they will now watch a video in which Sue acts as mediator. First, ask students to read the list of items. Tell them to watch the video and tick each item they see or hear.

ANSWERS
All except: holds one-on-one meetings and gets the parties to sign an agreement.

MANAGEMENT SCENARIO

🎥 E2

Sue: Let's get started then. I'm sorry I couldn't speak to you all yesterday. As you know, I was just leaving for Geneva when you asked me to mediate. First of all, a few ground rules. I'd like everybody to explain their point of view, without interruptions, and then we'll try to generate different options and see if we can't find a compromise that's acceptable to everyone. I'm not going to get involved, I'm just going to chair the discussion and help you to find an agreement. Is everybody comfortable with that?

All: Yeah that's fine, Sue. Okay that's fine. Sure.

Sue: Good. So, Ed, could you summarize the meeting you had in Kampala?

Ed: Well if Blue Rock don't support me on this, we can forget about the village wells project!

Sue: Let's stay positive please Ed; tell us about the benefits rather than the negatives?

Ed: All right. Well, Africa desperately needs highly trained water resources engineers. There's a lot of pressure on us to sponsor engineering students. Our local partners are very keen on the idea …

Cassie: Especially if their children are the students!

Sue: Cassie? We'll come to you next, okay? But let's hear Ed out first, all right?

Cassie: Sorry Ed.

Sue: So basically you're saying if we support the education project, we're sure to be able to continue to provide clean water to villages, have I got that right?

Ed: Exactly.

Peter: But the point is, Ed, you should at least have talked to us first, and …

Sue: Peter, can we try to use 'I' rather than 'you'? You know, 'I'd like' rather than 'you should'?

Peter: Oh, er, sure. Um, Ed, I'd like us to talk this through together before making any kind of commitment …

Cassie: Personally I just find this really disturbing! I mean, it's like they're trying to blackmail us!

Sue: Cassie, let's leave judgements aside for the moment, all right? That's rather a broad generalisation: can you be more specific?

Cassie: Well, Amos Jeffah's son wants to go to Brunel University. It just seems too much of a coincidence that they're suddenly asking us to fund engineering students!

Jack: Er, can I just come in here?

Sue: Yes, Jack, go ahead.

Jack: Frankly, that's a load of rubbish!

Sue: Let's not get too abrasive here. You're saying that's not a good example?

Jack: Right, sorry. Amos Junior is already at Brunel University; his course is being funded by the European Union. All the Africans want is for other bright young people to have the same opportunities.

Sue: So, are there any other options?

Emma: Couldn't we help them with the education project without actually funding it ourselves?

Jack: You mean get someone else to raise the money?

Emma: Exactly. That way, we'd ensure their continued cooperation with the wells project without upsetting our donors.

Sue: Ed, does that make sense?

Ed: I suppose it's worth exploring. Maybe we could ask the lottery people to get involved?

Cassie: We could try talking to the universities too?

Sue: All right. Let's look at that idea in more detail …

Sue: Peter, are you happy with that?

Peter: As I said, as long as it's clear that our donors' money is only being spent on building wells, yes, I can live with that.

Sue: Okay. So, shall we ask Ed to float the idea with the Africans?

All: Yeah.

Sue: Let us know how they react. I'll summarize what we've agreed by email – and I suggest we all meet again when I get back to London.

All: Okay. Thanks, Sue. All right.

9 🎥 **E2** Before playing the video again, check that students know some of the more complex vocabulary, such as: *disturbing, coincidence, abrasive*. Ask students to read the questions and play the video so that students can write their answers.

ANSWERS

a Because Sue was in Geneva and Peter was in Birmingham.
b Sue sets up the meeting by laying down some ground rules, i.e. first everybody explains their point of view, they generate different options and try and find a compromise.
c Assertively. For example, she asks Ed to talk about benefits, and not to make threats; she prevents an interruption from Cassie by promising to let her speak next; she asks Peter to use 'I' rather than 'you'; she asks Cassie not to make judgements and to be specific when she claims the Africans are 'blackmailing' Blue Rock; also, she asks Jack to use less strong language.
d Emma suggests they help the Africans to find an alternative source of funding for the Educating Engineers project.
e Ed will suggest the idea to the Africans; Sue will summarize what they have agreed by email; they will all meet again in London

10 Ask students to complete the gaps in the phrases from the video. Put students in pairs to discuss which assertiveness tips they refer to.

ANSWERS

a positive	Incentives, not threats
b talk, through	'I' not 'you'
c judgements	Description, not judgement
d specific	Specific, not general
e abrasive	Assertive, not passive or aggressive

11 Divide the class into small groups. Assign each student with a letter, A, B or C. Ask As to turn to page 134, Bs to page 138, and Cs to page 128. Give them a few minutes to prepare. When the meeting is finished, ask the participants to look at the mediation and assertiveness checklists on page 132 and complete them in order to evaluate their performance.